Lift Every Voice

The African American History Series

Series Editors:
Jacqueline M. Moore, Austin College
Nina Mjagkij, Ball State University

Traditionally, history books tend to fall into two categories: books academics write for each other, and books written for popular audiences. Historians often claim that many of the popular authors do not have the proper training to interpret and evaluate the historical evidence. Yet, popular audiences complain that most historical monographs are inaccessible because they are too narrow in scope or lack an engaging style. This series, which will take both chronological and thematic approaches to topics and individuals crucial to an understanding of the African American experience, is an attempt to address that problem. The books in this series, written in lively prose by established scholars, are aimed primarily at nonspecialists. They focus on topics in African American history that have broad significance and place them in their historical context. While presenting sophisticated interpretations based on primary sources and the latest scholarship, the authors tell their stories in a succinct manner, avoiding jargon and obscure language. They include selected documents that allow readers to judge the evidence for themselves and to evaluate the authors' conclusions. Bridging the gap between popular and academic history, these books bring the African American story to life.

Volumes Published

Booker T. Washington, W.E.B. Du Bois, and the Struggle for Racial Uplift
Jacqueline M. Moore

Slavery in Colonial America, 1619-1776
Betty Wood

African Americans in the Jazz Age
A Decade of Struggle and Promise
Mark Robert Schneider

A. Philip Randolph
A Life in the Vanguard
Andrew E. Kersten

The African American Experience in Vietnam
Brothers in Arms
James Westheider

Bayard Rustin
American Dreamer
Jerald Podair

African Americans Confront Lynching
Strategies of Resistance
Christopher Waldrep

Lift Every Voice
The History of African American Music
Burton W. Peretti

Lift Every Voice

The History of
African American Music

Burton W. Peretti

ROWMAN & LITTLEFIELD PUBLISHERS, INC.
Lanham • Boulder • New York • Toronto • Plymouth, UK

ROWMAN & LITTLEFIELD PUBLISHERS, INC.

Published in the United States of America
by Rowman & Littlefield Publishers, Inc.
A wholly owned subsidiary of The Rowman & Littlefield Publishing Group, Inc.
4501 Forbes Boulevard, Suite 200, Lanham, Maryland 20706
www.rowmanlittlefield.com

Estover Road
Plymouth PL6 7PY
United Kingdom

British Library Cataloguing in Publication Information Available

Library of Congress Cataloging-in-Publication Data

Peretti, Burton W. (Burton William), 1961–
  Lift every voice : the history of African American music / Burton W. Peretti.
    p. cm. — (The African American history series)
  Includes bibliographical references and discography.
  ISBN-13: 978-0-7425-5811-3 (cloth : alk. paper)
  ISBN-10: 0-7425-5811-8 (cloth : alk. paper)
  eISBN-13: 978-0-7425-6469-5
  eISBN-10: 0-7425-6469-X
   1. African Americans—Music—History and criticism. I. Title.
  ML3556.P45 2009
  780.89'96073—dc22   2008025181

Printed in the United States of America

∞™ The paper used in this publication meets the minimum requirements of
American National Standard for Information Sciences—Permanence of Paper
for Printed Library Materials, ANSI/NISO Z39.48-1992.

For Catherine and Elizabeth

Contents

Glossary of Musical Terms

The following terms might be unfamiliar to readers. They are highlighted in **bold** type on the pages on which they first appear.

antiphony—European musical term for the effect in which one singing group repeats or responds to the phrase of another group. It is roughly similar to call and response (see below).

atonality—The quality of music that is not in a standard key or does not use a standard harmonic system.

call and response—A common practice in African and African American music, as well as in oratory and religious services, in which a lead musician or other leader calls out words, and the group repeats them.

close harmony—The practice of playing or singing the notes in a chord (such as C, E, G, and B flat in a C major seventh chord) in their closest proximity to each other. Barbershop quartets, for example, gain their distinctive sound by almost always singing in close harmony.

field holler—A kind of agricultural work song, originating in slavery, often sung in call and response fashion, loud enough to be heard across distances and often sung in rhythm with the repetitive work being done.

griot—often also called *djeli*—A member of a West African community who wanders from village to village and sings or speaks the news and history of the community.

heterophonic, heterophony—The quality, notable in much African music, produced by a melodic line and variations when they are sung or played simultaneously. Differs from *polyphony*, more commonly heard in European music, which usually features different melodic lines sung or played by various musicians at similar points in the musical texture.

homiletic spirituals—A genre of sermons, originating among African American preachers of the 1800s, in which spoken oratory changes into singing.

melisma—Sliding from note to note, or within a note, especially in singing. Common in African and African American music.

modes—Ancient European seven-note scales (Dorian, Ionian, etc.) in which the notes are separated by different combinations of half steps (a short jump from one note to the next highest note) and whole steps (about twice the distance of a half step). The standard major scale's notes are spaced like this, in ascending order: whole/whole/half/whole/whole/whole/half. This scale is only one of at least seven modes in western music.

modulation—Shifting from one key or tonal center to another within a musical work.

pentatonic —"Five notes." Pentatonic scales featuring five notes are predominant in traditional East Asian, Native American, and most African music.

polyrhythm—The overall sound created by multiple different beats produced by musicians, especially by percussionists. African ensemble music often features ample polyrhythm.

ring shout—A slow, shuffling dance performed by African or African American worshippers in a circle, accompanied by sacred singing. An important African cultural survival in American slavery.

signifyin or **signifying**—The African American folk practice of using words, stories, songs, and humor to express new or hidden opinions and meanings.

syncopation—A term developed to describe the phenomenon in European music in which notes in between the usual beats of the time signature receive the most emphasis. White composers' perception of polyrhythms in African American music led them to represent it (e.g., in minstrelsy and ragtime) in syncopated written music (which simplified the polyrhythms).

timbre—The quality of the tone—its texture, roughness, and so forth—that is sung or played.

Chronology of Selected Dates

1740—South Carolina legislature, fearing rebellions, bans musical instruments among slaves.

1740–1761—Great Awakening revivals involve African Americans in Protestant hymn singing.

1801—First African Methodist Episcopal (AME) hymnal is published by the Reverend Richard Allen.

1821—The African Grove Tavern in New York City presents performances by black musicians.

1842—Charles Dickens observes famed dancer William Henry Lane, known as "Master Juba."

1845—*The Narrative of the Life of Frederick Douglass* describes the "sorrow songs" of slaves.

1859—Pianist Thomas Wiggins, known as "Blind Tom" Bethune, performs at the White House.

1867—*Slave Songs of the United States*, the first collection of its kind, is published.

1871—The Fisk University Jubilee Singers begin touring, which continues until 1878.

1878—James Monroe Trotter publishes *Music and Some Highly Musical People*.

1890—Singer George W. Johnson makes the first phonograph recording by an African American.

1892—Antonin Dvořák claims that spirituals can become the basis for America's classical music.

1893—Black ragtime pianists meet and share ideas at the Chicago Columbian Exposition.

1897—Bob Cole stages *A Trip to Coontown* in New York City.

1899—Scott Joplin's *Maple Leaf Rag* is published.

1900—James Weldon and J. Rosamond Johnson write "Lift Every Voice and Sing."

1903—*In Dahomey*, by Will Marion Cook and starring Williams and Walker, is the first black musical comedy to open on Broadway.

1912—James Reese Europe's Clef Club presents the first concert of black music at Carnegie Hall.

1910—Scott Joplin completes his opera *Treemonisha* and publishes it the next year.

1918—James Reese Europe's Hellfighters Orchestra fights in World War I and performs in Paris.

1919—Broome Records, the first African American-owned record company, is founded in Boston.

1920—Mamie Smith's "Crazy Blues" is the first blues recording.

1925–1928—Louis Armstrong's Hot Five and Hot Seven recordings are released.

1928—Paul Robeson appears in London production of *Show Boat*.

1932—Thomas A. Dorsey and Sallie Martin organize the National Convention of Gospel Choirs and Choruses.

1935–1936—Lionel Hampton and Teddy Wilson integrate Benny Goodman's big band and combos.

1939—Marian Anderson gives a recital before 75,000 people at the Lincoln Memorial.

1943—Duke Ellington's suite *Black, Brown, and Beige* premieres in Carnegie Hall.

1949—Anticommunist rioters disrupt a planned concert by Paul Robeson at Peekskill, New York.

1955—Marian Anderson is the first African American singer to appear at the Metropolitan Opera.

1959—Berry Gordy, Jr. founds Tamla Records; renamed Motown Records the next year.

1960—Black musicians hold an alternative festival to protest hiring at the Newport Jazz Festival.

1963—Marian Anderson, Mahalia Jackson, and Eva Jessye perform at the March on Washington.

1965—The Association for the Advancement of Creative Musicians (AACM) is formed in Chicago.

1972—Isaac Hayes is the first black songwriter to win an Academy Award, for "Theme from *Shaft*."

1982—Michael Jackson's *Thriller* is released; it becomes the best-selling album of all time.

1988—First nationally popular gangsta rap albums launch controversies over hip hop music.

2004—Jazz at Lincoln Center moves into a new concert space overlooking New York's Central Park.

Acknowledgments

I t has been a delight to work on this book. I am grateful to Nina Mjagkij and Jacqueline Moore, editors of the African American history series at Rowman & Littlefield, for their offer to contribute this volume to the series, and for their careful reading of the manuscript. Niels Aaboe, Asa Johnson, and Elaine McGarraugh guided the book to publication, and Ann Shaver copyedited the text. Completion of the manuscript was assisted materially by a grant from the Connecticut State University-AAUP research fund. Finally, as is always the case for me, this book is a testament to the love and support of Jenny and Catherine, and a gift to Elizabeth, our newest family member.

Introduction

African American music is one of the treasures of the United States. Spirituals, ragtime, the blues, jazz, rhythm and blues, gospel, soul, and hip hop—among other styles—are some of the richest and most distinctive products of our national culture. Developed in the face of centuries of racial discrimination, poverty, and other challenges, this music testifies to the resilience of African and Caribbean musical origins and the creativity of individuals, families, and communities. The biographies of people who make music are fascinating case studies of African American life from the 1700s to the present. In addition, the story of African American music's impact on nonblack listeners—who have played a role in making it one of the world's most popular cultural products—is a compelling chapter in the history of U.S. race relations.

This book is a brief overview of the complex history of African American music. It cannot devote much space to any particular important style, musician, event, or musical work that deserves extended treatment. Suggestions for more in-depth reading on some of the subjects are found in the bibliography. The goal of this book is to integrate the broad currents of the music's history into the history of African Americans and the United States.

Lift Every Voice defines the place of music within African American communities and the nation as a whole. Black music bears witness to the horrors of slavery, the first years of emancipation, the burden of segregation and second-class citizenship, the striving for civil rights, and efforts of the black middle class to pursue prosperity and security. Our topic is deeply embedded in African American social history. Families, neighborhoods, larger city communities, and groups of children, adolescents, and adults all found music to be an important part of their self-expression and group cohesion. Music often was swept up in the great social and political struggles that affected black Americans, such as abolitionism, the Great Migration to the North, and the civil rights movement. Today, in the early twenty-first century, we find that hip hop and other black musical expression have become implicated in debates about African American identity and status.

To a great extent, any music history is also a story about musicians—people who dedicate their working lives to music. This book will thus trace the evolution of African American musical specialists. Past and present, peoples of the African diaspora (the global dispersal of Africans due to the slave trade) have identified and nurtured individuals with musical talent and have honored those who reach the pinnacles of creativity. Musicians held distinct roles in African cultures which were undermined dramatically by American slavery, but by the 1800s free black composers and performers had found footholds in churches and in the early commercial music business. These musicians were the precursors to the twentieth-century instrumentalists, songwriters, classical composers, vocalists, and music entrepreneurs who captured the world's ear. Their rise to prominence was not always smooth. Reflecting the racism in American society, white entrepreneurs and musicians often *co-opted* black music—copying musicians' styles and robbing them of their deserved earnings and fame. The co-optation of African American music by others, unfortunately, is a major part of our story.

Lift Every Voice is not a music textbook. It is intended for readers with little or no knowledge of musical techniques or terminology. Nevertheless, I hope that musicians and music students will also benefit from its narrative. Some less common musical terms are marked in **bold** in the text and are defined in the glossary.

This book benefits greatly from earlier syntheses of African American music history, particularly Eileen Southern's *The Music of Black Americans*. While the present book is much briefer and less detailed than Southern's, it also includes new information and perspectives on the subject, derived from innovative scholarship that has appeared in the past decade. Historians, for example, have only recently revealed the African American origination of barbershop quartet singing and the details of Scott Joplin's later career in New York City. Mellonee V. Burnim's and Portia K. Maultsby's *African American Music*, which was published during the preparation of this manuscript, offers a much lengthier and topically organized treatment of the subject, and is especially recommended to readers who would like to explore it in more depth. *Lift Every Voice* covers the same territory quickly and chronologically.

Chapter 1 covers centuries of experience in a brief space, tracing the general history of African music from prehistory to the beginning of the slave trade, the history of music in slave societies of the New World, and slave music and culture in the United States until the eve of the Civil War. This chapter introduces students to a way in which music can be understood within general history. Using the approaches of anthropologists, ethnomusicologists, and some recent historians, I view African American groups as *cultures* that are defined primarily by their shared, self-made behaviors and institutions. Music is a notable component of almost every culture. It is connected with other elements of the culture, such as economics, religion, folk tales, or ceremonial occasions, and it shares with them many of the "core" values and qualities found in the culture as a whole. This approach is valuable because it highlights the important continuities in African American music and culture over the centuries, despite wrenching and dramatic changes in their social and political status. These important cultural traits also affected music making in small free black communities.

Chapter 2 begins with an account of how the Union invasion of the South during the Civil War exposed Northerners to slaves' music and encouraged some Yankees to publish the first collections of spirituals. The chapter then explores the musical life of the first generation of African Americans after the Civil War, to about 1900. It contrasts the evolution of sacred black music, in which slave spirituals were transformed into concert fare by the Fisk University Jubilee Singers, with the rise of secular African American songwriting and performing in the publishing houses of New York City ("Tin Pan Alley") and in vaudeville theaters across the country. Nationally known figures such as the pianist Thomas Wiggins, the soprano Sisieretta Jones, and the composer James Bland emerged. In this era, also, the diverse impact of white Americans on black music—ranging from minstrel performers' co-optation of black music to George L. White's efforts on behalf of the Jubilee Singers—became apparent.

Chapter 3 describes the nineteenth-century roots and the rise to prominence before 1920 of ragtime and the blues, two distinct African American musical styles that broke decisively from the minstrel tradition and increased the expressive power and range of black musicians. Arriving during an era in which "Jim Crow" segregation and lynching curtailed black social advances in the South and racism pervaded the entire country, ragtime nevertheless captivated the mass public. Disseminated to a mass audience by the phonograph, the comic ragtime songs of Bert Williams, the piano works of Scott Joplin, and the Broadway revues of Will Marion Cook reflected the brashness and fast pace of life in a newly mechanized and urbanized America. Ragtime also became the theme song of the

"Great Migration" during World War I, when the first large numbers of southern African Americans made their way to the northern cities, searching for a future free from Jim Crow. The blues, a song style championed by itinerant male guitarists and female stage performers, made its way north with the migrants, and offered a gritty and poetic alternative to the urbane sounds of ragtime. W. C. Handy, Gertrude "Ma" Rainey, and Bessie Smith helped to make the blues the dominant secular music of black northern communities.

As chapter 4 shows, though, ragtime and the blues were eclipsed in the mass media by a "swinging" new instrumental music that came to epitomize the 1920s. Jazz reached its fullest early development in New Orleans, where Jelly Roll Morton, King Oliver, and Louis Armstrong blended ragtime with the blues to produce exciting new instrumental improvisations. In the 1920s many different popular styles claimed to be "jazz," and co-optation by white musicians reached a new high point, but the dynamic creativity of black performers such as Morton, Armstrong, Fletcher Henderson, and Duke Ellington also brought African American music to new heights of sophistication and critical esteem. Their brands of "hot" jazz were some of the signal achievements of the "Negro Renaissance" of the 1920s. Despite the ravages of the Great Depression, black jazz persisted and became the foundation of the big-band swing music of the late 1930s and early 1940s, which brought unprecedented fame and profitability to popular music.

Chapter 5 explores a tradition in African American music that is neglected in earlier chapters: the tendency of musicians to seek elite status and a home in the concert hall. In the late 1800s, white and black composers began to advocate the use of African American music in classical composition, both to "lift up the race" and to create a distinctive American classical music out of a distinctive and rich ethnic tradition. Thus began an important tradition of African American composition for the concert hall, the ballet, and opera stages that continues to this day, largely outside the spotlight of the music business. Performers such as Roland Hayes, Paul Robeson, Leontyne Price, and Jessye Norman and composers such as Ulysses Kay, Nathaniel Dett, and Olly Wilson receive well-deserved attention in this chapter. In jazz also, especially after 1940, African American players (who often were also composers or arrangers) sought to make major musical statements that displayed complex and groundbreaking thinking and technique. Innovators such as Duke Ellington, George Russell, and Anthony Braxton brought jazz in league with the avant-garde (or "cutting edge") of classical composers, despite the eagerness of some younger musicians of the 1960s to ally modern jazz with the average black people who rebelled in the inner cities.

African Americans of "average" education and income shaped the popular mainstream of black music, through their own creative activity and their choices as musical consumers. In chapter 6 we return to sacred music, which after 1900 was transformed along with black organized religion. The rise of black gospel music in the early twentieth century in the Holiness and Sanctified churches, and its conquest of the more established Protestant denominations, inspired hymns, quartets, and solo careers that rivaled jazz and the blues in popularity and influence. Thomas A. Dorsey, Mahalia Jackson, and Sam Cooke were celebrities on a par with Louis Armstrong and Duke Ellington. Gospel worked in tandem with northern "urban" blues to inspire new popular music in the 1950s, including styles such as doo-wop and rock 'n' roll. Gospel songs and traditional spirituals, meanwhile, joined to inspire the musical arsenal of the southern civil rights movement of the 1950s and 1960s, the decisive African American mass action that ended segregation once and for all. "Soul" music, a vibrant new style of the 1960s and 1970s, brought the gospel sound into the secular mainstream.

The final chapter of this book explores currents in African American popular music since 1970, against the background of the mixed legacy of integration. Many black people fled poverty and the inner cities for middle-class suburbia, but others remained trapped and saw their condition worsen. Internal debates about African American identity, coupled with increased interracial tension and the new national dominance of conservative politics, created instability and conflict in black culture. All of these tensions influenced black music. Amid the rise of Motown Records and such stars as Michael Jackson and Prince, many argued that too much heritage and authenticity was being sacrificed in the name of success in the white-dominated market. The debates and the tensions have carried over into the era of hip hop, since the late 1980s, in which older notions of black music have been both honored and challenged and in which African Americans have debated the proper path to the American dream with renewed intensity. These debates today, more than anything, justify a historical survey such as the one I have attempted here.

Like other volumes in Rowman & Littlefield's series in African American history, this book contains a short collection of documents. This sampling of images, lyrics, reminiscences, opinion pieces, and manifestos is designed to encourage students to consider how verbal and pictorial evidence helps us to understand the history of music. A few questions for study or discussion are attached to each document. Nothing, of course, can equal actually hearing the music itself. I hope that this book will inspire readers to attend live musical performances, but recordings are also rich and exciting documents, which are especially valuable as the legacy of artists no longer living. The discography at the end of the book provides readers with suggestions for many hours of great listening.

I hope that this book will introduce readers to lives and achievements that will enrich their knowledge of the African American and American past, and that it will give them a new appreciation of how music reveals the emotional and intellectual life of a people over the course of many years and decades.

1

From West Africa to Slavery

The story of music in slavery tells of a rich culture, dating from prehistoric and ancient times, that adapted to the dislocation and despair inflicted by the slave trade and European colonialism. It also relates the amazingly rich and vital transplantation of music and African values to the New World. In the United States from 1790 to 1860, black slavery in the Americas reached one of its highest—and last—peaks of profitability for white masters. In the antebellum (or pre–Civil War) South, white observers were fascinated with the music and culture of slaves, and they described in detail what they heard and saw. At the same time, during the decades before the Civil War, music also helped African Americans, free people of color as well as slaves, to conceptualize freedom and to explore spiritual and secular self-expression.

AFRICAN ROOTS

In 1796, on completing an expedition through the interior of Africa, the British physician Mungo Park headed toward the Atlantic coast to search for passage home. From a town called Kamalia, in present-day Senegal, Park traveled with a coffle, a party that marched enslaved Africans to the coast. It "consisted of twenty-seven slaves for sale," later joined by others, "making in all thirty-five slaves." Also present were fourteen free black African men, each of them accompanied by "one or two wives and some domestic slaves." In addition, Park noted the presence of "six *jillikeas* (singing men), whose musical talents were frequently exerted either to divert our fatigue or obtain us a welcome from strangers."[1]

Park's recollection reveals some of the social conditions in West Africa during the transatlantic slave trade. Slaves "for sale" were destined for the markets on the Atlantic coast and for the fearful "middle passage" across the ocean to the Americas. Other Africans remained free, perhaps because they were complicit in the trade. Some slaves did not leave for America, but toiled in households of African elites. Park also tells us that "singing men" joined the travel party. Their social identity seemed to derive from their musical skill. As Park notes, the singers entertained travelers but also performed a crucial social function, advertising the coffle's arrival to strangers.

Park's story is part of a tapestry of fragmentary evidence about black Africa and its music during the international slave trade (between 1500 and 1850). Most black African cultures did not preserve their heritages in written records. We may never achieve a conclusive history of this time. The historical record of enslaved populations in the middle passage and in slave communities in the Americas is also far from complete. With a few exceptions, the names and stories of these millions have been lost.

Nevertheless, the testimony of travelers such as Park, along with other historical records, allows us to piece together a general story. Sub-Saharan Africa remains a rich repository of cultures and musical traditions that give evidence of their ancient roots. Present-day African American cultures also provide us with tantalizing evidence about the African past. Scholars of music have compared modern recordings and performances with the historical record to deduce some of the musical traditions of Africa centuries ago. It especially helps that the growth of the "cotton South" in the United States after 1800 is comparatively well-documented. Pursuing a myriad of clues, researchers have discovered many elements of the story of music's transition from Africa to American slavery.

Nineteenth-century stereotypes of Africa as the primitive "dark continent" have long since been demolished. The world's second largest land mass cradled the first human settlements, and at least a millennium ago it held a cultural diversity and sophistication surpassed only by Asia. The population of Africa was dynamic, migrating with changes in the weather, food supplies, and trade. The Bantus of the equatorial region, for example, launched a major migration in about the fourth century BCE, spreading their language and farming methods—and their musical instruments—for hundreds of miles to the east and south. Cities and empires rose and fell with the discovery and exhaustion of metal ore supplies and changes in manufacturing. As Europe struggled with poverty and disunity in the early Middle Ages (circa 600–1100), North Africa led the world in mathematics, scientific knowledge, and maritime innovation, and Islam swept across the Sahara desert to create extensive new intellectual, political, and trade networks.

After 1100, West Africa—at the southwest edge of Islam's realm—saw the successive rise and fall of the Songhay, Mali, and Senegambian empires, which etched sophisticated trade routes and political networks across the lower Sahara, into the savannah grasslands, and further south into the rain forests near the equator. Arts of all kinds flourished, although only the influx of Arabic provided a written culture. As in medieval Europe, local wars raged and villages were plundered for human booty; slavery in Africa resembled the oppression of peasants in Europe. However, Africans' cuisine was far more diverse and rich than those of Europeans, their clothing and adornments were more colorful, and their social rituals were more varied and vigorous. Thanks to continent-wide trade, the relative abundance of gold, metals, rice, beans, ivory, coffee, and other items enriched the lives of West Africans.

Music did as well. The behavior of the most isolated indigenous groups of our time suggest that all prehistoric humans made music in imitation of the sounds around them, produced instruments out of the materials in their midst, and integrated music into their daily life and significant rituals. Archaeological and pictorial evidence tells us that music in West Africa sprang from deep roots and flourished as its people migrated and traded. The bow, possibly the first invention that enabled humans to store and release energy, may have been used first as a plucked instrument, and only later was converted into a weapon. Rock paintings in the Sahara from about 6000 BCE show dancers with body painting and masks that resemble those found in traditional African dance of our time. Egypt, the world's wealthiest and most complex ancient culture, absorbed lutes from Arabia and exported harps westward into central Africa. Around the seventh century CE, the vibrant Jewish and Coptic Christian communities of Ethiopia developed notation systems of sacred music that are still in use today.

Similarly, pots from the 1100s and 1200s unearthed in Nigeria depict types of drums and other instruments that are still used by the Yoruba peoples. Instruments migrated along with humans; over a thousand years ago, the log xylophone accompanied Southeast Asian traders to the island of Madagascar, in East Africa, and spread along with the banana plants whose trunks were used to make the instruments. A millennium ago South African "pygmies," as Europeans misnamed some grasslanders, developed a complex singing style. This style was **heterophonic**, in which singers overlaid versions of a melody to create a dense musical texture. This heterophony was adopted by neighbored Bantu speakers, who then migrated and spread it far to the north. Along the southern coast of West Africa, the evidence suggests that while a few basic types of instruments (wind, percussion, and stringed) and general approaches toward singing (either unison vocal lines or **call and response**) were shared, across the centuries migration and interaction created thousands of local variations. Materials, customs, and political and social history and structure all helped to shape the distinctive music of each African community.

We do not know why, but it seems clear that from very early times sub-Saharan Africans integrated music making into more social activities, and thus made music more frequently, than peoples in most other regions of the world. This does not mean that black Africans were always making music; in fact, as observers past and present have noted, groups often went for weeks without singing and dancing. Rather, it indicates that West Africans developed numerous elaborate singing and playing rituals, tailored to many occasions that invited virtually all village residents to participate. After the eighth century Islam brought North African oboes and other hard-to-play instruments into West Africa and encouraged the appointment of professional court musicians, but on the coast beyond Islam's influence there were no such professionals, and almost everyone got involved in singing and playing instruments. The call and response style of singing found across West Africa might seem authoritarian, with a leader giving out a line that the crowd then repeats, but the calls and responses often overlapped a bit, which gave all the singers a more equal stature in performances.

The centrality of dance helped to shape the extraordinary rhythmic qualities of the music. West African music and dance both display what schol-

Photo 1.1.   An ensemble of traditional West African musical instruments, photographed in the early 1900s. Source: General Research and Reference Division, Schomburg Center for Research in Black Culture, The New York Public Library, Astor, Lenox and Tilden foundations.

ars confidently call the most sophisticated and intricate sense of rhythm in the world. On the southern coast of West Africa, drummers overlapped contrasting individual rhythms to create **polyrhythm**. African music lacked "downbeats" that mark European time signatures such as the "oom-pah-pah" triple meter of waltz tempo. Instead, polyrhythms overload the ear and create the illusion of an irregular master beat. As early European observers noted, a community could fall into this master beat, moving their heads, shoulders, and limbs to it, often with great subtlety. The complexity and elusive qualities of polyrhythm are unique features of African music, and they became foundations for African American music. These sophisticated sounds were accompanied by equally intricate body movements in West African dance. White observers marveled at how Africans shook their pelvises and locked and unlocked the joints of their limbs with exuberance and ease, dancing in ways that were alien to Europeans.

Not all music was particularly complex or public. Musicians used some instruments with limited expressive ranges, such as rock gongs, mostly for ceremonial effect. Musicians often played and sang alone; workers sang in unison in the fields; secret societies, which were common, nurtured their own music; and men, women, and children often had their own styles of singing. But weddings, funerals, state occasions, circumcision rites, ritual insults of royalty (a special West African tradition), and other events—such as the arrival of intriguing or important strangers—produced the most colorful and elaborate music and dance. Mungo Park in 1796, for example, found four drummers and four singing men accompanying a delegation from one town that sought to purchase grain from another. Beats on the large *tabala* or kettle drum accompanied a Muslim wedding feast, followed by whistling and singing by the women that lasted "all night." On one feast day, residents arrived in the village square in pairs, dancing and welcoming Park to the accompaniment of "simple and very plaintive airs" on "a sort of flute."[2] Ensembles of "thumb pianos," called *oompoochwas* or *mbiras*, produced long melodic lines that enchanted early European visitors to the equatorial region. They and more recent observers noted that the polyrhythms and diverse instrumental color of West African music, shifting in complex and exciting patterns over time, evoked the interwoven patterns and color schemes of indigenous cloth and basketry.

Like music elsewhere in the world, West African music was often deeply spiritual. Groups in the region recognized a division between secular and sacred music, even though the genres had much in common. Ancient African beliefs revolved around the worship of spirits, including those of ancestors and of the animal and natural world. Possession by spirits was not a typical result of spiritual practice, but particular singing styles associated with spirit possession became subsets of religious music. Islam brought dramatic changes both to spirituality and to sacred music in the inland regions of West Africa. Musically speaking, the Muslim call to prayer (of Arabian origin) is a solo recital with improvised melody and frequent **melisma**, or sliding between notes. This style, along with Islam's many restrictions on music and dance in everyday life, altered African music widely. Christian missionaries, arriving in West Africa in the 1500s, changed it further, as European clergy imposed hymns on converts. Ancient belief in spirits, and the music that expressed this belief, thus bent to the practices of the major monotheistic religions that arrived in West Africa.

THE SLAVE TRADE

The traffic in human beings across the Atlantic cut off enslaved Africans from much of their old way of life. The evidence of music in slave communities in the New World, though, is a major indication that African culture and values could survive and adapt to enormous hardship.

In the 1400s, contact with Europeans began to drive West Africans into enslavement and colonization. Portuguese navigators, followed by soldiers and merchants, established trading posts and Catholic missions and bartered for the rich local commodities. The Portuguese purchase of African slaves began almost immediately, but the market for them in Europe remained small. The growing demand for cheap labor in "the New World" across the Atlantic, though, changed everything. Portugal built the first transatlantic slave galleons and sent thousands of enslaved people to Brazil, its colony in America. Later Portugal earned riches by selling humans to Spanish colonies in the Caribbean and Central America. The wealth of the New World, the obsessive demand for cheap labor, and the huge profitability of the slave trade made it a central early phenomenon of modern capitalism—and over the next three centuries, Africa was raided and millions of kidnap victims were sent across the Atlantic.

One complexity of the early slave trade that eventually helped shape African American music concerned the ethnic origins of the enslaved Africans. While it is true that West Africa, with ready access to the Atlantic, supplied the vast majority of slaves, many Africans from other parts of the continent—particularly the South and the interior grasslands—were also sent to the Americas in chains. By the 1700s, as supplies of victims on the west coast were exhausted, slavers struck south into present-day Angola and negotiated for captives as far east as Mozambique. Sizeable shipments from these areas to Brazil, especially, brought new regional dialects, music, and other attributes to plantations. For example, the samba, Brazil's national dance, probably originated among slaves from Africa's east coast. Even among West Africans, cultural differences were pronounced. In the colonies of the Caribbean, and later in North America, diverse Africans were forced to live together. Differences among equatorial African peoples—for instance between the Yoruba, Hausa, or Bantu language groups—ensured pluralism and tensions that slowed the creation of an African American "melting pot." Strange new features in American locales—especially their plants and animals—diversified these makeshift cultures further.

All African American communities, though, developed in the context of the oppressive environment of modern slavery. "Chattel" status relegated the slave to the legal identity of cattle, making persons into property. The kidnappings in Africa, the horrors of the Atlantic crossing, dehumanizing slave auctions in America, and the backbreaking forced labor on plantations were so hostile to human existence that observers long assumed that enslaved people were completely cut off from their African roots. Especially in the Caribbean and in Brazil, almost all enslaved Africans toiled on large plantations which grew the staple crops for Europe and Asia's evolving diet: sugar cane, coffee, and rice. Here owners found it most profitable to work slaves to death in one or two years (most succumbed to the intense heat or tropical diseases, others to violence from overseers) and replace them with fresh slaves.

Slavery, one scholar has argued, was a state of "social death."[3] Plantation colonies did not recognize slave families and deemed all offspring to be the owner's property. From predawn hours to sunset, slave labor was coerced. To compel obedience, overseers imposed mutilating punishments for perceived infractions. Uneasy white populations—who were outnumbered by slaves as much as twenty to one in some plantation colonies—used military, vigilante, and judicial tools to crush any hint of revolt, but slave rebellions were numerous. Taking their cue from Native Americans, who had resisted Europeans' first attempts at enslavement, blacks in Jamaica, Santo Domingo, and Brazil fled into nearby mountains and created well-armed fugitive societies that survived for decades and served as inspirations for those still in bondage.

In the sixteenth and seventeenth centuries, the plantation systems of the West Indies sugar colonies created the model for slave life on plantations in English North America. Scholars have only been able to infer how African traditions such as music were translated in the hostile New World plantation climate. They use the term *survivals* to indicate a "living" cultural transplant from Africa to America, and the term *syncretism* for the blending of compatible African, European, and Native American cultural traits. Until the 1930s, when the pioneering work of the anthropologist Melville Herskovits appeared, white scholars and others accepted the often ignorant or hostile testimony of white observers of slave music and culture, which they claimed were degraded imitations of European originals. Since Herskovits's revisionism, though, anthropologists, historians, and others have revealed the survival and adaptation of many elements of African culture in American slave societies.

They have found, for example, that music was central to whatever social life and free time that masters permitted slaves to enjoy. In fugitive communities such as Palaces in Brazil and Accompany in Jamaica, Africans could most freely express themselves musically. The polyrhythmic sophistication of African music and dance persisted, and call and response remained the standard organizing principle for musical performance. The intimate tie between music and spirituality remained strong. In Cuba, a popular religious cult called *Santería* fused Yoruba spirit worship and drumming with devotion to Catholic saints, while a similar Brazilian worship practice called *candomblé* drew upon the primarily monophonic (or unison) singing of the Yoruba tradition.

Due to the trauma of slavery, though, African music was almost never transplanted whole to America. The basic structures of Old World music and its essential value to human existence, as a spiritual art form that could revive weakened bodies and minds, persisted, but specific techniques, instruments, musical genres, and social contexts were usually lost in the transatlantic passage. On plantations in the Americas, slaves were forced to start from scratch, constructing new communities and identities and creating music and culture out of local circumstances and materials. Old World practices remained part of the blend, but memories of Africa receded with the advance of generations, the mixing of African groups, and the ever-increasing dominance of the immediate New World environment.

In Brazil, for example, while secular songs showed Bantu influences and spiritual folk music exhibited Yoruba qualities, the actual songs are purely Brazilian, the product of centuries of cultural mixing. While certain rhythmic features and scales—specifically, five- and seven-note scales—and round dances are of African origin, Brazilian drumming generally lacks the complexity and the sophisticated "talking drum" techniques found in West Africa. In addition, hundreds of indigenous groups in Brazil, from the Amazon to the grasslands, introduced the nose flute and many other elements to African slave music. Scholars argue that the main currents of Brazilian folk music are a blend of African and Native American traditions.

Similar dynamics were at work further north, in the Caribbean and Central America, in the 1600s and 1700s. Even in the early years of Spanish conquest, African laborers brought to Central America mingled with native peoples, intermarrying and creating racially mixed communities. On Cuba, Hispaniola, and Jamaica, though, disease almost completely wiped out all indigenous people, and the mix of cultures was largely Afro-European. African survivals among the slave populations blended with elite Spanish, French, and English cultures, but also with working-class European ways shaped by peasant life and indentured servitude (a form of temporary bondage suffered by some white migrants to the New World). As in Brazil and other plantation colonies, African slave culture in Cuba or Jamaica involved forms of creolization, a term used by scholars to describe the syncretism of African, European, and indigenous ways of life that created Caribbean culture. Plantation slave communities, runaway colonies, and small free black neighborhoods in island towns remained isolated enough to perpetuate distinct music, speech, social relations, and other practices, but most African slaves probably interacted with natives and whites. There never was a rigid barrier between black and white cultures in the Americas. In the Caribbean, European colonial "masters" adopted African words, gestures, methods of rice cultivation, and artisan skills. This blurring of racial lines would have an important influence on the history of African American music.

In the French colony of Saint Domingue, or Haiti, the melding of Catholicism and spirit beliefs created religious devotions similar to those in Cuba. The label *vodun*, from the Beninese word for spirits, became attached to one such practice. In the early 1700s, Haiti's cultural creolization spread to French settlements in North America, notably New Orleans, a prosperous port and the leading French Creole community in the New World. New Orleans law recognized *gens de couleur* (people of color) as a group with an intermediate status in society, which enjoyed some legal and economic rights. The Catholic leadership in Catholic Creole societies tolerated the intermarriage of blacks and whites, and while priests disparaged interracial offspring from extramarital relationships, they could not stop them from becoming a large and visible social class. In New Orleans, this social phenomenon ensured that the city possessed a Creole identity that British settlements in North America did not have, and which would give rise to unique black musical expressions.

Musical instruments and practices in the Caribbean displayed obvious African traits. A British observer found slaves in Jamaica using drums, "a box filled with pebbles, the jaw-bone of an animal," and "Caramantee-flutes . . . made from the porous branches of the trumpet-tree" to make music. He also witnessed a bow instrument that was plucked by hand and which resonated in the player's mouth—another African-style artifact. A witness in Jamaica noted the presence of "bonjoes, drums, and tomtoms." "Bonjoes," of course, would become one of Africa's most important contributions to U.S. music. Two- or three-stringed lutes from Senegambia with gourd bodies and animal skin faces were direct ancestors of the Caribbean banjo. Observers noticed the virtuosity of skilled early players. Caribbean plantation owners banned drumming and dancing by slaves for religious reasons and to prevent gatherings that might lead to rebellious plotting, and slaves also were forbidden to take part in the annual celebrations of Carnival. Such restrictions encouraged secret religious practices such as *Santería* and *vodun* and the music and dance they inspired. Still, in cities such as Havana, slaves and free blacks could sing, play, and dance a special sacred dance, the "tango congo," on Epiphany. African Americans were generally allowed to celebrate the completion of harvest. On the sugar plantations of Jamaica, "the negroes assembled in and around the boiling house, dancing and roaring for joy, to the sound of the gumba," a square drum, "in the true African fashions."[4]

SLAVERY AND MUSIC IN BRITISH NORTH AMERICA

At first glance, the social landscape of the British colonies in North America might not seem very similar to the Caribbean. In the 1700s and 1800s, the African slave trade directly supplied only a few of the black people who lived in the British colonies and later the United States. In the tobacco-rich Chesapeake region, English indentured servants made up the bulk of the workforce until the late 1600s. In cities such as New York and Philadelphia, slaves worked on docks and in trucking carts and taverns, not on plantations. After 1700, plantations in the Chesapeake, the Carolinas, and Georgia became reliant on black slave labor, but nearly all of these individuals were the product of unusually high natural increase and not the result of importation. In most of British North America, slaves were more often exposed to Protestant Christianity than to the Roman Catholicism that dominated the Caribbean. In northern cities, small free black communities prospered in a few trades and service industries, and they provided fragile models of a life beyond slavery.

Nevertheless, the British colonies were harsh slave societies that reproduced much of the dehumanization that was found further south. Racist attitudes and economic practices ensured that slaves and free black people alike would be social outcasts. Dealing more harshly with mixed-raced persons than their counterparts in Creole societies, the English and Dutch in North America imposed the "one-drop" rule that declared any individual with African blood to be a "negro."

Evidence of African American music in the thirteen British colonies indicates that this music shared some features of slave music in the West Indies, but also displayed some important differences. African instruments made their way to North America, as did Caribbean musical traits. Senegambian flutes and lutes appeared in Virginia before 1700, along with a drum whose head, in West African fashion, was tightened by cords and pegs. The banjo made its way to the Chesapeake Bay region, although it remained more prominent on plantations further south. One African American banjoist, as one of his lyrics put it, made his left hand "go like a handsaw" along the instrument's fretless fingerboard. A scholar has suggested that an instrumental trio common in Senegambia—involving a plucked lute, a bowed lute, and "a tapped calabash" or hollow squash gourd—was reconstituted in America as fiddle, banjo, and tambourine bands. In Virginia in the 1600s, black fiddlers apparently played on instruments made from gourds. As in the Caribbean, slaves danced surreptitiously, after work, and on Sundays—a fact that offended English clergymen. One noted that slaves danced on Sundays to bring rain, while another, the famed evangelist George Whitefield, complained to American planters about how slaves "prophaned the Lord's Day, by their Dancing, Piping and such like."[5]

Colonial African Americans were influenced somewhat by the music and culture of Native Americans. In the South, slave plantations often abutted the territory of indigenous people. Little is known of Native American influences on African American music before 1800, but similarities between the music of the two groups probably initiated the cross-fertilization that became more evident in later years. Like African music, Indian music commonly featured descending melodic lines, **pentatonic** or five-note scales, call and response singing, and the use of drums and rattles. By contrast, though, while Eastern Woodland Indians employed **antiphony** or call and response, they rarely created a heterophonic singing sound. They also usually strung together brief, repeated phrases, a practice rare in African music. Native Americans almost never used stringed instruments, and their dances differed dramatically from African models, in form if not in function. Still, blacks and Indians were often thrown together, and musical contact and mixing between the two groups was inevitable.

The slave population of the thirteen colonies grew explosively in the decades before the American Revolution. By 1776, one in four residents of the colonies—over a half a million people, almost all enslaved—were black. A natural environment that was far healthier than the Caribbean and a greater reproductive rate helped to stimulate a myth among whites that North American slavery was benign, an enlightened corrective to the lethal heat and harsh life of the tropics.

In the years leading to up to the Revolution, white and black colonists alike were subjected to a process of Americanization which alienated them profoundly from their Old World roots and provided them with the elements of a common culture. This process included a melding of white and black cultures. For many in plantation areas this melding began early, since white adults generally allowed their children to play with black counterparts until they reached puberty. White colonists across North America adapted the King's English to their local needs. This adaptation included incorporating African-derived words such as "tote" and "O.K." into the American language. Most enslaved people blended African syntax and English words into Black English. The African-influenced Gullah dialect, which flourished in the Georgia Sea Islands, was an exception to the general linguistic blending that took place.

The Great Awakening of the 1740s and 1750s—the series of evangelical Protestant religious revivals that rolled through the thirteen colonies—

played a crucial role in the creation of African American culture. Clergymen brought a new physicality, emotion, and spontaneous songfulness to preaching and to the behavior of congregations and revival-meeting crowds. In the southern colonies, slaves flocked to revivals. The evangelical phenomenon of the "second birth" in Christ evoked the Afro-Caribbean experience of possession by spirits. Preachers encouraged ecstatic bodily movements among possessed worshipers of all races. English hymns, which translated the majesty of the King James Bible to singable form, galvanized revival gatherings. As black people joined in the hymns at revivals—and as they encountered European song in other settings—they adopted measured time signatures, European major and minor **modes** or scales, and the harmonic progressions that were common to British hymns. Enslaved persons such as Newport Gardner of Newport, Rhode Island (a native of Africa), "Frank the Negro" of New York, and the Philadelphian John Cromwell attained the title of singing master and would lead their communities in the hymns of the Awakening.

European influences assisted in the emergence of African American vernacular or grass-roots musical culture. Afro-Caribbean influences such as *vodun* persisted only in the lower South, but elements of Creole culture also appeared in the North. Slaves celebrated "Negro election day" (in which black "candidates" were celebrated in parade) and Pinkster ceremonies (featuring dancing and singing) on colonial election days in New England and on Pentecost in New York, respectively. These resembled some Creole rituals, but African Americans in northern colonies generally were more acculturated to English styles and ways. In the late colonial era, black musicians became proficient in popular European instruments such as the fiddle, fife, and military drum, which were widely available and highly portable. These players became ubiquitous at celebrations, taverns, and military musterings and campaigns.

During the American Revolution and the early years of the new nation, thousands of African Americans served in the Continental Army and helped to found the new nation. The rhetoric of human rights and liberty rang in speeches, pamphlets, and newspapers and some northern states passed laws that provided for the gradual abolition of slavery. Free black communities especially reflected the optimism of African Americans at the outset of the founding of the nation. Like their white neighbors, black men and women formed voluntary associations to provide charity, social activities, and other forms of mutual aid. Black Masons, excluded from white mens' lodges, created their own chapters, which bore a rough similarity to the secret societies of West Africa.

The key development that shaped African American music in the new nation was the establishment of the first autonomous black churches. Discrimination by white Methodists encouraged black parishioners in Philadelphia, New York, and Baltimore to create their own churches, which became the nucleus of the African Methodist Episcopal (AME) denomination. In 1801, the Reverend Richard Allen, the major figure in the formation of the AME, published his own volume of Methodist hymn texts. Singing in the new churches seems to have been a revealing mixture of old and new styles. White attendees at AME services were struck by the "moaning" singing of parishioners, which probably derived from the **melismatic** singing that had migrated from Africa and the Caribbean. The tradition of call and response also was carried forward in the practice of "line reading," in which the minister read printed psalm verses and parishioners (often alternating between male and female) sang the lines in response. Some individual singers, moved by the spirit of the worship, also modified and personalized hymns. More genteel black ministers and deacons considered such variation an embarrassing lapse of formal church behavior and tried to prohibit it in their parishes. Other African American denominations in free black communities in the North and the South joined the AME in publishing hymnals and developing formal church music traditions.

BLACK MUSIC IN THE NEW REPUBLIC

African American optimism during the revolutionary era would, for the most part, be cruelly rebuffed. While slavery was phased out in the northern states, it gained a new vitality in the South thanks to the arrival of the cotton gin and the massive demand for cotton by the textile industry on both sides of the Atlantic. As their profits multiplied, the planter class came to view slavery not as a necessary evil, but as a positive force, the foundation of the prosperous cotton South.

Simultaneously, white people across the United States increasingly championed ideas that characterized black people as intellectually, biologically, and socially inferior. Educated white people used science and medicine to "prove" their assumptions about nonwhites' inferiority, while working-class whites rallied around claims of racial difference to deny jobs, housing, and social status to black rivals. The new racism of the late 1700s and early 1800s threatened the physical safety of African Americans, slave and free, and mocked the ideals of the American Revolution. The racial discrimination by white-controlled churches that gave birth to the AME was only one facet of the hostility to blacks found in American society. Northern states deprived free black men of the vote, forced them to post bond before taking residence, and legally segregated schools and public facilities. In the years immediately preceding 1861, when the Union collapsed from the political tensions over slavery, some black leaders expressed despair about the fate of African Americans, and plotted the emigration of free blacks to Canada and Africa.

The history of black music in this era offers powerful evidence of this new kind of oppression. In *Notes on the State of Virginia*, Thomas Jefferson noted the African origins of the "banjar" and paid tribute to black musicality: "In music they are more generally gifted than the whites with accurate ears for tune and time, and they have been found capable of imagining a small catch." Aside from this tribute, though, Jefferson showed no appreciation for African American creativity or intelligence. "Whether they will be equal to the composition of a more extensive run of melody, or of complicated harmony, is yet to be proved. . . . Never yet could I find that a black had uttered a thought above the level of plain narration; never see even an elementary trait of painting or sculpture. . . . Among the blacks is misery enough, God knows, but no poetry."[6] For half a century Jefferson retreated from his ringing declaration, "all men are created equal," claiming that slavery had reduced blacks to an unequal social condition that would take centuries to remedy. Jefferson's tribute to black musical abilities was typical of most white attitudes toward African Americans for the next eighty years: fascination with their music and alleged "incoherent" mentality coupled with a near-total denigration of their fitness for modern society and citizenship.

For African Americans, music served as a healing self-expression in the face of hostility. Additionally, after 1800, black performers increasingly used their talents to extract favors and payments from white listeners. This development was most evident in the North, where segregation and discrimination against free black people was accompanied by the first African American presence in the burgeoning music business.

Commercial music making grew with the young nation. In the early 1800s, American printers produced many hymnals, ballad broadsides, and other musical publications, but existing print technology kept quantities limited, and rudimentary transportation limited their distribution. Most printed music was imported from Europe. The War of 1812, accompanied by a British blockade of ports, cut the United States off from European printed matter and encouraged the growth of the domestic industry. In the 1820s, American music publishers came into prominence, aided by innovations in transportation—such as the steamboat, toll roads, canals, and later the railroad—new printing technology, and the growth of a piano-playing middle class. Simultaneously, as U.S. cities grew they became religiously diverse and more tolerant, and moralistic laws that banned stage performances were repealed. Singers and dancers catered to audiences of all classes. Meanwhile, small elite circles became intent on cultivating opera, choral singing, and other forms of classical music, to show that Americans could perform European compositions ably and also develop their own refined musical tradition.

Educated and prosperous urban African Americans patronized black classical performers such as the soprano Elizabeth Taylor Greenfield, the tenor Thomas Bowers, and the trumpet player and conductor Francis "Frank" Johnson. The AME and other churches produced concerts of sacred music, and some trained composers wrote classically inspired works. In addition to Johnson, who enjoyed an international career until his death in 1844, a few talented African American performers were among the first musical and dance celebrities of modern popular entertainment.

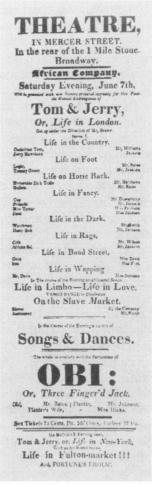

Photo 1.2. Broadside advertising free black musical performers at the African Grove Tavern, New York City, 1821. Source: Photographs and Prints Division, Schomburg Center for Research in Black Culture, The New York Public Library, Astor, Lenox and Tilden foundations.

These dignified performers struggled in the face of a new form of stage entertainment that was founded on the premises of racism: blackface minstrelsy. Minstrelsy's huge popularity after 1830 heralded the advent of the crude imitation and exploitation of African American music and dance by white performers. European performers and audiences had long been attracted to exotic nonwhite cultures, and white stage singers in America had blackened up their faces with burnt cork since the 1780s. The practice attained new popularity, though, when Thomas D. Rice introduced the song "Jump Jim Crow" in 1828. Rice claimed to have based his Jim Crow persona on the singing and dancing of a handicapped black performer he had observed on a river boat. This persona was caricatured further by white imitators, who honed the image of the carefree, uneducated black man who mangled the English language and engaged in grotesque stage dancing and skits. Employing elementary, but appealing bits of **syncopation** in their melodies, song composers such as Stephen Foster provided the minstrel stage with energetic musical material. The minstrel show congealed into a two-act formula involving dancing, singing, skits, and exchanges between the master of ceremonies or "interlocutor" and a corps of minstrels. Minstrelsy was popular among working-class whites, especially Irish immigrants, who enjoyed both the symbolic humiliation of blacks, who competed with them for jobs, and the feeling of liberation from conventional manners that the wild singing and dancing expressed. Northern cities, the sites of antiblack riots and segregation laws, were the natural homes of blackface minstrelsy, but the genre spread nationwide, creating a powerful new caricature of African American culture and music.

Before the Civil War, only one African American performer became a star of the minstrel stage, conquering it with his sheer dancing talent. William Henry Lane, a native of Rhode Island, was still in his teens when he became the dancing sensation of New York City minstrelsy. Lane was known to white audiences largely by his rather ironic stage name, Master Juba. In 1842, during his American tour, British novelist Charles Dickens witnessed Master Juba's performance in Manhattan. The "lively young negro," Dickens later wrote, was "the greatest dancer known." To the accompaniment of a fiddle and a tambourine, Juba performed the "single shuffle, double shuffle, cut and cross-cut; snapping his fingers, rolling his eyes, turning in his knees, presenting the backs of his legs in front, spinning about on his toes and heels like nothing but the man's fingers on the tambourine; dancing with two left legs, two right legs, two wooden legs, two wire legs, two spring legs. . . . He finishes by leaping gloriously on the bar-counter, and calling for something to drink. . . . "[7] Master Juba helped to invent modern tap dancing, which blended Irish and black dance styles. Black dancers nationwide referred to the virtuosic, high-stepping dance movements as "pattin' Juba." Lane gained international fame by touring Europe and appearing before royalty. He settled in London just prior to his death in 1852. Master Juba's career indicated that despite white prejudice, black people with unique abilities to adapt African music or dance to modern popular entertainment could achieve extraordinary fame and have great cultural influence.

SLAVE MUSIC IN THE ANTEBELLUM SOUTH

In the decades before the Civil War, the culture and music that served as the purported inspiration for blackface minstrelsy remained rooted in the southern states. Ninety percent of African Americans lived in the southern slave states. All but one-tenth of these three and a half million people lived in slavery. Virtually all of them were born in the United States. Across the Cotton Belt stretching from North Carolina to Texas, most slaves resided on large plantations, but many also lived on small farms or in cities, where they worked as laborers, artisans, or servants. The vast majority of white southerners owned no slaves at all, but they also imbibed the intoxicating myth of white racial superiority and endorsed slave ownership as the best path to individual economic advancement. A few thousand free African Americans also owned slaves, often spouses or children they had purchased from whites.

White and black observers recorded the life and culture of the slaves in the antebellum era. Even sympathetic whites such as abolitionists usually rendered Black English in a degrading manner and rarely transcended racist attitudes and preconceptions. Still, white observers often captured the vitality of slave culture—and especially black music—under the heel of oppression. This fact reflected the central paradox of the slave South. Enslaved people were chattel and property under the law, but even judges and legislators were compelled to admit that they were human, possessed of free will, and were accorded a right to the provisions of life. When whites observed slaves creating, feeling, and communing, they were confronted with the ambiguity surrounding the slave—a "thing" with a will, a subdued being who had the potential to act. This ambiguity made whites confused and uneasy.

Music, like all aspects of slave life, came under white regulation. Since the 1600s planters had been convinced that slaves used drumming as a code to spread calls to insurrection over long distances. Laws in the West Indies banned the "talking drums" of recent African arrivals and restricted mass gatherings of slaves. After the Stono Rebellion of 1739—the largest slave rebellion ever to take place in British North America—South Carolina passed a similar law, prohibiting slaves' use of "drums, horns, or other loud instruments, which may call together, or give sign or notice to one another of their wicked designs or purposes."[8] By the 1800s all slave states had such laws. Tensions stirred by the discovery of various slave insurrection plots, as well as exaggerated fears of northern abolitionism, created a virtual paranoia among southern whites about potential slave insurrections. Owners and overseers increasingly monitored slaves during their leisure hours.

No study of slave music, and very few transcriptions of songs and other melodies, appeared in America before the Civil War. Nevertheless, observations by curious northern and European white visitors, contemporary illustrations, and narratives of escaped slaves provide a rich portrait of southern African American music in the antebellum era. This music was constantly changing. The slave South was a large and varied region, and African and West Indian arrivals continued to introduce new cultural expressions. Nevertheless, by the 1800s chattel slavery, plantation agriculture, and Protestantism had helped to shape an identifiable slave culture and music that was distinct from that of the Caribbean. No contemporary observer failed to note the differences between the two traditions.

Slavery was by definition a labor system, and slaves were usually forced to work six long days every week. In the South, work songs became a central component of the forced labor and a much more central part of musical culture than they had been in Africa. Not all slaves worked in the cotton fields. Dock workers, rowers and paddlers, factory employees, and masons created their occupation-specific variants of agricultural work songs. The creative shouts of slave stevedores, who bellowed improvised verses to fit the rhythm of their back-breaking work on the docks, especially interested observers. Most work songs, however, emanated from the plantations. In many instances plantation slaves were forced to sing against their will to the same extent that they were compelled to work for no pay. Overseers and their team bosses, who were often slaves themselves, often considered silent workers to be conspiratorial and believed that singing on the job improved their productivity and morale. Due to this coercion, the "**field holler**" or "shout" did not merely provide rhythmic assistance to the performance of monotonous work. It also was laced with cries of despair. As Frederick Douglass—the escaped slave who became the leading black abolitionist—memorably said of slaves, "it is a great mistake to suppose them happy because they sing. The songs of the slave represent the sorrow, rather than the joys, of his heart; and he is relieved by them, only as an aching heart is relieved by tears."[9]

Whether or not whites coerced slaves to sing, field hollers and shouts did divert their thoughts from the drudgery of plucking cotton, threshing grain, swinging picks and axes, and countless other field labors, and they became a fertile genre of black music. Call and response, in which the leader creates one to three lines of verse and is met with a chorus-like response, was widely practiced. Some borrowed stories from popular trickster tales, telling of the exploits of Br'er Rabbit and other animals who outwitted powerful oppressors. Other chants, in which the chorus might precede the leader, blended Biblical imagery with references to local and contemporary conditions. Old Testament figures such as Moses who had led people out of bondage figured heavily in field hollers. Many work songs, though, expressed a loss of hope and a sense of exhaustion and spiritual abandonment. Hollers that protested the agonies of work and bondage strikingly subverted overseers' demands that they sing optimistically. They confirmed Frederick Douglass's observation about "sorrow songs," as well as a former slave's assertion that her favorite work song "can't be sung without a full heart and a troubled spirit."[10] Thousands of persons sold to new masters west of Appalachia made their treks on foot in shackled coffles; they too sang intensely and at length about their miseries. No recordings and few transcriptions of slave work song melodies exist. If nineteenth-century examples were similar to the field hollers that were recorded after 1900, though, they would have exhibited African and Caribbean musical qualities such as pentatonic scales and melismatic sliding between notes.

Special seasonal events also inspired work songs. For the December corn shuckings, groups of local slaves traveled to various plantations under the eyes of overseers to tear off the husks of corn, an operation that took several days at each locale. The shuckings became a holiday occasion for wealthy whites, who gathered on the porches to picnic and listen to the slaves' songs. One white witness heard the singing of an approaching shucking team "more than a mile" away, commenting that they "make the forest ring with their music." During the shucking "I was never more amused than while watching their movements and listening to their songs." The verbal creativity of the work leader would evoke folk tales, the Bible, and often the social event itself:

All them pretty girls will be there, / [chorus] Shuck that corn before you eat.
They will fix it for us rare, / Shuck that corn before you eat.
I know that supper will be big, / Shuck that corn before you eat.
I think I smell a fine roast pig, / Shuck that corn before you eat.
A supper is provided, so they said, / Shuck that corn before you eat.
I hope they'll have some nice wheat bread, / Shuck that corn before you eat. (etc.)[11]

Such light-hearted lyrics hint at what slaves might have sung when they were *not* working. Sundays were rest days for almost all slaves, and dance and other secular music was as likely to be heard then as spirituals and other sacred music—although in many cases, devout masters forbade slave dancing as sacrilegious. Many plantation owners recognized that Sunday recreation helped slaves to be better workers during

the rest of the week. Some owners even made sure that a fiddler or banjoist was included in the workforce, and helped to provide them with instruments. White observers and illustrators, though, usually noted that
fiddles and banjos, made out of gourds and wood and strung with cat
entrails, and percussive instruments made from wood, bone, and stones
most commonly accompanied song and dance. Percussion playing
blended with dancing that featured hand-slapping on thighs and other
parts of the body—the "pattin' Juba" style that William Henry Lane
popularized on the minstrel stage. The fragmentary evidence indicates
that singing and dancing on such occasions drew from white lyrics and
dances (the latter including the jig and the hornpipe), but also bore the
unmistakable African American body movements and steps, such as
jerking or shuffling, as well as call and response and other musical elements. Song collections that appeared after the Civil War indicate that
songs borrowed plots from trickster tales and satirized the manners of
masters, and that slave children had their own genres of "play-party"
singing.

Masters and other whites often intruded upon the slaves' music making and dancing. Enslaved people always suffered from a lack of privacy
and basic disrespect for their family and community life. As a result,
songs sung in front of whites, describing the wily escapes of Br'er Rabbit
and Moses's defiance of Pharaoh's bondage, indicated that slaves expressed rebellious thoughts in coded lyrics and musical messages. Just as
blackface minstrelsy expressed latent white anxieties about coexisting
with free urban African Americans, coded slave songs indicated black
anger at "the peculiar institution" and the desire for a life of freedom and
free expression. These "codes" persisted and evolved long after slavery
was abolished, and continue to shape black music today.

Practitioners and scholars alike label the African American skill at expressing multiple meanings in songs and stories as **"signifying"** or **"signifyin."** The skill had deep roots in trickster tales, insult songs, and other
African American expressions (which had African origins), and it
emerged repeatedly in U.S. slave music to mystify white listeners. In a
memorable instance, in 1838 the British actress Fanny Kemble was puz-
zled when slave boat rowers at her husband's plantation in Georgia sang

Jenny shake her toe at me, / Jenny gone away.
Hurrah! Miss Susy, oh! / Jenny gone away.

"What the obnoxious Jenny meant by shaking her toe, whether defiance
or mere departure, I never could ascertain, but her going away was an unmistakable source of satisfaction," Kemble wrote. "I have never yet heard
the Negroes . . . sing any words that could be said to have any sense." The

scholar Chadwick Hansen has determined that the rowers—who were probably recent migrants from the West Indies—actually were using the African word *to*, of Kikongo origin, which generally means "body part or member" but specifically refers to "buttocks." Jenny, in short, was not shaking her toe. The rowers' "satisfaction," relayed to Fanny Kemble's party with "a good deal of dramatic and musical effect," apparently derived from their covert expression of provocative female sexuality in front of a genteel white woman.[12]

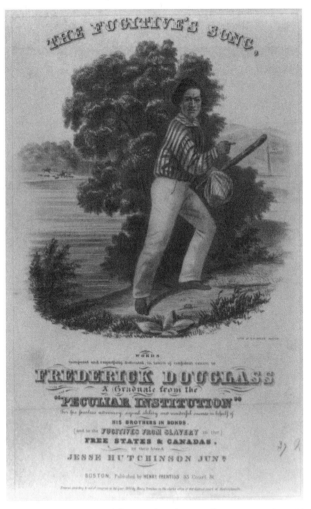

Photo 1.3. Sheet music inspired by Frederick Douglass's *Narrative*, 1847. Source: Prints and Photographs Division, Library of Congress.

The evidence indicates that there was a substantial quantity, and range, of secular music in antebellum slave life. Coupled with the rich song, dance, and concert music traditions that developed among free African American performers and communities in towns and cities across the United States, this secular music formed the basis for the black popular music genres that emerged in the next century. For decades after the Civil War, though, influential white advocates of African American music tended to argue that slave music consisted only of spirituals.

Black spirituals were an identifiable genre of sacred music, indigenous to the slave South, which expressed African Americans' emotional and sacred yearnings in an extraordinary manner. Spirituals originated when African American slaves borrowed from Baptist and Methodist hymnody. They combined lines and memorable phrases from hymns with their own favorite Biblical parables and folk legends. Slave preachers often broke into song during their sermons, repeating key phrases and lessons in a manner that evolved into makeshift call and response hymns. Scholars have named this genre of sermons **homiletic spirituals**. This creative reworking of standard hymns echoed the verbal skill of **griots** and other song specialists of West Africa.

More than any other variety of slave music, the spirituals won the attention and admiration of white listeners. Some of these listeners, convinced that they were witnessing the birth of an important genre of American music, carefully recorded the lyrics of spirituals, and some even notated the basic tunes. While whites usually overheard the spirituals during slave labor in the fields, the songs undoubtedly meant the most to slaves as an expression during their leisure time on Sundays and holidays. In mostly quiet rural settings, the mournful and rich singing carried along the valleys and over the hills and resounded hauntingly in listeners' memories. Like work songs, many of the spirituals were "sorrow songs," Biblical expressions of grief, longing, and supplication that were all too applicable to the slave's life. The famed titles of some of them convey these deep sentiments: "Sometimes I Feel Like a Motherless Child," "Trouble in Mind," "O Rocks, Don't Fall on Me," "And the Moon Will Turn to Blood," "I've Been Rebuked and I've Been Scorned," and "Let My People Go."

The early published collections notated spirituals as simple and unadorned songs. This practice obscured the fact that each spiritual was sung in many different ways across the South. As even the collectors noted, slaves rarely sang in unison, but entered the song at different points and created overlapping renditions of the melody. This reveals the transmission of **heterophony** from African vocal music to the singing of African Americans in the antebellum South. Sympathetic listeners such as the white poet Sidney Lanier were thrilled when individuals stretched syllables and emotionally embroidered the basic melody. As in African and Caribbean music, clapping and vocal interjections enhanced the elevation of the group's spirits. The release of tensions often occurred in the "jubilee" songs, a genre roughly opposite from the sorrow spirituals. Jubilee songs celebrated the Hebrews' release from bondage, Jesus's resurrection, and other triumphant tales from scripture, or provided more general feelings of elation. "Swing Low, Sweet Chariot," "Roll, Jordan, Roll," "My Lord, What a Morning," and "Sabbath Has No End" represented the powerful sentiments of the jubilee repertoire.

Although the spirituals were praised by many white listeners, they were part of a religious expression by slaves that many masters sought to suppress. Widespread slave participation in revivals and camp meetings continued into the 1800s, but in the wake of slave revolts in the Caribbean and the United States, southern state governments increasingly restricted preaching, singing, and assemblies by free and enslaved black people. The fact that Nat Turner, the leader of America's deadliest slave revolt, was a preacher added to the fear that slave religion was inherently abolitionist. On the plantations, therefore, expressions of faith went underground. Sunday services, baptisms, and even weddings and funerals, which were major events in slave culture and contained strong African overtones, took place in forests, swamps, and other hidden places out of the earshot of the slave owners.

Especially in these clandestine settings, known as "hush arbor," Afro-Caribbean religious traditions thrived. The most important of these was the "**ring shout**," a singing and dancing ritual that usually followed a formal Christian service. "Shouting" in black music encompassed both the pain-filled hollers of the laborer in the fields and the cries of exultation that may accompany the release of the spirit through dance and communal participation. Shouts are one of the main devices that link verbal and musical inflections in African and African American musical traditions. Dancing in a circle, in shuffling or in elaborate steps, taking care not to cross their legs as in secular dance, members of the slave community used ring shouts to situate Biblical stories in African American culture. Since drums were banned by law, slaves used bones, wood, pattin' Juba (hands on the hips and thighs), and the heavy treading of their feet to supply the hypnotic rhythm. As in revival meetings, some participants were overcome with the spirit and fell unconscious. More than any other musical expression in slavery, the ring shout revealed the powerful, often latent survival of the African foundations of slave music and rituals.

Spirituals, ring shouts, and work songs that mocked white masters were profound expressions of the discontent and rebelliousness that led thousands of slaves to escape the South by means of the Underground Railroad. Articulate former slaves turned abolitionists such as Frederick Douglass and William Wells Brown vividly described the horrors of the "peculiar institution" and won northern white converts to abolitionism. In their lectures to pious whites, Douglass and Brown often cited the spirituals as evidence of the slaves' Christian faith and humility. As the abolitionists fought a seemingly hopeless battle in the 1840s and 1850s, they continued to present a simplistic view of slaves and their music, emphasizing a sentimental image of piety and sorrow. The variety and richness of slave music would only begin to emerge after the Civil War destroyed slavery and offered African Americans some avenues for free and open expression.

The music of the slaves and free African Americans before the Civil War was a rich testament to an ancient, resilient, and transatlantic heritage. Even while the slave owners' empire seemed unassailable, spirituals and field hollers spoke of freedom and the liberation of souls. Even as laws and social institutions strove to bind human beings as property and deprive them of a social existence, music helped them to re-create semblances of their ancestral communities and to retain their fundamental cultural rituals. In slave quarters and in the cities, music was at the center of black identity. After the Civil War, African Americans sought to take advantage of freedom, and their music achieved a new national prominence. Dangers and oppression persisted, but great change occurred, and the future would never again seem without promise.

NOTES

1. Mungo Park, *Travels in the Interior of Africa* (London: W. Bulmer, 1799), chap. 24.

2. Park, *Travels in the Interior of Africa*, chap. 9.

3. Orlando Patterson, *Slavery and Social Death: A Comparative Study* (Cambridge, MA: Harvard University Press 1982).

4. William Beckford, *A Descriptive Account of the Island of Jamaica* (London, 1790), I:217–218; *Lady Maria Nugent's Journal of Her Residence in Jamaica from 1801 to 1805*, ed. Philip Wright (Kingston, Jamaica: University Press of the West Indies, 2002), 218; and a quote in Dena J. Epstein, *Sinful Tunes and Spirituals: Black Folk Music to the Civil War* (Urbana: University of Illinois Press, 2003), 53.

5. Quotes are from Gerhard Kubik, *Africa and the Blues* (Jackson: University Press of Mississippi, 1999), 8–9, 11.

6. Thomas Jefferson, *Notes on the State of Virginia*, ed. David Waldstreicher (New York: Bedford, 2002), 177.

7. Charles Dickens, *Notes on America* (1842), quoted in Eileen Southern, *The Music of Black Americans*, 3rd ed. (New York: Norton, 1997), 95.

8. Quoted in Epstein, *Sinful Tunes and Spirituals*, 59.

9. Frederick Douglass, *Narrative of the Life of Frederick Douglass, an American Slave* (1845; New York: Barnes & Noble, 2005), 30.

10. Quoted in Southern, *The Music of Black Americans*, 166.

11. Mrs. R. H. Marshall, "A Negro Corn-shucking" (1852), quoted in Roger D. Abrahams, *Singing the Master: The Emergence of African-American Culture in the Plantation South* (New York: Pantheon, 1992), 229.

12. Fanny Kemble, *Journal of a Residence on a Georgian Plantation in 1838–1839* (Athens: University of Georgia Press, 1984), 163; see also Chadwick Hansen, "Jenny's Toe Revisited: White Responses to Afro-American Shaking Dances," *American Music* 5 (1987), 1–19.

2

Jubilee and Tin Pan Alley

Contrasting Sounds of Freedom

In the decades from the Civil War to 1900, African American music displayed a people's extraordinary pride and promise, but it also reflected
their suffering under continuing victimization. The dreams of emancipa-
tionists were at best only partly fulfilled and black musicians—whether
they were elite concert artists, church singers, or popular performers or
composers—had to reckon with persistent white prejudice, violence, and
segregation. The distortion and exploitation of black music by white performers and audiences that began in antebellum minstrelsy intensified in
the postwar years. These years, though, also brought an expansion of the
ranks of celebrated and commercially successful African American performers and composers, as well as praise for black music from influential
white musicians who considered it to be an essential expression of American culture. These contrasting trends of the late 1800s set the stage for the
dramatic evolution of black popular, sacred, and concert music in the
early decades of the twentieth century.

THE JUBILEE

The beginning of the Civil War inspired a thrill of anticipation among
African Americans, slave and free. Although Abraham Lincoln repeatedly
insisted that the war had nothing to do with slavery, in the North would-
be black soldiers drilled in city squares, and in the South, advancing
Union forces were met by slaves who had deserted their masters in
droves to assist the Yankee cause. The duels between the major armies

ground on for years, along and between the vast valleys of the Mississippi's eastern watershed and the Virginia Tidewater region. These campaigns displaced hundreds of thousands of enslaved people from Memphis to the Potomac. Expressing both their rich traditions and the excitement of rapidly changing times, the refugees made the "contraband" camps reverberate with sacred and secular song. The camps were overcrowded and undersupplied, and many Union officers and soldiers were openly hostile to the escaped slaves—difficulties that suggested the hard road ahead facing the freed people. When the war ended some even returned to the plantations they had fled, reassured by familiar sights and faces and hopeful that their former masters would afford them respect.

The Union's naval blockade of the Confederacy and subsequent invasions of its major ports had brought northern troops to the Virginia coast and into the Deep South, to New Orleans and the Carolina and Georgia shores. Here, more than anywhere else, white and black abolitionists began immediate and radical experiments in creating free societies. While northerners attempted to construct free black farming communities, complete with schools, churches, and businesses for the former slaves—most notably in Port Royal, South Carolina, and Hampton Roads, Virginia—they were exposed to the power and vitality of music in slave culture. One white observer in Louisiana in 1862, for example, was struck by the "melodic speech" heard in a black congregation, where the newly liberated slave "pours out a stream of words as fast as he can utter them, or rather *sing* them, for the voice rises and falls in the cadence of a rude song, the congregation accompanying his voice, the men in a groaning voice and the women and children in all sorts of wailings and whinings."[1]

In the Sea Islands of South Carolina and Georgia, the Union's invasion vanguard came into contact with a unique African American community. The Gullah dialect, widespread fictive kinship—in which non-blood relations became "family"—and fine handcrafts struck observers as novel, but the music of the Sea Islands made the strongest impression on them. Charlotte Forten of Philadelphia, a black abolitionist, and the white Colonel Thomas Wentworth Higginson of Boston began to record "spirichels"—a term for sacred songs of the islands that would come to designate all religious slave songs. Higginson commanded the 1st South Carolina Volunteers, the first unit of freedman soldiers in the Union army. He recalled that during one night in camp, "a feeble flute stir[red] somewhere in some tent, not an officer's,—a drum throb[bed] far away in another." A ring shout took place in "a regular native African hut, . . . crammed with men, singing at the top of their voices, in one of their quaint, monotonous, endless, negro-Methodist chants, with obscure syllables recurring constantly," while they stamped their feet and clapped their hands in rhythm. Dances begin "monotonously round some one in the centre; some 'heel and toe' tumultuously, others merely tremble and stagger on, others stoop and rise, others whirl, others caper sideways, all keep steadily circling like dervishes."[2] Freed people concocted their own lyrics for the soldier's tune "John Brown's Body," instead of using Julia Ward Howe's popular setting, "The Battle Hymn of the Republic."

In 1862, hoping to turn the tide of the war, Abraham Lincoln allowed black soldiers to take arms and transformed the war into a crusade against slavery. His announcement of the preliminary Emancipation Proclamation in September created waves of anticipation among African Americans everywhere. Religious freed people welcomed the event as the long-awaited jubilee, God's response to their prayers. The news was greeted in contraband camps with songs of faith and joy. On New Year's Day, 1863, when the proclamation took effect, the 1st South Carolina and local African Americans on the Sea Islands held a gala ceremony and feast. As Colonel Thomas Higginson waved an American flag, an elderly black man and two women began an impromptu rendition of "My Country, 'Tis of Thee" "so simple, so touching . . . it gave the keynote to the whole day. Firmly and irrepressibly the quavering voices sang on, verse after verse; others of the colored people joined in. . . . I never saw anything so electric; it made all other words cheap; it seemed the choked voice of a race at last unloosed."[3]

Like other wars before it, the Civil War featured military bands that accompanied soldiers during marches and goaded them into battle. African American drum, bugle, and flute players were represented in both the Union and Confederate army band ranks. Black musicians playing for rebel armies were required by Confederate law to be paid—an unusual provision for slave laborers in the South. African American music and singing greeted the advance of Union armies in many southern cities and towns. When General William Sherman's soldiers captured Savannah, Georgia in December 1864, black residents sang, "Glory be to God, we are free!" In January 1865 the U.S. Congress passed the Thirteenth Amendment to the Constitution, abolishing slavery, and in the following weeks the Union completed the conquest of the Confederacy. The collapse of Robert E. Lee's army and the fall of the Confederate capitol of Richmond, Virginia inspired a final musical celebration by newly freed black people. Ecstatic men still behind bars in Lumpkin's slave auction pen in Richmond sang, "Slavery chain done broke at last . . . I's goin' to praise God till I die," and were joined by blacks on the outside, who liberated them. Others in the streets sang "Richmond town is burning down, High diddle diddle inctum inctum ah."[4] The next day the visiting President Lincoln was greeted by freed people with wild cheers and jubilee songs.

Emancipation would affect the course of African American music in the South in deep and unexpected ways. In the weeks and months after the fall of slavery, four million freed people transformed their lives. They traveled across the South to reunite families that had been broken up by slave sales. They replaced "slave names" with first and last names of their own choosing. They sought paid employment and the rudiments of education, and they built their own communities. "We have progressed a century in a year," the northern black missionary Jonathan Gibbs exulted.[5]

New African American churches proliferated. In addition to serving as musical centers for free black communities, they were also political, social, and charitable institutions. Ministers such as Henry Turner, who later became the AME bishop in Georgia, became model "race men"—tireless, principled, and eloquent defenders of black people's rights and dignity in American society. Their example of black masculinity became a model for political and legal activists. New laws, they argued, must provide African American men with paid work, their own homes and farms, legal marriages and parenthood, and the vote. The emphasis on manhood explains why the Fifteenth Amendment to the Constitution, ratified in 1870, protected the vote for black men, but not for women of any color.

An interesting difference arose between two groups of black churches, a difference that helped to shape African American religious music after the Civil War. Many congregations kept the folk religion of slavery alive. In many AME and Methodist churches, Sunday gatherings began with a formal service, in which an elder "deaconed" a hymn, reading two lines at a time, which the congregation repeated. Often, still, according to the white observer William Francis Allen, when this service was over a ring shout followed: "the benches are pushed back to the wall, . . . old and young . . . all stand up in the middle of the floor, and . . . the 'sperichil' is struck up." However, some southern black ministers, influenced by the white middle-class Protestants who brought charity and schools to their communities, rejected the ring shout. Believing that the former slaves had to be "lifted up" to the cultural level of genteel middle-class whites and blacks, these churchmen advocated formal sacred singing as part of a strict new code of church behavior and morality. As early as 1867 Allen observed that spirituals were "going out of use on the plantations" of the Sea Islands and being replaced in some churches by more formal hymn singing. That same year Harriet Beecher Stowe regretted that black church singing was becoming "a closer imitation of white, genteel worship . . . solemn, dull, and nasal."[6]

William Francis Allen did not merely observe changes in postwar black sacred music; he also played a central role in notating and publicizing it. From 1863 to 1865, Allen, Charlotte Forten Grimké, Lucy McKim Garrison, and Charles Pickward Ware compiled an extensive portfolio of slave songs, and in 1867 they published *Slave Songs of the United States*, the first collection of its kind. Allen's preface intelligently differentiated slave songs from the "spurious imitations" of minstrelsy and attempted to tease out the Africanisms in various texts and musical qualities. He identified heterophony by noting that "there is no singing in *parts*, as we understand it, and yet no two [people] appear to be singing the same thing." Allen also cautioned that while most of the ninety songs in the collection were "taken down by the editors from the lips of the colored people themselves," the transcriptions are "but a faint shadow of the original. The voices of the colored people have a peculiar quality that nothing can imitate; and the intonations and delicate variations of even one singer cannot be reproduced on paper. And I despair of conveying any notion of the effect of a number singing together."[7]

Slave Songs and similar collections that followed it, such as Thomas P. Fenner's *Cabin and Plantation Songs*, made black songs, especially spirituals, conform to white middle-class tastes. In published form, spirituals exhibited only hints of the pentatonic scales, syncopation, and heterophony that could be heard in southern black singing. Their presentation on paper made them more accessible to middle-class whites, who considered even the simplified versions of the tunes to be exotic and fascinating. In addition, in the uncertain years after the war, when no one could safely predict future race relations, this simplification of African American music helped many white Americans to perceive black culture as genteel and nonthreatening. For similar reasons whites often rendered southern black dialect comically, as in the version of the Uncle Remus tales published by the white Atlanta journalist Joel Chandler Harris.

The Fisk University Jubilee Singers rose to fame within this context. Colleges were second in importance only to the church in representing southern African American aspirations in the aftermath of the Civil War. These colleges strove to train the black educators who would prepare the four million freed people for the future. Fisk University in Nashville, Tennessee was a modest and struggling institution, existing from year to year on the verge of bankruptcy. In 1871, George L. White, a white northerner who was the school's treasurer and music instructor, with the assistance of Ella Sheppard, a former slave who was a Fisk student and a pianist, honed the school's glee club into a fund-raising attraction. The nine men and women in the choir—seven of whom were former slaves—first appeared in churches near Nashville, where they performed songs from the classical repertoire.

Prior to this, no African American vocal ensemble had ever appeared in a formal concert setting. Rampant white hostility discouraged George White from continuing local engagements and led him to plan a long tour through the northern states, which he thought might be more amenable to black performers. However, discrimination and prejudice also met the Jubilee Singers in the North, and months of meager concert earnings and

The Nine Jubilee Singers who left Fisk University. October 6, 1871.

Minnie Tate. Green Evans. Isaac Dickerson. Jennie Jackson. Maggie Porter. Thos Rutling. Ella Sheppard. Benj. M. Holmes. Eliza Walker.

Photo 2.1. The Fisk Jubilee Singers. Source: General Research and Reference Division, Schomburg Center for Research in Black Culture, The New York Public Library, Astor, Lenox and Tilden foundations.

wearisome traveling took a toll on the students' spirits and health. Near the end of 1871, though, the Singers' fortunes changed. The group had been singing published spirituals only as encores at the conclusion of concerts. For an appearance at Oberlin College in Ohio, though, White and Sheppard decided to present an entire concert of spirituals. The audience, largely consisting of white ministers, responded enthusiastically, and invitations from churches across the North began to pour in. A triumphant appearance at the Reverend Henry Ward Beecher's prestigious Plymouth Congregational Church in Brooklyn, New York, brought the Jubilee Singers national renown. In 1872, the group performed at the White House before President Ulysses S. Grant, and they then visited Great Britain, where they sang for Queen Victoria. At the end of their tour the Singers returned to Nashville with $50,000 in earnings. The money financed the construction of Jubilee Hall, a fortress-like building at the center of Fisk University that was designed to protect students and teachers from the local Ku Klux Klan.

Like the white editors of the first spirituals collections, the Fisk Jubilee Singers simplified slave songs. They also arranged them in multipart harmony that conformed to European classical music. Most of the spirituals' Afro-Caribbean characteristics, such as call and response, heterophony, and pentatonic scales, were eliminated, and the song texts steered clear of any hint of despair or protest. The Singers' presentation of the spirituals was perhaps the most notable example in the 1870s of freed people conforming to the cultural values of the white middle class. Approving white observers claimed that the Singers were helping to "lift up" the entire African American race. The Singers appeared in idealistic settings such as the World Peace Jubilee, a festival in Boston that featured tens of thousands of performers. The group's success bred imitation, as many spirituals choirs, some of them from other black colleges such as Hampton Institute, others passing themselves off as bogus "Fisk Jubilee Singers," began to tour the United States. The Fisk ensemble made additional tours of North America and Europe and continued to raise money for the university until 1878, when the exhausted George White and Ella Sheppard suspended most of its operations.

In addition to spirituals, African Americans expressed the message of racial uplift through concert music. "Classical" music, which had originated in the cathedrals and courts of Europe, was promoted by genteel nineteenth-century critics and educators as the music of intellectual and spiritual cultivation, and the middle classes in America, white and black, followed their lead. In 1821, black performers in Manhattan opened a concert garden called the African Grove, and in the 1840s, New Orleans's Creoles of color performed French opera in the Théâtre de la Renaissance. In the 1870s, short-lived black-run opera houses operated in Washington,

D.C. and Brooklyn. The bandleader Walter Craig became a mainstay of white and black high society functions in Manhattan for more than four decades. Elizabeth Taylor Greenfield and other antebellum African American concert singers had embarked on tours, and after the Civil War their examples were followed by the sopranos Marie Williams, Mamie Flowers, and Ann and Emma Hyers, and the tenor Sidney Woodward. Most notable in this postwar group was the soprano Sisieretta Jones, a gifted native of Virginia who grew up in Rhode Island and received conservatory training. The vogue for black classical recitalists peaked in the early 1890s, when Jones performed at the White House.

A pioneering African American writer, James Monroe Trotter, promoted black concert musicians by advocating cultural uplift through classical music. Trotter's life story dramatically summarized recent black history. After his family escaped from slavery in Mississippi, he served with distinction in the Union army during the Civil War and afterward became a respected civil servant in Boston. In 1878, Trotter published the first history of music in the United States, *Music and Some Highly Musical People*. In a reflection of Trotter's endorsement of black integration with the genteel white middle class, the first part of his book barely mentions African Americans. Instead it explores "the beauty, power, and uses of music" and advocates its cultivation in America. The second part of the book chronicles the activities of black concert singers, bandleaders, pianists, choruses, opera companies, and pedagogues, roaming from Portland, Maine to New Orleans, through byways such as Chillicothe, Ohio, and Helena, Arkansas. Trotter only briefly alluded to the obstacles presented to these musicians "by color-prejudice, the extent of whose terrible, blighting power none can ever imagine that do not actually meet it."[8] *Music and Some Highly Musical People* displays Trotter's fierce pride and optimism, molded by his extraordinary passage from slavery to freedom, social respectability, and political prominence.

Trotter's sentiments were echoed by a distinguished musician from Europe, whose visit to the United States would transform the opinions of many whites and blacks about the potential of African American music. As native of Bohemia, Antonín Dvořák had risen from modest origins to become one of the most celebrated composers of his day. In 1892, he accepted an offer to become the first director of the National Conservatory of Music in New York City. Among Dvořák's best students were gifted African American musicians, including Will Marion Cook and especially Harry Burleigh, who performed many spirituals for the composer. Captivated by the hints of Africa and the rich emotion in the music, Dvořák spoke words to a reporter that immediately became famous: "I am now satisfied that the future music of this country must be founded upon what are called negro melodies. These are the folk songs of America, and your composers must turn to them. . . . In the negro melodies of America I discover all that is needed for a great and noble school of music."[9]

Dvořák did not make an idle statement. He had studied black music, as well as Native American music, as closely as he could, given the total lack of scholarship on the subject at the time. He included some of the elements of both styles in his own compositions written in the United States, such as the symphony "From the New World." Most white American classical composers, who tended to equate black music with minstrelsy, sneered at Dvořák's pronouncement, but musicians like Cook and Burleigh—who went on to notable careers and inspired generations of future black musicians—were emboldened by the Czech master's endorsement. Within a few years, some younger white composers also began to appreciate and study African American music. Dvořák's assessment of black music gave an important stamp of approval to the efforts of promoters such as George L. White and James M. Trotter on behalf of African American concert performers, and offered a vision of the music's future development.

African American concert performers, though, could not escape the realities of everyday life in America. For black as well as white performers and audiences, the division between classical and popular music in the nineteenth century was not strict. Classical music and opera were not yet assisted by wealthy benefactors, so performers supported themselves by appearing in commercial theaters and on tours that were designed to attract customers from all walks of life. In these surroundings, the entertainment of the audience, not its spiritual "uplift," was usually the highest priority. The Hyers sisters formed a company in the 1870s that performed African American-themed shows that were precursors to musical comedy, such as *Out of Bondage, Colored Aristocracy*, and *Underground Railroad*. Sisieretta Jones, whom promoters billed as "the Black Patti" in a reference to a famous Italian soprano, toured with a crowd-pleasing stage ensemble called the Black Patti Troubadours. Bandleaders such as Francis Johnson of Philadelphia and Walter Craig of New York always performed the songs that were most popular with their audiences. Even James M. Trotter's *Music and Some Highly Musical People*, despite its pervasive rhetoric of gentility and cultural uplift, discussed popular African American performers with the same admiration and respect that concert artists received.

For African American spokespersons such as Trotter and Frederick Douglass, uplift and monetary advancement were indivisible. Singers and instrumentalists who labored in poorly paid jobs in black neighborhoods aspired to prominent and lucrative careers both to "lift up" black Americans culturally and to improve their own fortunes. "Race leaders" such as Douglass and the Reverend Henry Turner argued that individual achievers in all fields would improve African American culture and earn the respect of many white people. As a result, almost every appearance by the Fisk Jubilee Singers or Sisieretta Jones was acclaimed by these leaders as a "first," a demolition of a barrier in a particular theater or town in which a black performer had never before been accorded respect.

The achievements of black musical performers stood out in part, though, because of the general bleakness of the postwar American racial scene. The inescapable, brutal fact underlying the concert triumphs and racial uplift of the postwar years was that life for African Americans generally differed little from the antebellum era. African American dreams for equal rights and status after the Civil War were largely dashed. Republicans in Congress implemented Radical Reconstruction, which provided military protection and civil rights for southern African Americans and gave black men the vote and the opportunity to hold public office. Reconstruction, though, failed to provide southern blacks with the education, paid work, and property ownership they needed to achieve social equality. In the 1870s, northern white voters and politicians lost interest in Reconstruction and did not resist the Ku Klux Klan and white supremacists regaining control of southern politics. Poverty, illiteracy, and the indignity of sharecropping became the lot of the majority of southern African Americans, and new segregation laws and restrictions on voting relegated them to second-class citizenship.

The careers of even the most celebrated black musicians of the Reconstruction era were affected by the revival of racism. Fisk University was an endangered institution for years after the Civil War, suffering attacks from the Klan that compelled the school to build the citadel of Jubilee Hall for the protection of its students and faculty. Its graduates, working as teachers, also faced intimidation by the Ku Klux Klan in their rural classrooms. Even in the North, the touring Fisk Jubilee Singers were described by unsympathetic newspapers as "trained monkeys" who sang "with a wild darkey air." Whites banned the singers from better hotels and forbade them from entering the front doors of the concert halls in which they appeared.[10]

The career of Thomas Greene Wiggins, known as "Blind Tom" Bethune, powerfully illustrates the limits of progress for musicians in the postwar South. Born in Columbus, Georgia, in 1849 to slave parents, Wiggins had only limited sight in one eye and exhibited symptoms of severe autism, but he was also a musical savant. He taught himself to play the piano, after which his master provided him with a teacher. At the age of eight Wiggins gave his first recital, displaying an advanced technique and a mastery of complex classical compositions. James Bethune, Wiggins's master, sent him on concert tours to help pay the Bethune plantation's debts. Hundreds of appearances earned nothing for Wiggins and his family, but enriched James Bethune and the concert promoter who assisted him. At the age of ten, "Blind Tom," billed as "the Mozart of his race," appeared at the White House before President James Buchanan, and during the Civil War he toured the South to raise money for the Confederate war effort. Wiggins could play a work from memory after a single hearing, perform two different tunes with his hands while singing a third one, and execute difficult finger work with his back to the keyboard. Wiggins was a nineteenth-century American incarnation of a kind of musician valued by cultures in West Africa, where visual impairment often accompanied or stimulated musical gifts.

Even after the Civil War, James Bethune continued to maintain total control of Wiggins's career and earnings. When the pianist turned twenty-one, his former master persuaded the state of Georgia to declare the former slave insane and appoint James his guardian. Wiggins continued touring until the 1880s, when a custody battle erupted between Bethune

Photo 2.2.   Piano virtuoso Thomas Greene Wiggins, billed as "Blind Tom" Bethune. Source: Prints and Photographs Division, Library of Congress.

family members. After a brief reunion with his long-estranged mother, Wiggins was entrusted by a judge to James Bethune's daughter, who continued to send him on tours, marketing him as "the last slave set free." Biographers have estimated that Wiggins earned the Bethune family $750,000 during his half-century of performing.

While Blind Tom's life was shaped by white exploitation, the career of John William Boone shows how another visually impaired black musician negotiated difficult racial conditions with more success. "Blind Boone" was born in Missouri, the son of an escaped slave. Although his eyes were removed during a childhood brain operation, he retained his mental faculties and mastered singing and classical piano. Boone's manager was a sympathetic black promoter who sent him on a series of tours across the Midwest. Before his death in 1927 Boone performed 8,000 concerts across North America and Europe. Boone's business success, owing to techniques similar to those the Bethune family used to market Tom Wiggins, suggested ways in which canny and talented African American performers might carve out respectable careers in a racially hostile society.

During Reconstruction, in fact, black performers and managers craftily exploited racial stereotypes in music and the theater to achieve professional success. In this era, the lyrical content of songs was often offensive; the stereotypes of black on stage were vicious caricatures; and black earnings were almost always less than those of white performers. These conditions undoubtedly were emotionally and psychologically stressful for all black performers, but tough, ambitious, and talented individuals made the most of the centrality of blackness in American popular music. In the 1870s and 1880s they initiated a tradition of black commercial success that blazed trails for future generations of African American musicians and performers.

STEREOTYPES AND COMMERCIAL SUCCESS

The first popular genre in which black musicians made their mark was blackface minstrelsy. Minstrelsy remained a pillar of American popular entertainment after the Civil War, despite the fall of slavery. The survival of this genre—dedicated to the grotesque parody of black speech, song, and dance—illustrates the continuity of racism throughout the nineteenth century. Before the Civil War, minstrelsy had been most popular in northern cities, where working-class whites were concerned about the social mobility of free black people; it was in these cities where segregation laws, and their minstrelsy-derived nickname "Jim Crow," originated.

After the war the nature of minstrelsy changed. Jim Crow, in both its legal and musical guises, traveled south. By the 1880s, white supremacist southern state governments embraced systematic public segregation as their "solution" to racial tension. At the same time, the Southern market became far more central to the business of minstrelsy than it had been prior to the war. Most blackface shows following the Civil War became dominated by African American performers, who, like their white predecessors, covered their faces with burnt cork to look "black" in the way that audiences expected them to look.

Black minstrel troupes became popular in the South almost immediately after the end of the Civil War. In April 1865, a white man in Macon, Georgia, designated fifteen of his former slaves the "Georgia Minstrels." Many other musical groups later adopted the same name. Most of them originated in the North, such as Sam Hague's Slave Troupe of Georgia Minstrels, founded in Indianapolis by Barney Hicks, an African American. Hicks later sold his troupe to a new owner, who renamed the group Callender's Georgia Minstrels. This organization became the most successful black minstrel group in the United States. In their performances, black minstrel troupes perpetuated the format that white performers had created before the Civil War.

The first nationally known African American popular performers emerged from these black minstrel shows, including the performer-songwriters Sam Lucas and James Bland and the singing comedians Wallace King and Billy Kersands. At the height of his popularity, Kersands, the best-known black minstrel performer of his time, earned as much as the leading white blackface performers, about $100 a week. While the Fisk Jubilee Singers and their comparatively small audience of genteel white patrons, who despised minstrelsy, hoped to lift up African Americans culturally and spiritually, minstrelsy offered black performers a means for making considerable sums of money before millions of customers. The profits generated annually by minstrelsy dwarfed the sums that the Jubilee Singers earned for Fisk University.

The most lucrative job opportunities for black performers of the post-Civil War era were in stage roles that grotesquely parodied African Americans. The Fisk Jubilee Singers had striven to replace the minstrel stereotype with a dignified stage presentation of black performers. Even at the height of their fame, though, after their appearance at the Reverend Henry Ward Beecher's church in Brooklyn, the Singers were identified in the newspapers for a time as "Beecher's Negro Minstrels." Unlike the Singers, minstrels such as Billy Kersands welcomed such treatment in the press. Throughout his nearly fifty-year career, Kersands prospered by presenting a freakish display on stage, filling his enormous mouth with saucers or billiard balls and moving his huge frame to his signature dance, which he called the "Virginia Essence."

While postwar minstrel shows perpetuated old racial stereotypes, they also portrayed society and race in ways that reflected changing conditions in America. Skits increasingly portrayed city life as dangerous and un-healthy, and depicted the rural South as a refuge of peace and quiet. Black and white minstrelsy took part in the romanticization of the antebellum plantation that became common in the late 1800s. Northern and southern audiences alike shed their anxieties about contemporary America—a land of industrialization, heavy immigration, racial violence, and class con-flict—and embraced images of kindly white "colonels" and "belles," faithful elderly slaves, and harmless, foolish young "pickaninnies" and "coons." This nostalgia reinforced southerners' pride in the lost Confed-erate cause, reaffirmed northern white prejudices against blacks, and helped Yankees and Rebels to overcome the bitterness of the Civil War and Reconstruction. In the 1890s, as theatrical showmanship became more highly developed, some minstrel troupes were absorbed into much larger touring "spectacles," most notably an extravaganza whose title summed up the essence of its appeal: *The South before the War*.

The introduction of African American performers to blackface min-strelsy coincided with the postwar expansion of commercial popular mu-sic. Economic integration and expansion during the Civil War caused mu-sic publishing in the North to expand dramatically, as company owners marketed and distributed millions of pieces of patriotic sheet music across the region. Professional songwriters honed their ability to produce best-selling new songs, such as "Pop Goes the Weasel," "Jingle Bells," and "Camptown Races," whose simple and catchy musical qualities were de-rived from antebellum minstrelsy. Federal laws offered copyright protec-tion to songwriters and allowed some of them to become wealthy. Newly published songs were publicized in concert saloons, a new urban institu-tion that presented variety shows, and then on touring circuits. Touring shows made some of the songs national "hits." By 1890, the family-friendly shows that troupes performed in theaters along these circuits came to be known as vaudeville.

As in minstrelsy, African American musicians who sought careers in songwriting or vaudeville had to conform to the racial stereotypes of the postwar era. The prevalence of demeaning black stage caricatures and plantation nostalgia ensured that even black people in the popular music business who avoided minstrelsy had to write songs or create stage rou-tines that featured these themes.

James A. Bland, Sam Lucas, and Gussie L. Davis were among the edu-cated black musicians of the 1870s who exploited prevailing racial stereo-types to succeed in Tin Pan Alley, the New York City songwriting indus-try. Bland, born in New York and educated at Howard University, was a prolific songwriter and one of minstrelsy's most celebrated banjoists. His songs were firmly in the nostalgic minstrel vein, such as "Pretty Little South Carolina Rose," "Father's Growing Old," "In the Evening by the

Moonlight," and his most famous creation, "Carry Me Back to Old Virginny." In 1881, Bland made London his home, and he successfully toured
Europe—out of blackface—for the next twenty years. Lucas, also born in
the antebellum North, first gained fame as a minstrel singer, and then as
a lead in the Hyers sisters' productions and as the first black man to play
the title role in a stage production of *Uncle Tom's Cabin*. Davis, born in
Cincinnati in 1863, was refused admission by a local music conservatory
because of his color until he agreed to work as a janitor to pay his tuition.
He later wrote songs for his own troupe, the Davis Operatic and Plantation Minstrels, and relocated to New York City. Davis's sentimental ballad
about a father on a train mourning his son, lying in a coffin "In the Bag-
gage Coach Ahead," became one of the biggest hits ever to come out of
Tin Pan Alley. In the half decade preceding his death in 1899, Davis was
the most successful black songwriter in the United States.

MUSICAL THEATER AND THE PHONOGRAPH

Historians have noted that after the Civil War, national industries helped
to tie Americans in small towns and on farms more closely together into
a national culture. The commercial music industry and nationally known
genres such as minstrelsy and vaudeville played important roles in the
creation of this culture. Secular popular music and stage shows also encouraged African Americans to associate music less often with the church.
Many black commentators in the 1860s and 1870s noted a steep decline in
churchgoing among men, as well as a diminishment in the religious fervor of black communities. The pews in churches increasingly held old
men, children, and a dominant cohort of female worshipers. These parishioners provided most of the passion in black spirituality and church music in later decades, for example during the Holiness or Sanctified church
revival of the 1890s. They also stimulated a new interest in spirituals in
the early 1880s, when the composer Marshall Taylor released his *Collection
of Revival Hymns and Plantation Melodies* and a second incarnation of the
Fisk Jubilee Singers began to tour. While African American culture was
secularizing in many ways, black churches adapted and endured, and sacred song remained a vital element of African American music.

The 1890s proved to be a momentous decade in the history of African
American music. For the first time, popular performers rejected the minstrel persona and created their own stage presences; black composers and
producers mounted their first major stage productions; the phonograph
offered an intriguing new mass medium for black music; and profitable
new styles such as the cakewalk and ragtime emerged. By 1900, African
Americans had earned a much greater presence in popular music.

In social and legal terms, the 1890s was a grim era. The U.S. Supreme Court gave states the permission to maintain their segregation laws, ruling that "separate but equal" facilities were permitted under the Constitution. The federal government considered race relations to be a purely local problem. For African Americans living more than a generation after the end of slavery, lynchings, racist rhetoric, vicious caricatures, and denial of justice seemed to indicate that white America had severely limited the scope of their freedom and opportunity. The white majority nationwide relegated black people to an ironclad, second-class status. In a sign of the times, Booker T. Washington gained fame by advocating education for black people in the practical trades and urging a passive response to segregation and lynching.

Racial discrimination and the threat of violence profoundly affected African American musicians in the 1890s. As we have seen, the popular entertainment genres in which they worked imposed blackface on them and employed them in nostalgic stage fantasies about a mythical Old South. In addition, black musicians were reminded that, because of their color, they risked physical endangerment.

Successful African Americans in all occupations were prime targets for white mob hatred, and musicians were among the most conspicuous members of this group. In July 1900, the father of the early jazz clarinetist Big Eye Louis Nelson was among the many African Americans killed by white mobs in New Orleans. The killings occurred in the aftermath of the capture and murder of Robert Charles, a black man blamed for the deaths of several whites. The following month, rumors that a black man had wounded a police detective set off white violence in Manhattan's theater district. African American entertainers became targets of the mob's wrath. George Walker, half of the famous vaudeville duo of Williams and Walker, was knocked unconscious and dragged down a street by the mob. Walker was saved from a likely death by intervening police officers. The songwriter and performer Ernest Hogan also was injured and rescued by a patrolman. Walker and Hogan enjoyed levels of unprecedented fame and fortune for black entertainers, yet American society could not ensure their physical safety. A Negro spiritual had spoken of the slave's "trouble in mind." A generation after emancipation, the handsomely paid, highly educated, and well-dressed descendants of the freed people still endured such trouble.

The turn of the century, though, also witnessed major changes in American culture which offered opportunity and hope to black musicians seeking recognition and the freedom to express themselves. Historians consider the 1890s a "watershed" period in American history. Industrialization now dominated the urban landscape. A severe depression stimulated class conflict and demands for government regulation of the economy. The United States expanded its diplomatic and military adventures overseas.

Culturally, America was transformed by urbanization and by the new kinds of people, institutions, and ideas found in the cities. Enormous immigration from Eastern and Southern Europe turned northern cities into polyglot sites of diverse worship, languages, politics, and cuisine, and began to undermine the Anglo-Saxon Protestant dominance of American culture and expression. Urban entrepreneurs devised new leisure institutions that hastened cultural change. Saloons and dance halls undermined middle-class traditions of courtship and youthful restraint. Boxing rings and baseball parks played host to an explosion in spectator sports. Department stores turned city residents of all classes into consumers in the mass market. Amusement parks such as Coney Island created vivid and fantastic havens of escape from everyday reality. Novelties such as the bicycle and the telephone introduced new notions of recreation and sociability, especially for young women. Although the idealized nineties "new woman" was still expected to marry by a certain age, she also threw off her mother's reserved demeanor, partook in sports and exercise, enrolled in college, and visited theaters and dance halls.

Music reflected the excitement and cultural change of the 1890s. The most dramatic manifestation of this was the emergence of ragtime, which gained notice only late in the decade. Before then, though, established genres such as minstrelsy, vaudeville, and popular songs also changed with the times, adopting less formal and more energetic qualities and celebrating the brash ways of city dwellers. African American innovators were at the center of all of these innovations in popular music.

James A. Bland's and Gussie Davis's success as Tin Pan Alley songwriters was representative of the rising and large new cadre of professional African American performers. Billy McClain, a white minstrel veteran, became the impresario of the massive nostalgic revues *The South before the War*, *Darkest America*, and *Black America*, which employed hundreds of black musicians and singers. In 1890, the U.S. census recorded a total of 1,490 "Negro actors [and] showmen"; ten years later, 530 were counted in New York City and Chicago alone. Show business trade papers such as the *Freeman* advertised job opportunities. At the same time, urbanization in the 1890s caused black stereotypes in popular music to evolve. The presence of African Americans in service occupations in wealthy white households and the prominence of this group in the black middle class inspired stock portrayals of servile but elegant butlers, maids, and cooks. In minstrel shows and nostalgic revues, tuxedo- and gown-clad black performers performed the ubiquitous new cakewalk routine, a dance competition accompanied by minstrel tunes for which the winners were awarded a cake.

The cakewalk reputedly had its origins among slaves in Florida. Influenced by the dancing of Seminole couples, these slaves held competitions that mocked their masters' social dances in competitions, offering the winners rare confections as awards. Like corn-shucking ceremonies, cakewalks fascinated white observers, who apparently encouraged its spread among plantation slaves across the South in the late 1850s. Accounts of the competitions published during the war led minstrel troupes to incorporate the dance into their shows. By the 1890s the cakewalk was a stylized exercise in "high stepping" and "strutting." It allowed pioneering black vaudevillians such as Dora Dean, Charles Johnson, Bob Cole, and Stella Wiley to express themselves creatively, in respectable clothing, for good pay, and before appreciative audiences. Simultaneously, the cakewalk had become the newest rage in the ballrooms of affluent white people—the first sign that African American musical culture was beginning to influence the leisure behavior of urban white elites.

In the 1890s, the influential New York City entertainment scene showcased striking new achievements by African American performers. These innovators broke with the traditions of minstrelsy and plantation nostalgia and looked to vaudeville and the European operetta as models for a new musical genre. Bob Cole, a talented multi-instrumentalist from Georgia, made his biggest mark as the most stylish stage proponent of non-stereotypical black dance. In 1897, after touring with Black Patti's Troubadours, Cole helped to create *A Trip to Coontown*, the first show created by African Americans to appear on Broadway. As its title suggests, this musical comedy exploited the current vogue for "coon" songs, which used particularly virulent stereotypes to portray mammies, pickaninnies, razor-wielding "bucks," and other black characters in humorous situations. It was a sign of the times that even innovative young black musicians had to work within the boundaries of humiliating racial caricatures. *A Trip to Coontown*, though, did not feature blackface and the usual minstrel dances. It proved to be a popular success. Cole's troupe toured the nation and revived the show in New York in later years.

In the summer of 1898, the outdoor "roof garden" stage of the Casino Theatre in Manhattan welcomed another unexpected hit, a loosely plotted show entitled *Clorindy, or the Origins of the Cakewalk. Clorindy* was both a culmination of the cakewalk craze and a harbinger of a new theatrical genre: musical comedy. It brought a measure of fame to its creator, Will Marion Cook. A product of Washington, D.C.'s black elite, Cook had studied performance and composition with leading musicians in Berlin and with Dvořák in New York. Cook recalled that his mother "thought that a Negro composer should write just like a white man," but his failed efforts at a classical career brought him to the brink of poverty. His new show at the Casino Theatre, like *A Trip to Coontown*, was rich in stereotypical fare such as "Darktown Is Out

Tonight" and "Who Dat Say Chicken in Dis Crowd?" Cook noted that such songs prompted his college-educated mother to lament, "Oh, Will! Will! I've sent you all over the world to study and become a great musician, and you return such a nigger!" but he had scored a success.[11] Cook also gained attention by conducting the all-white pit orchestra. Later in 1898, he collaborated with Paul Laurence Dunbar, the fiercely proud young African American poet, on the revue *Senegambian Carnival*.

There were other beneficiaries of *Clorindy's* success as well. Its lead performer was the popular comedian Ernest Hogan, whose billing of himself as "the unbleached American" reflected the new assertiveness of younger African American performers in this era. Bob Cole contributed songs to a new edition of *Clorindy* in 1899, which starred the performers for whom Cook had originally intended the show: the peerless comedy team of Williams and Walker. George Walker, from Lawrence, Kansas, first teamed with Bert Williams, a native of the Bahamas who was raised in California, in 1893. Billing themselves as "the Two Real Coons," Walker played the city slicker and Williams the sad blackface victim of bad luck in comedy routines laced with songs. In future shows that succeeded *Clorindy*, such as Will Marion Cook's *Sons of Ham* and *Policy Players*, the duo rose to fame. George Walker's dancing skills and good looks gained much notice, but Bert Williams's understated vocal delivery, more spoken than sung, haunted audiences. In musical comedy settings, Williams's wistful singing conveyed something of the suffering that African Americans endured. Southern audiences were rarely able to experience it, though. Pioneering an important new policy, Williams and Walker avoided the Jim Crow South whenever possible.

In 1903, Williams and Walker's stardom was confirmed with their success in a show called *In Dahomey*, the first full-length all-black stage production on Broadway. *In Dahomey* told the story of two confidence men, played by Williams and Walker, who hope to defraud a group of African Americans seeking to recolonize West Africa. Superficial portrayals of Africa and the Caribbean, which avoided the corrosive stereotypes of the American South, were common in these musical comedies. Musical comedy was a new genre, inspired by the success of Gilbert and Sullivan's English operettas, which wove songs into the fabric of coherent plots. Will Marion Cook provided the music for *In Dahomey*, as he would for subsequent Williams and Walker successes. The comedy duo then toured Europe, where they appeared before royalty. Back home they created their own music publishing business and forced some large white-owned theaters to drop their racially exclusive policies.

In the meantime, Bob Cole teamed with the brothers J. Rosamond and James Weldon Johnson to produce a series of musical comedies that contained songs performed in nonderogatory African American dialect. In

Photo 2.3.   Entertainer Bert Williams. Source: Prints and Photographs Division, Library of Congress.

these shows pianist J. Rosamond Johnson appeared with Cole in a stage act, dressed in white tie and black tails. The Johnson brothers, natives of Jacksonville, Florida, were well educated and committed to the advancement of black civil rights. James Weldon Johnson—a novelist, diplomat, and later the first black secretary of the National Association for the Advancement of Colored People (NAACP)—particularly embodied the post–Civil War generation's dual commitment to authentic black artistic expression and the struggle for racial equality. In 1900, the Johnson brothers celebrated the anniversary of Lincoln's birth by composing "Lift Every Voice and Sing," a song that blended their musical and social concerns.

Two decades later, during the Harlem Renaissance, the song became known as the unofficial "Negro national anthem."

Also beginning in the 1890s, a momentous technological innovation, the phonograph, helped to transform the careers of many African American musicians. In that decade, Thomas Edison's wax cylinders and Emile Berliner's shellac disks competed for a small but rapidly growing audience, presenting recordings of up to three minutes in length. From the very beginning, white people controlled the American recording business. Black artists, limited by prevailing stereotypes and a racial hierarchy that rigidly dictated their repertoire, made little money in the emerging recording industry. In May 1890, Edison Records released George W. Johnson's "The Whistling Coon," probably the first recording ever made by an African American. Johnson was a Manhattan resident who sang songs at the ferry docks to collect coins from passengers. His remake of "The Whistling Coon" in 1891 became a best-seller, and it was followed in later years by "The Laughing Coon" and "The Whistling Girl." Johnson never made much money from his records, and his notoriety largely derived from his trial and acquittal in 1899 on the charge of murdering his common-law wife. In the 1890s, phonograph companies recorded virtually no African American musicians of repute. Black vocal quartets made some interesting recordings in New York and in New Orleans, but other records featured white minstrel singers who were marketed as black people—a trend that typified the often informal and scattershot nature of the phonograph business in the early years.

Bert Williams and George Walker, though, paid careful attention to recording as a component of their careers, and they were among the first performers of any race to use records to extend their fame. In doing so, they brought a major African American musical presence to early records. Bert Williams in particular approached recording sessions with great care, to ensure that his intimate and moving voice was captured accurately. A century after he made his first records, the clarity and immediacy of his singing remains striking. After 1900 black vocal groups also made inroads in recording studios. "Down on the Old Camp Ground," recorded in 1901 by a quartet from the Dinwiddie Normal School in Virginia, sold well enough to earn the group a vaudeville contract. Church ensembles also began to record, as did the reconstituted Fisk University Jubilee Singers, who in 1909 committed to disk two songs with texts by Paul Laurence Dunbar. At a time when phonographs were something of a novelty that only affluent persons could afford, record companies made no effort to market to African American consumers. Aside from Bert Williams, the first generation of black recording artists had little impact on the listening public.

In the four decades between the Civil War and the dawn of the twentieth century, African American musicians had become the primary performers in minstrelsy, created lucrative careers in songwriting and in urban performing venues, and had adapted slave genres such as spirituals and the cakewalk into stage entertainment that helped to define American culture in the industrial age. They accomplished this in the face of the virulent racism of the postwar era, which saw civil rights erased and a regime of segregation and racial violence descend on the South. Performers paid a price by conforming to the stereotypes of this era, performing in blackface and writing and singing "coon" songs. It is impossible to divorce the creativity and hard-won success of black musicians from the poisonous context of these decades.

Nevertheless, the post–Civil War era also showed the Fisk Jubilee Singers and African American churches preserving and promoting the sacred music of the antebellum years. Black music won praise from influential musical elites such as Antonin Dvořák, who were also astonished by the technical abilities of instrumentalists such as "Blind Tom" Bethune and vocalists such as Sisieretta Jones. The bitter failure of Reconstruction and the campaign for black equality in U.S. society was countered in African American music by the resilience of the church and other community institutions and by the innovations of talented composers and performers. In 1903, the sociologist and activist W. E. B. Du Bois prophetically declared that "the problem of the Twentieth Century is the problem of the color line."[12] For African American musicians, the challenge of the new century would be to use music as a central tool for recalling their rich transcontinental heritage and establishing a healthy and prosperous identity.

NOTES

1. Quoted in Jon Michael Spencer, *Sacred Symphony: The Chanted Sermon of the Black Preacher* (New York: Greenwood Press, 1988), 1.

2. Thomas W. Higginson, "December 3, 1862," in *Army Life in a Black Regiment* (Boston: Fields, Osgood, 1870), located at www.gutenberg.org (accessed January 2007).

3. Higginson, "January 1, 1863 (evening)."

4. Leon F. Litwack, *Been in the Storm So Long: The Aftermath of Slavery* (New York: Knopf, 1980), 167–169.

5. Eric Foner, *Reconstruction: America's Unfinished Revolution, 1863–1877* (New York: Harper & Row, 1988), 102.

6. William Francis Allen, Charles Pickard Ware, and Lucy McKim Garrison, *Slave Songs of the United States* (1867; repr., New York: Arno Press, 1971), viii, xx.

7. Allen et al., *Slave Songs*, i, iv, v.

8. James M. Trotter, *Music and Some Highly Musical People*, (1878; New York: Johnson Reprint, 1968), 352.

9. Quoted in Joseph Horowitz, *Dvořák in America: In Search of the New World* (Chicago: Cricket Books, 2003), 72.

10. *New York World* (1873), quoted in Llewellyn Smith and Andrew Ward, *The American Experience: Jubilee Singers*, www.pbs.org/wgbh/amex/singers/filmmore/transcript.html (accessed January 2007).

11. Will Marion Cook, "Clorindy, the Origin of the Cakewalk," *Theatre Arts* (September 1947), 62.

12. W. E. B. Du Bois, *The Souls of Black Folk* (1903; New York: Modern Library, 2005), 9.

3

The Rise of
Ragtime and the Blues

The entry of African American musicians and performers into black-face minstrelsy, popular songwriting, cakewalks, and stage revues is only part of the story of black music in the late 1800s. Away from the bright lights of Broadway and vaudeville, average people perpetuated musical traditions from the days of slavery that were far more relevant to their daily existences than music in the commercial marketplace. For example, Afro-Caribbean practices persisted in children's play, which included chants and verbal contests, as well as the use of simple instruments such as the bow diddley or diddley bow, a single-stringed bowed instrument that had changed little in its transition from the central African grasslands. Other African survivals such as mouth-resonated musical bows, as well as the practice of sliding knives or trinkets on strings, persisted among rural African Americans.

In the late 1800s, these "hidden" musical practices began to be developed by African American professional musicians into new popular music styles. A newspaper story published in the 1910s related the testimony of an English performer who visited St. Louis in 1888. In the city he heard an elderly black woman improvise a little song about a popular racehorse: "I-za gwine tuh Little Rock, Tuh put mah money on-a Proctuh Knott." The extra syllables were the key additions, creating a vivid syncopation in the tune. "That sounds so ragged," a witness supposedly said, and, the journalist proclaimed, "the name 'ragtime' was born."[1] In his autobiography published in 1941, the African American composer, musician, and publisher William Christopher Handy offered a story about the origins of another new musical style. In 1892, when Handy was a young black minstrel performer in Memphis, he heard a strange kind of singing on a street, in which the singer slid his voice between the five or so notes that made up the tune. Here, Handy proclaimed decades later, was one of the original statements of the blues.

Ragtime and the blues became prominent and even revolutionary musical genres in African American music. Their origins are less clear than the previous statements suggest, but the evidence indicates that both styles were shaped by old musical traditions of the African diaspora and were directly inspired by musical practices of poor southern African Americans after 1865. Beginning around 1900, ragtime became the big new musical rage, bringing fame and influence to musicians such as Scott Joplin and James Reese Europe. Ragtime accompanied a cultural shift in America from the relatively rigid behavior and morality dictated by the Victorian middle class toward more relaxed social relations, and in some white circles, toward a new respect for African Americans and their music. By 1910 the blues, not ragtime, was probably the secular music of choice of African Americans in the rural South, but it had a slower path to acceptance among the white mainstream and the urban black middle class.. During World War I and the 1920s, when southern blacks began to move north in large numbers for the first time, they brought the blues with them. Touring shows and the phonograph made the blues a successor to ragtime, as well as the first widely broadcast secular musical expression of authentic African American emotions and tribulations.

RAGTIME

Ragtime music occupies a central and vivid position in the evolution of African American music. As it rose in popularity in the late 1890s, it echoed the lively syncopation of minstrel songs, the emphasis on notes off of the main beat that set feet to tapping. At first ragtime was almost indistinguishable from some of the cakewalk and "coon" songs that were in vogue in the late nineteenth century. By the 1920s, after it had matured as a distinct style, ragtime almost imperceptibly gave way to jazz, which in its earliest incarnations shared ragtime's intricate syncopations, rich chord progressions, and opportunities for technical virtuosity, especially on the piano. During the twenty-year reign of ragtime, African American musicians moved away from the limited career horizons of the minstrel era, associated their work with the struggle for racial equality, and carved out lives outside the South. This generation of musicians, almost entirely born after emancipation, actively sought to put the legacies of slavery behind them.

In particular, young black piano players were bringing new energy and complexity to their performances. Their new musical ideas gained the biggest exposure at entertainment venues near major fairgrounds. The late nineteenth century was the heyday of the public exposition—the regional, national, or world's fair that presented the wonders of the modern age to large numbers of paying attendees. Over time, unofficial entertainment districts outside official fair sites, offering the visiting masses informal leisure, became an important part of the fair phenomenon. African American performers in medicine shows, minstrel troupes, or "gilly" wagons (which presented vaudeville-style shows on a small scale), as well as brass bands and tavern piano players, provided entertainment in these venues. Some attendees of the New Orleans Cotton Exposition of 1885 later claimed to have heard some of the earliest ragtime music there. The much larger congregation of black musicians outside the 1893 Columbian Exposition in Chicago—the most celebrated fair held in the United States at that time—exchanged new musical ideas from across the nation. The piano "professors" in attendance probably gave ragtime its most important early exposure.

By the 1890s, the piano had become a central component of American middle class culture. Domestic manufacturers created the largest and most efficient piano industry in the world, and the growing, mostly white middle class made the instrument a symbol of their status and refinement. A handsome piece of furniture as well as a musical device, a piano in a home told visitors that its owners had achieved prosperity and possessed a cultivated sensibility. The reputation of the great European composers was never higher, and music education, centered on piano pedagogy and appreciation courses, touched millions of youngsters and adults.

African Americans with middle-class pretensions shared this interest. In an 1898 short story, the African American writer Charles W. Chesnutt depicted the snobbish head of a "Blue Vein Society," the light-skinned black town elite. His home, "handsomely furnished, contain[ed] among other things a good library, especially rich in poetry, a piano, and some choice engravings."[2] Young members of such households who studied the piano would have absorbed the rich harmonic language of the great composers, a language marked by progressively complex harmonies and tonalities shifting between major and minor keys. Most of these same young pianists, though, would discover that the formidable racial barriers of this era included widespread discrimination in conservatories and concert halls. Thus young black pianists gravitated toward accessible piano jobs in taverns, the popular stage, and touring shows.

As a result, less genteel black urban settings such as taverns and social clubs employed talented young pianists who were bursting with musical ideas but had little opportunity for social advancement. One such setting was Tom Turpin's Rosebud Saloon in St. Louis. In the mid-1890s, Turpin, a pianist, gathered other skilled players, such as a teenager named Louis

Chauvin, and nurtured one of the earliest and most important centers of ragtime piano. St. Louis, the self-proclaimed gateway to the West, was at the height of its regional dominance and prosperity in these years. Especially for its large African American population, St. Louis provided a meeting place for rural and urban, Yankee and southern, and eastern and western styles and ideas; its rich German-American musical culture also was a resource.

Sedalia, in southwestern Missouri, was a lesser city in the state, but it nevertheless provided a fertile niche for creative black pianists. In 1892, twenty-five-year-old Scott Joplin had moved with his family from Texarkana, Texas, up the route of the Sedalia cattle trail, which had helped to make the town a musical crossroads. A strong musical education and employment at Sedalia social clubs, including the Maple Leaf Club, gave Joplin experience and encouraged his lofty aspirations. He also toured with minstrel shows in the 1890s. St. Louis pianists helped him to refine his piano playing, and late in the decade he signed a contract with John S. Stark, a Sedalia music publisher. In 1899, Stark published some of Joplin's first compositions, including the *Maple Leaf Rag*, launching a mutually respectful and ultimately highly profitable relationship. As ragtime became a national rage in the early twentieth century, Joplin's compositions sold by the tens of thousands; the *Maple Leaf Rag* alone sold half a million copies in a decade.

Joplin's expressive and nuanced piano rags, which also included *The Entertainer*, *The Cascades*, and *Easy Winners*, are now among the most famous pieces in American music, but they were only one element in the rise of ragtime, and Joplin was one of many important figures. His compositions encapsulate what is commonly called the classic trait of ragtime: the "ragged" or syncopated melody, played by the right hand over a steady walking bass line, played by the left. While popular songs usually had two sections, a main body and a chorus, Joplin's rags usually consisted of three to five alternating parts. Drawing techniques in **modulation**—moving from one chord or key to another—from classical models, Joplin also expanded the harmonic richness of American popular music. His compositions were complex musical statements that often unfolded at three times the length of the average Tin Pan Alley song. Joplin cowrote best-selling rags with younger pianists such as Arthur Marshall and Scott Hayden and helped launch them on their own careers. The important piano rag composer James Scott, whom Joplin met after he and John Stark moved to St. Louis in 1900, also wrote piano works quite similar to Joplin's.

In the ragtime era, though, these innovative small masterpieces were often obscured by other songs and performers that flooded the genre. The first publication to call itself a "rag" was an 1896 piano arrangement by Max Hoffmann of part of the song "All Coons Look Alike to Me," which was not a rag at all but the quintessential "coon song" and signature tune

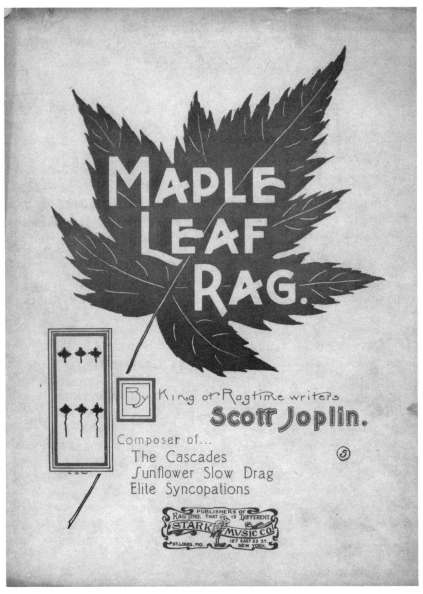

Photo 3.1. Sheet music cover, *Maple Leaf Rag*, 1899. Source: New York Public Library Digital Image Library.

of the black stage performer Ernest Hogan. The song's crude harmonies, syncopations, and racial stereotypes have little to do with the classic ragtime of Joplin and others, but thousands of transitional songs of this sort increased the popularity of ragtime at the turn of the century. Contrary to the claims of some historians, ragtime was never exclusively or even primarily piano music. Up-tempo musical theater numbers by Bob Cole and Williams and Walker were similar enough to piano rags to also be considered ragtime pieces. Any melody that modulated between a major and minor key bore a ragtime characteristic. Urban minstrel shows, which mostly vanished after 1900, vaudeville acts, brass bands, circus ensembles, medicine shows, and society dance orchestras all incorporated ragged rhythm in their music.

Much of that "ragtime" music was written by white Americans. As in minstrelsy, white composers made disproportionate profits and gained fame from a style that was based on African American musical sources. When John Stark relocated his publishing business to New York City in 1905, he paid special attention to promoting the rags of the white composer Joseph Lamb. Scott Joplin and Lamb became good friends, but the former also decided to end his relationship with Stark. Stark had often disappointed Joplin by refusing to publish certain works, including a grand opera that the composer had worked on for years. Joplin had other worries as well. In 1911, a Russian Jewish immigrant named Irving Berlin scored the greatest success of his short songwriting career with "Alexander's Ragtime Band." According to Stark's descendants, Joplin accused Berlin of stealing the tune from him. Ironically, Berlin's song bore few elements of the classic ragtime style. It did not console Joplin that many white composers far from St. Louis had mastered the basic ragtime style and had successfully published their songs in local markets. Like minstrelsy and the cakewalk, ragtime encouraged some genuine white admiration of black music, but it mostly fell victim to co-optation by white musicians. Some of them, such as Irving Berlin, easily outearned Scott Joplin, James Scott, and other major black ragtime composers.

In the ragtime era, though, African American musicians also expressed a new assertiveness and rebellion against racial inequality. They rejected the old minstrel stereotypes that had been imposed on their predecessors. Scott Joplin shared the strong racial pride of his contemporary, the New York composer and conductor Will Marion Cook, but unlike Cook, Joplin refused to portray stereotyped characters and employ comical black dialect in his musical works. Also, unlike Bert Williams, Joplin and other recognized black ragtime musicians refused to perform in blackface.

Black ragtime composers also associated their works with classical music and sought some of the prestige of that tradition. They pointed out that rags demanded piano playing skills that were also required in the classical repertoire. For the first time, the white audience heard black musicians repeating Antonin Dvořák's claim that African American music could be the foundation of a true art form. Even though Joplin had received little formal musical education and might have been satisfied with writing commercially successful piano rags for the rest of his career, he decided to write operas, in an effort to incorporate black music into an elite genre. The subject of Joplin's lost first opera, *A Guest of Honor*, was Booker T. Washington's dinner at the White House with President Theodore Roosevelt in 1901. Despite the growing controversy among blacks about Washington's social and educational views, the dinner—and the outrage it sparked in the white South—inspired pride and hope. Washington had encouraged black Americans to advance themselves through self-help and entrepreneurship within their communities, and Scott Joplin followed this advice. After his break with John Stark, he began his own publishing company in New York City, and for a few years it was moderately successful.

Ragtime presented to white listeners a new generation of dignified black performers, but it also heralded a new era of race relations. Young white ragtime fans used the music to help erode Victorian formalities regarding leisure and behavior in public. Middle-class white youth enjoyed rags in their home parlors and in leisure settings of all kinds: carnivals, circuses, restaurants, dance halls, and vaudeville. College students embraced ragtime as the sound of their unique brand of campus leisure, an early form of youth culture in the twentieth century. Some middle-aged and wealthy whites also embraced ragtime. In the cities, affluent white people began to patronize restaurants, known in New York City as "lobster palaces," that served theater audiences after the shows, and intimate cabarets in which they mingled with "exotic" Latin American and African American dancers and musicians. In cabarets, the physical proximity between white women and black men seemed especially daring to traditionalists who feared interracial romance and sexual activity. In the ragtime era of the 1900s and 1910s, this interaction in the new urban nightlife led many white contemporaries to claim that a revolution in American leisure and behavior was under way.

THE GREAT MIGRATION

African Americans in the 1910s who migrated from the South to northern cities experienced a revolution in their expectations, daily life, and self-expression. Thanks to the Great Migration, the assertiveness and racial pride expressed by black musicians in the North before 1910 would be amplified, and legions of talented southern performers and composers would arrive in the cities.

In 1900, African Americans made up only about 2 percent of the population of most major northern cities. Black communities were outnumbered by immigrants and rural white migrants. Since most industries, in collusion with labor unions, refused to hire black workers, few rural black migrants made the journey to the urban North.

In the South, though, black America had already begun to urbanize. Rural black migration to southern cities began soon after the fall of the Confederacy. Despite the effort of Union forces during Reconstruction and white-supremacist state governments to keep them "on the farm," freed people moved by the thousands to towns and cities, seeking relief from the poverty and drudgery of plantation labor. After 1880, African Americans made up the majority of workers in Birmingham, Alabama's new steel mills. New Orleans more than doubled in size from 1870 to 1900, mostly due to black migrants from plantations in the lower Mississippi River Delta region. City life was difficult for most migrants. They remained poor and suffered from substandard housing and education. In addition, the new segregation laws applied to many more sites in the cities than in the countryside. But black urbanites also found strength in numbers: communities for worship, commerce, and sociability that supported leisure institutions, rich and energetic street life, and careers for entrepreneurs and talented performers.

Black musicians such as Bob Cole and J. Rosamund Johnson who migrated from the South to the North before 1900 were the advance guard for the Great Migration that took place two decades later. Musical professionals, in addition, were pioneers in affluence. They were among the few African Americans anywhere in the nation who earned something approaching a middle-class income. Migrants embraced the musicians' popular successes and musical expressions of optimism as symbols of their hopes in northern urban communities. Furthermore, performers who toured internationally were exposed to societies that did not habitually mistreat people of color. These experiences allowed them to return to America with a new cosmopolitan attitude and a sense that the world valued African Americans and their music. These perceptions further empowered black communities in the North.

Amid the optimism, though, migrants also realized that discrimination and disadvantages existed in northern cities, and even before the Great Migration musicians suffered from those conditions. Some of them were the target of a white mob during the race riot in Manhattan in 1900. In addition, the lack of good medical care for northern African Americans made them more vulnerable to communicable diseases. Syphilis, the most common sexually transmitted disease of the era, was poorly treated in black communities. It took the lives of the vaudevillian George Walker and the ragtime composer Louis Chauvin, among others, and it was rumored also to have caused the death of Bob Cole in 1911. Most tragically, syphilis gradually deprived Scott Joplin of his physical and mental health. In the late 1900s and early 1910s, Joplin was active in New York as a music publisher, performer, and composer. His obsession was to produce on stage his full-length opera, *Treemonisha*, which he completed in 1910 and published the next year. Joplin's story told of Monisha, who as an abandoned infant had been found under a tree. After becoming educated, she struggles against the superstitions of her neighbors in a black rural community in Arkansas and tries to share her learning with them. The music of *Treemonisha* is firmly in the style of Joplin's short piano rags, but it succeeds in helping to tell a dramatic and involving story that lasts nearly two hours. Joplin could only marshal enough forces to stage the ballet from Act II of *Treemonisha* in a single performance, and to rehearse a single reading of the complete score. The work would be neglected for sixty years. Meanwhile Joplin's syphilis entered the tertiary stage, weakening him physically and inducing paranoia and dementia. He died on April 1, 1917, two weeks before the United States entered the First World War.

The years leading up to World War I, as well as the conflict itself, had a much more positive impact on James Reese Europe, thirteen years Joplin's junior. Like Joplin, Europe was a southern migrant. Born in Mobile, Alabama and raised in Washington, D.C., he came to New York City in 1900. Here Europe, in his early twenties, almost immediately became professionally successful. He wrote some well-received songs and became a sought-after conductor of musical shows, working with Bert Williams, Bob Cole, and others. In this era the musicians' union in New York, Local 803 of the American Federation of Musicians, excluded African Americans. In response to this, in 1910, James Europe helped to create the Clef Club, an organization that provided black musicians with regular bookings and union-style benefits such as insurance and unemployment relief.

Leading the group's flagship band, the Clef Club Orchestra, James Europe became one of the city's busiest and most successful conductors. Concerts in Carnegie Hall and other major venues brought the first dignified large-scale presentations of black popular music to the general public. One of these presentations brought together the works of Harry Burleigh, J. Rosamond Johnson, and Will Marion Cook, encompassing the sweep of recent black music from spirituals to musical comedy. In 1913, Europe's group became the first all-African American band ever to be recorded by a commercial American label. His ragtime recordings displayed imaginative arrangements, with colorful percussion effects, heavy use of violins, and various exotic international styles. Europe also became a musical director for the white ballroom dancers Vernon and Irene Castle. Their collaboration won Europe some of the most lucrative performing engagements in New York. Europe and the Castles popularized versions of African American "barnyard" dances such as the turkey trot for the middle-class white public.

James Reese Europe lived and worked in Harlem, which in the 1910s became black America's cultural mecca. Slow sales of newly built brownstones in this predominantly Jewish neighborhood led developers to sell to affluent blacks in the early 1910s. The tuxedo-clad James Reese Europe, king of New York society orchestras, was a symbol of Harlem's rising fortunes. World War I made Harlem, and other northern cities, the destination for hundreds of thousands of working-class southern black migrants. American industries needed many more workers to fill orders coming in from the Allies and, after America entered the war in 1917, from the U.S. government. Manufacturers dropped their ban on hiring African American workers and sent agents to the South to recruit them, offering them signing bonuses and free transportation to the northern industrial centers. From 1915 to 1920 nearly half a million black people migrated to the North.

African Americans and their music also were enlisted in the U.S. military campaign in France. The New York 15th Infantry, the first black volunteer unit activated for service in 1917 was perceived by many observers to be representative of the confident new spirit of African Americans in Harlem. James Reese Europe was commissioned a captain, serving both as director of the "Hellfighters" regimental band and a field officer. When the regiment arrived in Paris in 1918, the Hellfighters caused an instant sensation among French devotees of ragtime music, who had never before heard such a large and skilled black ensemble. Rushed into combat by the Allies during Germany's massive spring offensive, Europe was virtually the first American company commander to lead troops in the trenches of World War I. Europe, the future bandleader Noble Sissle, and most of the unit's other members survived the war and earned military honors, as well as one of the most tumultuous welcome-home parades that New York City had ever seen. Much of Manhattan turned out to watch the Hellfighters march down Broadway, and when the soldiers reached Harlem the procession dissolved into a joyous street party. In 1919, James Europe's civilian band began another round of touring and recording. During a break in a performance in Boston, a mentally unstable member of the group stabbed Europe in his dressing room. The bandleader died from his wounds at the age of thirty-nine. Like his return from military service in France, James Europe's funeral was a major public event in New York City.

During World War I, ragtime had begun to be overshadowed by a musical newcomer called jazz. When James Europe had returned from military service, he had embraced the new trend by calling his new group a "jazz orchestra." This turn away from the ragtime designation, as well as Europe's premature death, indicated that ragtime's reign as America's most important popular music was coming to an end.

THE BLUES

As ragtime rose and fell in popularity, many other new styles of nonreligious music were brewing in black America, particularly in the South. For example, in southwest Louisiana, African Americans were deeply influenced by Cajun music. Black musicians blended Afro-Caribbean traits with the French-American fiddle and accordion dance music of their white neighbors. In 1928 the accordionist Amédé Ardoin recorded influential black Cajun, or *la la*, dance numbers. This was the origin of what was later known as zydeco music.

Another tradition originating in the late 1800s, that of small groups singing in **close harmony**, profoundly affected vocal music nationwide. For generations, groups of three to five African Americans, usually men, had harmonized by singing notes in chords in their closest formation, usually only two or three steps in the scale away from each other. Such group singing also featured individuals "sliding" or "snaking" from high and low notes toward the middle of the register—in other words, moving from widely spaced ensemble voicing into close harmony.

Close harmony influenced the singing of white minstrel ensembles, and among African Americans the practice continued to thrive in "schoolyards, lodge halls, barrooms, shoeshine stands, railroad stations, and street corners"—as well as in barbershops.[3] Before the Civil War, the majority of professional hair cutters in the United States were free African American men, and after the war their shops in black neighborhoods were hubs of social activity. Men and women waiting for haircuts often sang in close harmony to amuse themselves, and in the 1890s, the all-male close-harmony quartet, based in the barbershop, became a distinct musical genre. James Weldon Johnson, as well as others, argued that it emerged in Jacksonville, Florida. "Barbershop" harmony was soon co-opted by white quartets, who also adopted black standards such as "Way Down Yonder in the Corn Field," which was originally a slave work song. White publicizers of barbershop singing ignored the African American origins of the genre. In the twentieth-century barbershop singing was eclipsed in black communities by the blues and gospel singing, although groups in the latter genre especially retained barbershop numbers in their repertory.

Developing African American popular styles such as zydeco and barbershop ensemble singing showed the dynamism and diverse inspirations of working-class black musicians in the decades after emancipation. At the turn of the nineteenth century, these styles were secular counterparts to equally dynamic black church music, which we will examine in a later chapter.

The blues became the most important of the new secular musical styles. In the decades after 1900, the blues became a powerful new statement of the mentality of southern African Americans living under Jim Crow. Blues songs were documents of black life and thought that fused traditional musical materials and the forms and themes of recent commercial songs. The blues' emotional power and close ties to black spoken culture ensured that after 1920, it would be far more influential than ragtime in stimulating the grass-roots musical creativity of future generations of African Americans.

Scholars most regularly associate the blues with the plantations in the Mississippi Delta and the Atlantic tidewater regions and with the traveling singers, or "songsters" as they were called, who visited the plantations. After about 1890 these guitar-playing vocalists gained a sudden, new prominence in the South. As the historian David Evans has noted, "blues songs seem to turn up everywhere in the Deep South more or less simultaneously—in rural areas, small towns, and cities such as New Orleans and Memphis."[4] Reminiscences, such as those of W. C. Handy, suggest that a definite new song style was taking shape around 1890. However, it would be decades before blues songs were commercially published or recorded, so the early history of the blues remains obscure.

The blues is usually defined as a song style, sung by an individual with instrumental accompaniment, typically a guitar played by the singer. Blues song stanzas varied considerably, but the most characteristic form was the three-line stanza, in which each line took up four musical bars and the second line repeated the first (the "AAB" form). The three lines of this stanza are colored harmonically by chords rooted in the first, fourth, and fifth notes of the song's scale, respectively (the so-called I-IV-V chord pattern). This structure often made the blues sound pentatonic, suggesting its deep roots in the African American musical tradition. To white Americans, the most pungent characteristic of these tunes were their "blue" notes, which sounded to them like flattened tones, especially the second and sixth notes, in a western-style scale. The rhythm was stable, usually slow, and featured subtle distortions of tempo and displaced beats that contrasted strongly with the mechanical syncopation of ragtime.

The singer's inventiveness was a hallmark of the blues. The use of regular stanzas indicates that blues songs were structured on popular songs, and well-known lyrics from those songs appear in some blues. The influence of commercial music stops there, though. In a standard blues song, no two stanzas typically were played or sung the same. Rather, it featured variations in pitch, rhythm, and inflection. Unlike commercial minstrel, vaudeville, or ragtime singers, blues vocalizers utilized many effects, such as sliding between notes, moaning, growling, and "shouting," which helped to proclaim their individuality. Like pentatonic harmony, these effects suggested the blues' closeness to vocal traditions stretching back to Africa.

Blues lyrics encompassed a range of subjects that distinguished them sharply from the typical topics of earlier black-influenced popular songs. They are almost exclusively subjective, telling of the singer's perception of the world. Songs told of relationships—most often between the singer and a member of the opposite sex—and of sorrows and delights relating to work, misfortune, or broader social conditions. Some lyrics told their tales in a straightforward manner, while others were rich in metaphors and symbols. Variations of all kinds can be found in the blues of various artists and regions, but all traditions basically resembled this template.

In some important ways the blues differed from dominant black musical genres of the 1800s such as spirituals and close harmony singing. These genres were group vocal traditions that derived from the singing styles of the equatorial West African coast. Unlike the blues, these styles featured mostly group singing, as well as heterophony and rhythmic complexity accompanied by drumming and dancing. The musicologists Paul Oliver and Gerhard Kubik argue that the blues grew out of a branch of African music that had almost no influence on other African American musical traditions. The music of the western Sudan grasslands between the Sahara desert and the equatorial coast, they argue, inspired the blues, giving the latter style its unusual fixation on individual expression. Kubik claims that grasslands music, influenced by Islamic traditions from the Sahara to the north, endowed the blues with sliding vocals and its peculiar harmonic structure. He argues that the grasslands yielded a unique musical scale that accounts for the placement and frequency of the so-called "blue notes" in blues songs. We do not know how this unusual African tradition might have snuck into black music in nineteenth-century America. Kubik suggests that slave masters' restrictions on music making by groups and toleration of individual singing and guitar playing could have provided the opportunity for a charismatic, very unusual-sounding black songster, influenced by grasslands music, who planted the seed of the blues genre around the time of emancipation.

Scholars emphatically reject the once-popular notion that the particular misery of African Americans in the Jim Crow era inspired blues music. Blues songs certainly described the suffering caused by poverty and racism, as well as conflicts between members of the black community, but they were artistic creations, not the spontaneous emoting of aggrieved singers. In addition, the blues were part of a biracial southern musical culture. Blues singers borrowed from popular songs by white composers. Whites in Appalachia and the Deep South performed Celtic and English ballads and dance tunes which became the precursor to "hillbilly" or country music, but they acquired characteristics we associate with the blues, such as vocal melisma and flattened "blue notes." Despite Jim Crow, southern whites and blacks borrowed musically from each other.

The blues, in short, was not a "primitive" and unchanging product of an isolated people, but rather a complex new creation, which blended African American and white American musical traditions and lyrics in a deeply satisfying new way.

While the Mississippi Delta region, straddling the river from the Gulf of Mexico north to Memphis, can no longer be called the sole birthplace of the blues, it is impossible to deny the special musical and lyrical power of the blues tradition that emerged there. It is equally hard to imagine that oppressive social conditions in the region had no effect on the music. Like nowhere else, African Americans in the Delta were confined to impoverished existences as sharecroppers on large cotton plantations. By 1900, any black hopes that Reconstruction or civil rights could bring racial equality to the Delta had been crushed by white supremacists. Mississippi outclassed the rest of the South in its unequal administration of justice, lynchings, neglect of education for blacks, and vicious racist rhetoric. Musicians in the Delta may not have always "had the blues" when they sang, and their musicianship grew out of years of clear-headed musical adaptation and reworking, but their surroundings provided plenty of misery to explore in their singing. Prison work songs, field hollers, and the rhythmic songs of railroad "gandy dancers" or repairmen enriched their repertory, along with phrases and motifs from the Afro-Caribbean root medicine and spirit worship that persisted in the Delta.

Around 1907, Charley Patton, a man of mixed race, became the first notable guitar-playing blues singer to emerge from the ranks of workers on the mammoth Dockery cotton plantation in Mississippi. Patton performed in jook joints—small taverns, usually located in deserted houses or barns, which provided the main entertainment for tenant farmers on their rare free nights. Jook joints were often plagued by gambling and crime. The danger of sexual assault in jook joints precluded appearances by female singers, although there were exceptions, such as the future blues star "Memphis Minnie" McCoy. Patton's booming voice and guitar-playing tricks made him a popular performer, and he helped nurture other important blues singers such as his half-brother Sam Chatmon, Tommy Johnson, Son House, and the pianist Little Brother Montgomery, who illustrated that not all Delta blues musicians were guitarists. Although white patrols and posses made it risky, even in the Delta black men were free to travel, and Patton and others walked and rode the rails to jook joints across the region, in rural and urban settings.

For decades these blues musicians had no professional support and had to continue working as laborers on the plantations, the local railroads, or the levees designed to hold back the Mississippi River. Patton's most successful recording, "High Water Everywhere," presented a reaction to the great flood of 1927, a disaster that destroyed communities in the Delta and displaced hundreds of thousands of poor African American residents. Patton, Son House, John Hurt, and other early singers created the basic Delta blues style, full of sharply angular guitar attacks, **timbres** with moans and cries, and evocative, often surreal lyrical imagery. Their recordings, as well as those made by male performers of the next generation such as Robert Johnson, Howlin' Wolf, and Muddy Waters, became in succeeding decades among the most influential in American popular music.

Other regions in the South, differing in many ways from the Mississippi Delta, produced strong blues traditions well before Charley Patton's recordings began to circulate in the late 1920s. Eastern Texas, dominated by cotton fields, but also a land of lumber camps, ranching, and petroleum extraction, offered living conditions and hardship little different from those in the Delta. Huddie Ledbetter, born in the region in 1888, learned a number of instruments and a vast song repertory in his youth. Between his frequent stints in prison, "Lead Belly" helped to shape a distinct emerging Texas blues style, featuring strumming influenced by Mexican and "cowboy" guitarists and a richer, hollering mode of singing. It was a younger man, however, "Blind Lemon" Jefferson, who first brought fame to Texas blues through the recordings he made in the late 1920s.

The Piedmont, the long stretch of Appalachian foothills ranging from Virginia to Florida, produced a different kind of guitar-playing tradition, characterized by finger plucking and a large song repertory. The blues that emerged in the Piedmont region differed from those in Texas. In cities in that region, guitarist-singers could be found on central street corners and in other busy public places. In Atlanta, guitar ensembles were especially common. In the recordings that appeared in the 1930s, Piedmont blues were curiously dominated by singers such as Blind Willie McTell (Walter McTear), Blind Blake, and Blind Boy Fuller, who perpetuated the African American tradition of musical excellence among the visually impaired. Elsewhere, rural Louisiana gave rise to a slow-tempo "swamp blues" tradition, and St. Louis, Kansas City, and other southern cities nurtured their own blues singing traditions.

The relationship of early blues to the African American church was complex. Churchgoers could never entirely escape the troubles and tensions of the secular black world that the blues described: poverty, discrimination, personal demons, and interpersonal conflict. At the same time, the blues were influenced by religious songs. Despite the different musical qualities of the blues and spirituals that Gerhard Kubik has emphasized in his attempt to locate their origins in separate African traditions, the blues almost certainly derived their shouting and moaning qualities and "bended" notes in part from black sacred song.

Testimony from the early twentieth century often notes that the music heard in churches and in jook joints were indistinguishable. The blues singer T-Bone Walker recalled that as a youth in Dallas, "the first time I ever heard a boogie-woogie piano was the first time I went to church. . . . That boogie-woogie was a kind of blues, I guess. Then the preacher used to preach in a bluesy tone sometimes." The folklorist Zora Neale Hurston wrote that a blues pianist in Jacksonville, Florida gained "nearly as much of his business from playing for 'Sanctified' church services as from parties."[5] Some Delta blues pioneers, such as Son House, came from preachers' families and pursued that calling before becoming musicians. Thomas A. Dorsey, a minister's son in Atlanta, began his piano and guitar-playing career as blues singer "Georgia Tom," and only gradually made a transition into church music. The proximity of sacred and secular music and behavior, though, worried members of the black elite. After 1910, as the blues became a stable and popular genre, ministers in the South, and later in the North, castigated it as "the devil's music." For all of its affirmative spirit and beauty, the blues became a ripe target for devout African Americans, who associated them with the crime and sexual promiscuity around jook joints and taverns, as well as with vestiges of pagan spirit worship that were referenced in some blues lyrics. It was a tension that would persist for decades.

In the meantime, as the Great Migration brought southern African Americans to the North, the blues emerged as a new popular music. William Christopher Handy provided a familiarity with the music business, entrepreneurship, and a sense of showmanship that helped to lift the blues into national prominence. The son of a preacher from Florence, Alabama, the young Handy worked at various jobs in trades and industry and as a schoolteacher, but he found music, especially cornet playing, to be his passion. In the 1890s, Handy traveled across the South and Midwest with minstrel shows and with his own instrumental quartet, which performed at the Chicago Exposition of 1893. While teaching music at Alabama A & M College for Negroes, Handy began researching local black music. After returning to work as a bandleader, Handy was exposed to some of the first Delta blues. He recalled in his autobiography that in 1903, at the railroad station in Tutwiler, Mississippi, the silent night air was shaken by the guitar playing of "a lean, loose-jointed Negro, press[ing] a knife on the strings of the guitar. 'Goin' where the Southern cross' the Dog,' the singer repeated three times, accompanying himself on guitar with the weirdest music I had ever heard."[6] The singer might have been Henry Sloan, the musician who has been credited with teaching Charley Patton. The song referred to the intersection of the Southern and the Yazoo & Mississippi Valley, or Yellow Dog, railroads. Further exposure to such "weird," rough playing and singing in the region encouraged Handy to make arrangements of these songs for his ensemble.

In doing so, Handy, like the spirituals collectors in the emancipated South during the Civil War, codified black folk music in a straightforward but simplified manner that made it accessible to whites and the black middle class. In 1912, when Handy published his first hit song, "Memphis Blues," he introduced 12-bar blues and "blue notes" to a mass audience. Based in Memphis until he joined the Great Migration to Harlem in 1917, Handy launched his own publishing company and publicized his versions of the Delta blues. He adapted the basic harmonies of the blues to dance tempos, and soon songs such as "St. Louis Blues" inspired dancing in white-dominated halls and hotel ballrooms. Most important, Handy promoted them specifically as *blues* songs, imprinting the name in the memories of listeners. After he arrived in New York, Handy proved adept at locating capital and making his publishing and band offices a center of musical activity in Harlem. He had to contend with many unauthorized performances of his songs by white bands, but his tireless promotion of the blues, and of himself, kept him prosperous. Handy's efforts in the 1920s and 1930s as a historian of black music and owner of Handy Records, one of the first black-controlled record companies, helped him to earn the title he gave himself, "Father of the Blues."

Another factor in the commercialization of the blues was the vaudeville circuit—or, more specifically, the southern portion of the circuit overseen by the Theatre Owners Booking Agency (TOBA). This organization was begun in 1909 by S. H. Dudley, a pioneering African American theater owner, but was reorganized and expanded in 1920 by Milton Starr, a white impresario from Nashville. TOBA maintained a network of theaters for black audiences in the South and sent a variety of road shows along the circuit throughout the year. Some performers expanded their tours beyond the South and visited the Northeast, Midwest, and West, but the "chitlin' circuit" remained central to their careers. Performers on the circuit criticized TOBA for its low pay, poor accommodations, and arduous travel, and famously described its acronym as standing for "Tough On Black Asses." But TOBA also gave them steady work, and for African American audiences the constant stage offerings were a revelation, providing them with regular exposure to some of the most talented black singers, dancers, musicians, and comedians. In the South and elsewhere, TOBA raised black America's standards and expectations for high-quality entertainment and provided fertile fields for future innovators and entrepreneurs in African American music.

Female blues singers were among the leading attractions on the TOBA circuit. In contrast to jook joints, the circuit provided some safety for women performers, on and off the stage, as well as incomes and commercial promotion. Preeminent among the TOBA blueswomen was Gertrude "Ma" Rainey. Born in Alabama and raised in Columbus, Georgia, Rainey was a veteran of minstrel shows. In 1902, at the age of twenty, Rainey apparently heard her first blues song, performed by a youth in Memphis. With her husband, William "Pa" Rainey, Gertrude developed a specialty act in the Rabbit Foot Minstrels called the "Assassinators of the Blues," which popularized the term in the early years of TOBA even before W. C. Handy began to promote the music.

In the 1910s and 1920s, Rainey became one of the most famous and talked-about African American performers due to her talent, activism, and prolific sexual activity. Rainey's booming alto voice easily filled large halls, and while on the TOBA circuit she battled for fair pay and better treatment for black performers. In the process Rainey, along with her protégé Bessie Smith and other female singers, developed a blues style quite different from the drawling Delta blues and the genteel arrangements of W. C. Handy. Interpreting lyrics that proclaimed female woe and resolve in the battle of the sexes, Rainey, Smith, and other vaudevillians made the blues into an expression of black women's concerns.

Commercial female blues singers were the first to become nationally known through recordings. Mamie Smith was the pioneer, recording "Crazy Blues" in 1920. This song, the third one she sold to OKeh Records, unexpectedly became a hit. Mamie Smith, a contemporary of Ma Rainey's, was a Cincinnati native who was also a veteran of minstrel shows and vaudeville. She had lived and worked in New York City for a few years, however, specializing in the blues songs of her friend Perry Bradford, who, like Handy, was a promoter and publisher of such songs in Harlem. Until 1920, white-owned record companies rarely employed African American vocalists. Smith only appeared in the OKeh studio because the famous white singer Sophie Tucker had canceled her recording date. "Crazy Blues" went on to sell one million copies in a year and inspired the major record companies to pay attention to African American performers and consumers. Thus was born the phenomenon of "race records"—in which extraordinary and enterprising black talent in blues, jazz, and other genres were exploited to earn great profits for the white-run recording industry. Black-owned record companies such as Black Swan and Handy also took part, but they were minor partners in the race records phenomenon.

The popularity of recordings by female blues singers provided an overdue acknowledgment of the musical artistry of African American women. Since the antebellum era, white and black accounts of music making by slaves and free blacks had been skewed heavily toward male performers. This was a reflection of the social conditions surrounding African American music. The music business was a difficult arena in which to make a living, and despite the presence on stage of the Hyers sisters, Stella Wiley, and Sisieretta Jones, male performers and songwriters dominated the ar-

Photo 3.2. Blues singer Bessie Smith, photographed by Carl Van Vechten. Source: Prints and Photographs Division, Library of Congress.

duous tours, uncertain theater engagements, and low-royalty sheet music concerns that defined the musical profession. The African American church and its music increasingly were dominated by women, but, as in most white congregations, this dominance did little to pull women out of the traditional female domestic sphere. But black churchwomen usually worked outside the home as well, and their everyday difficulties, at the hands of society, their men, and their communities, became the subject matter of performances by female blues singers. The TOBA circuit and race records gave these singers prominent platforms for expressing the desires and troubles of a nation of black women, and the blues, abetted by techniques from other popular music, provided them with powerful expressive techniques and forms.

More generally, race records preserved and disseminated a huge array of black musical talent during the years of the African American Great Migration. For that reason, race records, along with live musical performances, were a central inspiration for the writers, artists, and composers of the "Harlem Renaissance." Their creative works in the 1920s expressed the optimism and newfound freedom of African Americans in the era of the Great Migration. The young poet Langston Hughes's most celebrated collection was entitled *The Weary Blues,* and Hughes's and Sterling Brown's pioneering experiments in "blues poetry" transformed black literary aesthetics, replacing the traditional exaggerated representations of dialect with more authentic renderings of Black English. In the early 1920s, race records preserved the female vaudeville blues style, making celebrities of Mamie Smith, Ma Rainey, Ida Cox, Ethel Waters, Bessie Smith, and a number of singers, renamed "Smith" by their managers, who hoped to repeat Mamie's success. After 1925, sales of the female singers' records declined somewhat, and producers such as OKeh's Tommy Rockwell began to seek out the male singers in the Delta and East Texas. Soon Charley Patton, Blind Lemon Jefferson, Blind Boy Fuller, and others were selling hundreds of thousands of records.

The blues' honesty about male-female relationships and, more rarely, about same-sex intimacy, inspired white listeners to consider it a morally degraded music. Thanks to the Harlem Renaissance, African American creativity and originality gained greater recognition from whites in the 1920s, but that recognition was often skewed by the persistence of old stereotypes and caricatures. Recording companies encouraged female blues singers to increase the suggestive imagery in their lyrics. Even serious white observers such as the novelists Carl Van Vechten and Thomas Wolfe, enamored of psychological theories inspired by Sigmund Freud, fixated on the lustful black woman as an emblem of the frank sexuality of their own literary works.

Whenever blues singers could break free from these harmful commercial distortions, their performances thoughtfully addressed the realities of African American life. These included the existence of tension in personal relationships, especially between adult men and women. In blues lyrics these relationships were usually described with almost no reference to stable family life. Much debate has taken place about the possible long-lasting impact of slavery on black families. While emancipation and legal marriage and parentage transformed many lives for the better, records show widespread domestic violence and upheaval in the Reconstruction South. The evidence about family life beyond 1877, in black communities nationwide, is sometimes contradictory. The percentage of stable two-parent families in many northern cities in the early 1900s, for example, is close to that of whites. However, poorer African American men and women suffered from difficult or scarce work, unsuitable housing, education, and medical care, and a lack of social services. This deprivation increased the frequency of parental desertion, domestic violence, pregnancy by single women (a cultural norm that derived from practices in West Africa), and other signs of apparent family instability. These conditions inspired ministers and others in the black middle classes to attack the blues' occasional glamorization of infidelity and sexual activity. But the blues also gave voice to the psychological and social conflicts of everyday African Americans, and thus helped to make the difficulties of black life a more prominent part of the public record.

CONCLUSION

By the 1920s, African American popular music had undergone a transformation that made it sound very different from the music recorded in the 1890s on paper and on cylinder wax. Ragtime had demonstrated that a large number of highly skilled black pianists could adapt African American polyrhythms to the harmonies and piano techniques of European classical music. The exciting syncopation that resulted, in turn, caught the fancy of younger Americans of all races who yearned for less restricted leisure and who defined themselves more fully through vigorous re-creation. Ragtime artists such as Scott Joplin, James Scott, and James Reese Europe found in the music and in the new professional associations they were creating a way to bury the caricatures of black music and musicians that were born in the era of slavery and minstrelsy.

The blues also allowed its creators to distance themselves from the shadows of the antebellum past. The greatest victims of Reconstruction's failure, the tenant farmers on the cotton plantations of the Deep South, developed a secular song form that borrowed the most effective solo music-making elements from the Afro-Caribbean tradition and combined them with lyrics that inspired individual boldness, frankness, and confession. Today, the blues singer is often compared to the griot of West African tradition, a spokesman and master poet for his society. The revival of the playful, articulate, and wise voice of the griot in the person of the blues singer provided African Americans with a musical voice that critiqued poverty and inequality in the industrial United States. Average black people would no longer be silent in the face of injustice.

After 1920, ragtime declined quickly in popularity. It was revived occasionally in later decades by groups of mostly white fans. The blues, by contrast, grew and diversified in succeeding decades, becoming the foundation for many new genres of black popular music. However, in those same decades jazz, a music that blended ragtime's instrumental virtuosity and rhythmic excitement with blues harmonies and timbres, as well as other ingredients, eclipsed the popularity of the blues for a generation. The practitioners of jazz became the most celebrated African American musicians in history up to that time.

NOTES

1. Edward A. Berlin, *Ragtime: A Musical and Cultural History* (Berkeley: University of California Press, 1980), 12.

2. Charles W. Chesnutt, "The Wife of His Youth" (1898), in *Charles W. Chesnutt: Stories, Novels, and Essays,* ed. Werner Sollors (New York: Library of America, 2002), 102.

3. Lynn Abbott, "'Play That Barber Shop Chord': A Case for the African-American Origin of Barbershop Harmony," *American Music* 10 (1992), 290.

4. David Evans, "Blues," in *African American Music: An Introduction*, eds. Mellonee V. Burnim and Portia K. Maultsby (New York: Routledge, 2006), 79.

5. Quoted in Lawrence W. Levine, *Black Culture and Black Consciousness: Afro-American Folk Thought from Slavery to the Present* (New York: Oxford University Press, 1977), 180.

6. W. C. Handy, *Father of the Blues: An Autobiography* (New York: Macmillan, 1941), 74.

4

The Emergence of Jazz

Louis Armstrong became one of the most famous musicians of the twentieth century, but for much of his life, the odds were stacked against him. Born in New Orleans in 1901, Louis rarely saw his parents for the first few years of his life. His father drifted away, and his mother could not afford to raise him and may have worked as a prostitute to make ends meet. Louis was raised by his grandparents. As a dark-skinned boy of pure African American lineage, Louis was at the bottom of New Orleans's complex racial hierarchy. Urban poverty surrounded him. He played in the streets, participated in petty crime, and witnessed more serious offenses committed by older men and women. After firing a pistol in public, Louis was taken from his mother by the police and placed by a court in the Colored Waifs' Home. Many young men in Louis Armstrong's situation became habitual residents of state facilities and faced the prospect of a stunted life, deprived of marketable skills, stable family lives, and even clear personal identities. Such young, poor African American males would struggle in the United States throughout the twentieth century, but some of them, like Louis Armstrong, found music to be their salvation.

Louis Armstrong beat the odds. His grandparents and the local churches provided him with values and self-esteem, and at the Colored Waifs' Home he received all of the formal instruction on the cornet that he would ever need. Not just crime surrounded him; music, played by bands and pianists in the streets, taverns, dance halls, and parks, and sung in churches, was part of his daily upbringing. And Armstrong, driven with a passion to escape the streets and attain a life of greater comfort, pushed himself to become the best band musician he could be.

Despite his ambition, he might not have dreamed that he would soon leave New Orleans and become the toast of the jazz scene in Chicago and New York City. It was even less likely that he would have foreseen becoming an internationally beloved entertainer, a star of stage and the movies, and the founding father of a musical style that reshaped popular culture around the world.

Louis Armstrong's story conveys much of the drama and excitement in the story of African Americans in jazz. Jazz is not purely a black music, but at every stage of its development the most significant innovators were African American. In addition, to an extent greater than in ragtime or the blues, jazz became the black musician's ticket to respect and prosperity in the eyes of the largely nonblack public, in the United States and in Europe. The rise of jazz took place during the tumultuous era of the two World Wars, which bookended the "roaring 1920s" and the era of the Great Depression. In those thirty years, from 1915 to 1945, the United States was transformed into a world power and a welfare state, in which the government committed itself to protecting its own needy citizens and the stability of the world. Americans' earlier concerns about local or re-

Photo 4.1. Louis Armstrong in the 1940s. Source: Prints and Photographs Division, Library of Congress.

gional status or social hierarchy seemed less important. In this era, intellectuals challenged the scientific racism of earlier generations, which had supposedly "proven" innate racial inequality, and black civil rights activists launched the first effective major movement since Reconstruction.

Like earlier popular music, jazz was affected by the larger context of racial inequality and discrimination, and some white musicians and audiences minimized the African American contribution. But black jazz musicians largely belonged to a new, twentieth-century generation that held greater expectations for their careers and their music. Also, to an unprecedented degree, white listeners respected their achievements. In many ways, the excitement generated by jazz symbolized the winds of change and progress that increasingly offered encouragement to African Americans.

EARLY NEW ORLEANS JAZZ

If we explore the relationship between two older musical styles, ragtime and the blues, and a newcomer, jazz, we discover an interesting example of how the old gives way to the new in African American culture. In a sense it is accurate to say that ragtime and the blues were blended together to create jazz, but such a simple recipe ignores the complexities of chronology, influence, and biography that the story of early jazz reveals.

Proud residents of New Orleans, as well as many others, have claimed that the city was the "cradle of jazz," the sole birthplace of the music. The claim is probably inaccurate. Many cities and towns nurtured styles similar to New Orleans jazz at about the same time, and some even assisted in the development of New Orleans jazz. Nevertheless, it is clear that musicians and listeners during jazz's early boom years in the 1920s and 1930s considered New Orleans to be supremely important. Regardless of its status as jazz's birthplace, New Orleans between 1900 and 1920 played host to the creation of an exciting and highly influential jazz style. The interaction of musicians and bands from other parts of the country with New Orleans jazz musicians helped to create the music that captivated the nation and the world.

By 1900, New Orleans's old identity as a French colonial city, populated in part by Creoles of color who covered a wide racial spectrum, had been modified by nearly a century of U.S. control. As in other southern cities, a primarily Anglo-Saxon white business and political elite ruled New Orleans—or, more accurately, misruled it, leaving the city without social services and infrastructure that other municipalities were developing. As the South's major port, New Orleans first attracted large numbers of internal migrants, including rural African Americans and some whites from the Mississippi River Delta, as well as immigrants from Ireland and Italy. A decade of recurring ethnic and racial violence, culminating in the Robert Charles riot of 1900 that led to the deaths of dozens of African Americans, showed New Orleans to be a cauldron of social discontent. The imposition of racial segregation at this time forced the Creoles of color, many of them virtually white-skinned, into the second-class status of black migrants from the plantations. New Orleans in this era seemed unlikely to give birth to a major artistic development. Despite social tensions and poverty, though, the city's streets and working-class leisure venues produced a musical revolution.

"American (non-Creole) Negroes," Creoles of color, and white New Orleanians all played a role in the creation of New Orleans jazz. The music was called "ragtime" by most practitioners until at least 1920, reflecting the dominance of the earlier genre in preceding years. The city's rich heritage of opera, dance orchestras, and brass bands, influenced by a long French tradition, blended with Hispanic influences from Mexico and the Caribbean. New Orleans's brass bands gained new renown from an appearance at the World Industrial and Cotton Exposition in 1885. Affluent Creoles of color had long supported formal musical instruction, employing French solfège (do-re-mi note learning) and other practices, while parades, funerals, and other traditions encouraged regular band performances. Black people were excluded from official parades on Mardi Gras and other festive occasions, but they created informal "second line" parades behind the white marchers. Meanwhile, in Storyville, New Orleans's legal prostitution district, black and Creole musicians, especially pianists, shared and stole each other's musical ideas.

In the 1890s and 1900s the music of rural black migrants, especially early blues, began to blend with the classical and ragtime elements of white and Creole music. The shouts and bugle blasts of street peddlers and junk dealers and hymn singing in the migrants' storefront churches displayed some characteristics of the Delta blues. Creole musicians and audiences, falling in social status due to segregation and resentful of the migrants' poverty, dark skin, and lack of formal education, largely rejected any musical assimilation, but some young Creoles, such as Ferdinand LaMotte and Sidney Bechet, were decisively influenced by the blues. LaMotte, a young pianist and occasional pimp who disdained his African American ancestry and billed himself as Jelly Roll Morton, left New Orleans in 1904 for a long nationwide sojourn as an itinerant pianist.

Among black musicians at that time, the term "ragtime" began to designate a new kind of band music, in which the melismas, vocal effects such as growling and moaning, and stanza-by-stanza improvisation of the Delta blues became melded with the standard repertory of minstrel, Tin Pan Alley, and ragtime songs. Twelve-bar blues songs became standards. Around 1905, the clarion call of the new style was sounded by a barber and cornetist named Charles "Buddy" Bolden. Bolden's band, one of dozens that played in dance halls, parades, and outdoor functions, stood out for its "ratty," blues-influenced inflections, and the leader's booming cornet-playing sent growls, yelps, and "blue notes" sounding across entire city blocks. Bolden's career was cut short in 1907 when he was committed to a mental institution, the victim of alcoholism and dementia, but his influence proved decisive. Cornetists such as Bunk Johnson, who was black, and Freddy Keppard, a Creole, followed Bolden's lead. Another young cornetist was Joe Oliver, a rural migrant whose musical training included stints in Manuel Perez's Onward Brass Band, a leading Creole ensemble. Oliver's ambition and ideas about collective improvisation made his band a force on the New Orleans scene by 1916. That year he offered tutelage to fifteen-year old Louis Armstrong.

By that time, New Orleans "jazz" had taken shape. Its musicians had mastered traditional European-American band instruments and had developed their own advanced playing techniques. The nimble clarinet, strumming banjo, blasting cornet, thumping bass and snare drum, and sliding "tailgate" trombone all had developed their characteristic qualities. Bands, which varied in size from three to twelve members, improvised collectively on a diverse repertory of tunes. Improvisers used their instrumental skill to create new melodies out of notes in a song's chords. They regularly worked "blue notes" and blues harmonies into their playing, especially when they improvised on the blues themselves. Jazz was performed ably in New Orleans by hundreds of male and female city residents, who rewarded the most expressive and technically skilled improvisers with applause and esteem. In the 1910s, local journalists and non-jazz musicians disparaged or ignored jazz, but its rise to fame had begun.

The origins of the term "jazz," like "ragtime" and "the blues," remain obscure. Historians have linked "jazz" to West African words relating to music and dance; a music promoter whose first name was Charles or "Chas"; jasmine-scented perfume; and "ass," slang for sexual intercourse, since the term was often spelled "jass" in the early years. The earliest published use of the term appeared in 1913 in a San Francisco newspaper, possibly planted by a New Orleans musician passing through the city. "Jazz" became a well-known term in 1917, when the Original Dixieland Jazz Band (ODJB), from New Orleans, made its first recordings for the Victor Company. The ODJB was an ensemble of white musicians of Sicilian, Irish, and English backgrounds who, despite segregation, had mingled in the streets and dance halls with blues-improvising black musicians. Despite their name, the band's performances sound like a particularly frenetic brand of ragtime, and the sliding whoops of clarinetist Larry Shields generally do not resemble slides in the blues. The

ODJB recordings broke sales records and encouraged a worldwide, largely white audience to think of jazz as frantic and comical dance music. The disconnect in American popular music between the mass market concept of jazz and the music performed in the blues-band improvisation style created in black New Orleans would persist for at least the next two decades.

CHICAGO AND NEW YORK CITY

Meanwhile, World War I encouraged the Great Migration of African Americans from the South to northern cities. Black New Orleanians of all statuses left the city to pursue better lives in the North, but only the few individuals who were trained in the skilled trades might have expected the brightest prospects there. Musicians were among their number. The pianist Tony Jackson, a veteran of Storyville, moved to Chicago and scored a hit with the publication of his song "Pretty Baby." Joe "King" Oliver brought his Creole Orchestra to the same city in 1918. Meanwhile, young Louis Armstrong expanded his horizons in a different way, winning a job with Fate Marable's Mississippi riverboat band. Marable's band did not play jazz, but performed popular standards. Armstrong and his friend, the drummer Warren "Baby" Dodds, had to learn to read sheet music and adapt their jazz style to the band's playing. On the riverboats, Armstrong traveled as far north as Wisconsin, spreading the New Orleans style and encountering jazz musicians in cities such as Memphis and St. Louis. Those cities lacked the particular musical heritage of New Orleans, but they had long been sites of extensive black musical activity, and now they were also witnessing the blues, ragtime, and band music blending into exciting new styles. Black jazz musicians remained unrecorded until 1920, when they provided instrumental accompaniment on some of the first records by female blues singers, and the first jazz band was not recorded until the next year, when the New Orleans trombonist Edward "Kid" Ory led a session in Los Angeles. In the meantime, though, jazz musicians worked together on theater tours and in cabarets. After performances, they met in taverns and other nightspots and challenged each other to "cutting contests," musical duels that helped them develop new ideas and hone their improvisational skills.

Chicago was the first major destination for many black New Orleans jazz musicians. The southern black migration to Chicago in the 1910s was a story of triumph and tragedy. The meatpacking plants and steelyards offered good pay, but also gave rise to hostility from white workers who feared job competition. A general housing shortage led to violent reprisals by whites against African American migrants who moved into previously all-white neighborhoods. In July 1919, white anger peaked in a major race riot, in which mobs of both races looted, burned buildings, and killed. The black South Side did not stop growing, though, and its vitality into the 1920s was a testament to the optimism of its residents. The broad avenues, spacious homes and yards, parks, and schools all spoke of a better life, as did the relentless boosterism of the nationally distributed South Side newspaper, the *Chicago Defender*. Commercial blocks and intersections became hives of nightlife, featuring restaurants, dance halls, theaters, and nightclubs serving the more-affluent members of the black community. During Prohibition (1920–1933) the liquor-serving establishments fell under the control of white organized crime, and some sites became swamped with thrill-seeking white customers, but on the whole the South Side of Chicago was a vast improvement over the jook joints of the Delta and the decaying dance halls in west New Orleans.

It was to this environment that Louis Armstrong migrated in 1922, when King Oliver invited him to join the Creole Orchestra in Chicago. Oliver's recruitment of a second cornetist was unusual, and a reflection of his pioneering efforts to tailor the New Orleans sound to northern audiences. In 1923, the group made the first important recordings by a black jazz ensemble. Practitioners such as Armstrong called the band's style "hot" jazz, rich in the harmonies and timbre of the blues and in skilled solo and group improvisation. Fans of hot jazz distinguished the style from the "sweet" or "crazy" music of popular white bands that most listeners of the 1920s considered to be jazz. In later years, admirers of hot jazz would define it as the wellspring of the entire mainstream jazz tradition. They argued that successive generations of blues-inspired improvisers all could trace their inspirations back to Bolden, Oliver, and Armstrong.

King Oliver's pianist, Lil Hardin, married Louis Armstrong and tutored him in the life of the urban professional musician. Throughout his life Armstrong remained an unpretentious man whose speech and manner reflected the streets of New Orleans—as well as his own gregarious and extroverted personality—but he also depended on and learned from people who were adept at business and northern ways, such as Hardin and his future manager, Joe Glaser. Armstrong enjoyed smoking marijuana for relaxation, a habit he picked up in Chicago, and suffered lip injuries from his imprecise use of his mouthpiece, but he was a very hard worker who polished his musical ideas relentlessly. He was also a voluminous letter writer, who commented with passion and intelligence on racial injustice and many other aspects of his experience.

By 1924, Louis Armstrong was able to break out on his own. In Chicago he had gained a reputation as the most brilliant blues stylist on the cornet, a master improviser who could string together dozens of variations on a twelve-bar tune. Armstrong, at his wife's urging, left Oliver and Chicago to join the Fletcher Henderson Orchestra in New York City. Arriving in the nation's largest city, Armstrong confronted a jazz scene far different from that of New Orleans or Chicago.

Fletcher Henderson, a native of Atlanta, was typical of black migrants to New York City in that he was from the Southeast, not the Mississippi River valley. In addition, he held a degree in chemistry from Atlanta University, the most important black college in the Deep South. While many migrants to Harlem were unskilled workers, an unusual proportion of them, like Henderson, were well-educated professionals. Henderson, though, abandoned graduate study at Columbia University for music, because scientific careers were still largely closed to African Americans. Similarly, professionals in Harlem such as the diplomat and activist James Weldon Johnson and the lawyer Paul Robeson were drawn to music as an expression of the black spirit during the Great Migration. As a result, black music in Harlem acquired a veneer of sophistication and polished professionalism. The urbane image of New York jazz would achieve its ultimate definition in the late 1920s in the work of a new young bandleader, Duke Ellington.

New York City's jazz scene was also shaped by its roots in black ragtime. In the taverns and apartments on the Upper West Side and later in Harlem, African American pianists challenged each other to create bolder improvisations of ragtime tunes. Two decades of intense competition in Manhattan produced a driving piano style known as "stride." In this style, the pianist's left hand played a measured beat that bounced in octave intervals, a loping effect that gave stride piano its name. Unlike in ragtime, though, the left hand also played bits of melody, which freed up the right hand to provide dazzling ornaments, leaps, and runs up and down the keyboard. Masters of stride such as Luckeyth Roberts, Willie "The Lion" Smith, James P. Johnson, and Thomas "Fats" Waller turned ragtime and other popular songs into improvisations that, in their counterpoint, rivaled the complexity of classical works. Older players such as Eubie Blake and Jelly Roll Morton, who migrated to New York from Baltimore and Chicago, respectively, also made the transition from ragtime to stride. The veteran pianists found acolytes such as Bill "Count" Basie, from nearby New Jersey; Edward "Duke" Ellington, a native of Washington, D.C.; and Art Tatum, from Cleveland. Earl "Fatha" Hines, a classically trained pianist from Pittsburgh who worked in Chicago for most of the 1920s, developed a similarly complex and sophisticated jazz piano style.

In the 1920s, New York City, with a population of six million, readily provided a huge array of entertainment venues. Fletcher Henderson's jazz band, which featured the skilled arranger Don Redman and the pioneering tenor saxophonist Coleman Hawkins, found lucrative work at two of them: the Club Alabam' and the Roseland Ballroom. Both establishments only admitted white customers, indicating the significant level of discrimination to be found even in America's most cosmopolitan city. Henderson's band was already successful when Louis Armstrong joined the group, but his addition created even more excitement among jazz fans. While the blues were known among black New York musicians through recordings and some personal experience, few of them were even aware of how much the Delta blues had influenced black New Orleans jazz. After working with Armstrong, Coleman Hawkins emulated the cornetist's booming, vocal-style delivery in his saxophone playing. The power and vivid personality of Armstrong's playing single-handedly made soloists the stars of jazz. Audiences glorified individual improvisers and neglected the collective improvisation that had been the basis of New Orleans jazz. Despite his success in New York, Armstrong returned to Chicago in 1925, where he worked in bands with his wife Lil and with pianist Earl Hines, who became an important collaborator. While in Chicago, Armstrong led a series of brilliant recording sessions with his Hot Five and Hot Seven ensembles. These records sealed his reputation as a bold innovator and helped to make recordings one of the central points of reference for devoted listeners of jazz.

These recordings displayed Armstrong's dazzling improvisational skill, which sometimes strayed far from the letter of the original melody but which constructed works of art within the constraint of sixteen-bar choruses and three-minute recording times. They also captured his inimitable singing style, a raspy and exuberant cousin to his trumpet playing, bluesy in sound and feeling, but featuring a swaggering joyousness that was alien to the Delta blues.[1] Jazz historians credit Armstrong with inventing wordless "scat" singing, which became a hallmark of jazz vocals, but some of them note that he also constructed this kind of singing out of earlier black folk practices.

Swinging was the word that, above all, distilled the essence of Louis Armstrong's, and jazz's, revolutionary impact on American music. "Swing" is the quality that is most frequently associated with jazz, but it is also the most difficult to define. Simply put, swinging means *not* to play or sing in the strict tempo or rhythm of a song. Instead, musicians place notes so that they lag behind or, less commonly, arrive slightly before the steady beat of the band's rhythm section or the pianist's left hand. This definition, though, does not capture the reason *why* musicians swing, which is to heighten the emotional appeal of the music and make it more conducive to satisfying bodily movement.

The roots of swing lay in sub-Saharan African music, where the absence of dominating time signatures and beats and the interweaving of parts in musical ensembles created highly flexible polyrhythms, which seemed to lag or push forward as the musical moment saw fit. This flexibility of

rhythm lent a general feeling of satisfaction, and even joy, to performances, a feeling similar to what African American musicians in the
twentieth century would call "being in the groove." Swinging probably
was one of the "delicate variations" in the singing of freed people in South
Carolina in 1863, that the white listener William Francis Allen insisted
"cannot be reproduced on paper."[2] In New Orleans, early jazz players applied swinging to traditional musical forms, turning marches into "slow
drags" and ragtime rhythms into "shuffles." In the 1920s, many white listeners, ranging from female striptease dancers to disapproving clergymen, associated the swinging quality of jazz with sexually suggestive
physical movements. In dance halls, though, swing allowed young
African Americans to transcend the mechanical syncopation of ragtime
dances and to incorporate subtlety, grace, and sensuality into the new
dance steps of the 1920s such as the Lindy Hop and the Charleston.

More than any other earlier black music, 1920s hot jazz popularized a
spirit that was alien to the dominant European model of comportment,
movement, and leisure. In the years when millions of Americans of all
races, especially youth, were yearning to escape the formalities of the
past, jazz was an irresistible call to cultural rebellion. In the 1920s,
teenaged white men such as Bix Beiderbecke of Davenport, Iowa; Jimmy
McPartland of Chicago; and Arthur Arshawsky (later Artie Shaw) of New
York found their entire mentality transformed by jazz music, and they
were all inspired to embark on careers as improvising "hot" musicians.

When the novelist F. Scott Fitzgerald looked back on the 1920s and
called it "the jazz age," he was probably thinking of the music of popular
white musicians such as Paul Whiteman and other "sweet" bandleaders.
The label, however, also accurately places African American jazz music at
the center of the decade's change in sensibility. By the end of the decade,
the popularity and cultural influence of jazz musicians such as Louis Armstrong easily eclipsed those of the black poets, novelists, and artists of the
Harlem Renaissance. During the Great Depression, many major figures of
the Harlem scene fell into obscurity, but the leading black jazz musicians
maintained their celebrity and expanded their following. Jazz continued to
be a dynamic music. Band musicians changed their instruments to accom-
modate advances in arranging and improvisation; banjoes and tubas gave
way to saxophones and complex arrays of drums and cymbals.

In general, all varieties of black popular music of the 1920s displayed a
special dynamism and confidence. Although African American stage mu-
sicals of the 1920s such as Eubie Blake and Noble Sissle's *Shuffle Along* contained more ragtime music than jazz, they also exhibited energy and fresh
ideas that brought them great success and popularity. The spectacular careers of stage performers such the tap dancer Bill "Bojangles" Robinson
and the short-lived singer Florence Mills also demonstrated the vitality of

African American music in the 1920s. Although white producers continued to feature these performers in plantation or jungle settings, their joyous intensity transcended the stale stereotypes that surrounded them.

Jazz's vitality may have been best illustrated by the rise of Duke Ellington as a bandleader and composer. As a youth Ellington had shown little promise as a musician, aspiring more toward a career as a commercial artist and relying heavily on the charm and aristocratic bearing that inspired his nickname. When Ellington, now a pianist and songwriter, made his second and final move to New York in 1923, he was not even considered the leader of his ensemble, the Washingtonians. In the next few years, though, Ellington took charge, honing his pianistic skills with the assistance of stride pianists such as Fats Waller and studying composition with arranger and bandleader Will Vodery and the elder statesman of African American stage music, Will Marion Cook. Four years of nightclub performing paid off when Ellington's band, now a resplendent ten-man group, was hired as the house orchestra for the Cotton Club. This gangster-owned nightclub brought the racist arrogance of elite Broadway to Harlem, excluding black customers and mounting caricatured "jungle revues" for its big-spending white audiences. Ellington nevertheless exploited his six-year engagement at the club by carefully choosing his band's personnel and composing numbers that showcased their individual sounds and blended them into a harmonious whole.

Largely ignorant of the Deep South, Ellington acquired his blues and New Orleans jazz secondhand, but no one captured the vivacious and audacious striving found in post-Migration black Harlem as effectively as he did. His band included gritty players such as the trumpeter Bubber Miley and the drummer Sonny Greer who were balanced by smooth, urbane stylists such as the clarinetist Barney Bigard and the trombonist Lawrence Brown. Brown's section mate Juan Tizol, the only nonblack band member, provided a Hispanic influence. In Ellington's early works, suggestive instrumental growls coexisted with gauzy tropical harmonies and chords that seemed to float in from French Impressionist music, while a swinging beat and cacophonous percussion kept the band firmly grounded in the black jazz mainstream. In addition, the bandleader developed an introspective style, best captured in pieces such as "Solitude," that echoed the poignancy of Scott Joplin's slower works and Bert Williams's vocals and modified jazz's reputation as a purely extroverted music.

Ellington was not the first great jazz band composer. Jelly Roll Morton committed arrangements to paper which his band, the Red Hot Peppers, preserved in classic recordings in 1926, and Don Redman pioneered arrangements for big bands while working for Fletcher Henderson in New York. But Ellington, through his innovative compositions and his association with a skilled and well-connected white manager, Irving Mills, realized his enormous ambitions even as the Great Depression ravaged the music business. In the early 1930s, he began writing extended compositions on major topics in the African American experience. He welcomed some critics' comparisons of him with Debussy and Ravel, and his band made very successful tours of Great Britain and Scandinavia.

JAZZ MUSICIANS ON THE MOVE

Jazz, to a greater extent than spirituals, vaudeville, and ragtime, enabled its African American practitioners to travel the world, expand the popularity of their music, and experience cultures outside the United States. Sidney Bechet spent much of the 1920s in Europe. Bechet, a clarinetist and soprano saxophonist from New Orleans, was probably Louis Armstrong's only real rival as a solo improviser. Bechet's elegant, passionate improvisations, laced with his signature heavy vibrato, were as innovative as Armstrong's more swaggering and powerful statements. Immediately after World War I, Bechet traveled with Will Marion Cook's ragtime orchestra to Europe, where he stunned cultivated listeners with solos that contrasted wildly with the band's rigid arrangements. Bechet repeatedly returned to Europe, where his combative temperament ultimately landed him in a British jail and caused his deportation back to the United States. Unlike Armstrong, Bechet was unwilling to submit to a manager's discipline, and he never achieved a successful show business career.

Other jazz musicians traveled overseas as well. The pianist Teddy Weatherford worked for many years in the Philippines, China, and India, and the trumpeter Valaida Snow, a rare female star on that instrument, also toured the Far East. In the 1930s, the saxophonists Coleman Hawkins and Benny Carter spent years in Paris. In that city, a rabid coterie of local fans wrote the first published histories of what they called *le jazz hot* and nurtured the careers of native jazz innovators such as Django Reinhardt and Stephane Grappelli. Thanks to these chroniclers and to the impact of the phonograph, black music's global reach expanded.

Within the United States, also, black musicians were on the move. Bands coveted months-long residencies at dance halls and nightclubs, but these gigs were rare, and even they did not provide a living or family wage for band members. Duke Ellington's band traveled for weeks, especially while the Cotton Club was closed during the summer. Irving Mills eventually was able to obtain a railroad car for Ellington and his musicians, but most other bands traveled by bus or car. In the 1920s, America became an automotive culture, and few in the nation logged as many miles on the road as band musicians. Recording royalties were negligible and radio, a new medium, benefitted few musicians, least of all African

Americans. The only reliable source of revenue came from dance halls and nightclubs, which demanded an endless supply of live musical talent. When they appeared in these venues, though, musicians often suffered at the hands of untrustworthy paymasters. Canceled engagements or car trouble stranded penniless bands far from home. Bands often suffered from break-ups and turnover in personnel, and musicians found that long road trips led to tensions with wives and other relatives back home.

In addition, traveling black musicians faced Jim Crow and discrimination in the South. These hazards had afflicted generations of touring black musicians, but by the late 1920s the automobile and the growth of the band business brought many more of them to the segregated states. Successful jazz musicians were well-connected professionals, usually from New York or Chicago, who earned much more than the average person, white or black, northern or southern, who attended their performances. The sizeable population of formally-trained, well-paid, and professionally-connected black musicians in the jazz age benefitted African American communities immeasurably, but racist white Americans also perceived them to be a threat to their concept of racial hierarchy. Most reputable hotels and restaurants only served white customers, so visiting jazz bands usually lodged and dined with families in African American neighborhoods. Many nightclub and theater owners reserved their main entrances for white customers, and forced black musicians to enter the buildings in which they performed through back doors. Laws in the southern states required that audiences either be all white or carefully segregated. In many settings, white hecklers taunted black musicians and even threatened violence.

The vast majority of traveling bands toured regionally, within a few states in the environs of their home city. Bandleaders such as Alphonso Trent and Andy Kirk of Dallas, Walter Page of Oklahoma City, Zack Whyte of Cincinnati, Charlie Creath of St. Louis, Eddie Barefield of Minneapolis, and Floyd Turnham in Los Angeles kept their bands on the road for months each year. The most celebrated and influential regional jazz market was the so-called Southwest or territory, the area bounded by the Rio Grande to the south, the Platte River to the north, the Mississippi River to the east, and the Rocky Mountains to the west. This large region benefitted from an extensive railroad network that aided travel by musicians. Itinerant pianists from lumber camps and speakeasies, for example, developed a blues-oriented regional piano style that came to be called "boogie-woogie." This style blended blues harmonies and jazz swing with a steady beat in the left hand. The Southwest held a diverse musical heritage. Missouri enjoyed a rich tradition in ragtime and east Texas was a major center for the blues. Musicians of mixed race, especially in Oklahoma, were influenced by widespread Native American music and culture.

Kansas City, Missouri, was the railway hub of the Southwest. The city's governing political machine permitted gambling dens and houses of prostitution that created job opportunities for musicians. More than any other town, Kansas City became a meeting point for boogie-woogie pianists and for jazz bands that worked boogie-woogie into their arrangements. The Blue Devils Orchestra, originally from Oklahoma City, was an early exponent of the new regional band style, followed in Kansas City by Benny Moten's orchestra and an ensemble led by a transplanted New Jerseyan, Count Basie. After Basie became a well-known performer, the boogie-woogie sound became one of the key stylistic forces behind the big-band boom of the late 1930s. Southwest blues singing also became a major influence on the use of vocals by jazz bands. Big Joe Turner and Jimmy Rushing, an original member of the Blue Devils and later a mainstay of Basie's ensemble, made the extroverted "shouting" blues a staple of the regional jazz style in Kansas City and beyond.

In urban black communities across the country, jazz bands became important institutions, although some residents did not automatically accept them. Echoing white critics, many ministers and social arbiters viewed jazz as being similar to the blues, tainted by its association with illegal speakeasies and sexually suggestive dancing. The music critic for the *Chicago Defender*, "sweet" bandleader Dave Peyton, admonished musicians to avoid the "ugly" and "raspy" sounds of jazz. This black opposition never disappeared entirely, but by about 1930 it had diminished. Eloquent supporters of jazz, such as the journalist Frank Marshall Davis and the trumpeter Rex Stewart, rallied communities to the music in the African American press. To the black middle class, the examples of Henderson and Ellington in Harlem, for instance, illustrated that jazz drew some of its key practitioners from its own formally educated ranks.

The bands, in turn, gave back to communities. All of the original members of the Oklahoma City Blue Devils came from families that ran businesses and contributed to the city's black institutions, and the band performed for social clubs, churches, at baseball games, weddings, and other local events. Jazz bands across America associated themselves with baseball teams in the Negro Leagues, traveling, lodging, and even performing with them. Increasingly, even churches availed themselves of the services of local or visiting jazz bands.

Jazz bands played a role in the social activism of black communities, especially in the North. At the humblest level in Harlem, jazz music, often performed only by a solo stride pianist, was often the main attraction at "rent parties." Attendees at such a party contributed admission fees that helped a struggling apartment tenant to pay the rent. Even at the height of Harlem's vogue in the 1920s, the great majority of African American residents were poor, the victims of widespread job and housing discrimination. Many employers in the city refused to hire black workers and landlords and home sellers elsewhere in the city excluded black renters and buyers. Rent parties helped to alleviate the discriminatory rates charged to black apartment dwellers, which often exceeded the average white tenant's payment by 40 percent.

The jazz age signaled the real beginning of popular music's role as a weapon for community pride and activism among urban blacks. Band-leaders such as Duke Ellington and Count Basie donated their services at fund-raising events for the NAACP, which continued to lobby for national civil rights legislation. Ellington and others also played at benefits for the U.S. Communist Party, which sought to win black support through its legal defense and labor organizing initiatives. In Harlem and other black districts, dance halls and nightclubs that regularly featured jazz music were also sites for political meetings and fund-raising events.

THE 1930S: THE SWING ERA

The Great Depression increased the urgency of community activism by African Americans. Well before the stock market crash of October 1929, riots, low-paying jobs, persistent hiring discrimination, ghettoization, and inferior schools and city services had diminished the optimism of black migrants in northern cities. The crash led to a cessation of credit and hiring that hurt the most vulnerable members of American society. A deep slump in crop prices compelled southern landowners to force sharecroppers off of their land, a practice that Franklin D. Roosevelt's well-meaning agricultural reforms of 1933 actually intensified. In southern cities, virulent white workers demanded the layoff of African Americans to ensure jobs for themselves. In urban black communities nationwide, unemployment exceeded 50 percent. Still excluded from most labor unions, black workers took part in strikes that were easily suppressed by governments, and gained little leverage in the general labor struggle of the early 1930s. Memories of movements for black self-help such as Marcus Garvey's Universal Negro Improvement Association (UNIA), strong in the 1920s, stimulated new calls for African American racial unity and cultural and economic separatism from whites. On street corners, black Communists, Jamaican activists in the Rastafarian movement, and members of the newly founded Nation of Islam spoke out against a hostile white-run society. Tensions exploded in Harlem in 1935, when a major riot caused the looting of white-owned businesses.

In these troubled times, most black jazz pioneers were not notably involved in political activism. During the Great Depression, black jazz musicians shared in the guardedly positive feelings of African Americans toward the Roosevelt administration. FDR's frequent consultations with his black "kitchen cabinet," First Lady Eleanor Roosevelt's passionate support for civil rights, and the fact that New Deal aid provided assistance to poor black people attracted strong African American support. Relief aid was not always distributed on a color-blind basis, and for political reasons Roosevelt hesitated to support civil rights legislation, but black voters still flocked to the Democratic Party. Jazz critics, promoters, and musicians, especially whites, portrayed African American music as a sort of theme song for the biracial New Deal coalition and its championing of the "common man." Duke Ellington expressed such sentiments in an article in a new jazz periodical, *Down Beat*, in 1938, rejecting communism in favor of FDR's moderate welfare state.

The cautious liberalism voiced by Ellington and other black jazz musicians marked them as spokespersons for their time, but in later decades it also exposed them to criticism from less patient African American activists. A few of these impatient voices did emerge in the black jazz scene in the late 1930s. The young pianist Teddy Wilson endorsed socialism, and Dizzy Gillespie and other young musicians spent some time at the Communist Party's summer gathering, Camp Unity, in upstate New York. A particularly startling indication of militancy among swing musicians occurred in 1939, when the vocalist Billie Holiday recorded "Strange Fruit." This song, which Holiday had cowritten with Abel Meeropol, a white member of the Communist Party, was a searing indictment of lynching in the South. Her performance of this song became a staple of the entertainment at Café Society, a left-wing nightclub in Manhattan that served as a gathering place for white and black leftist artists and intellectuals.

Racial conditions in the swing era continued to concern black musicians. It was clear that white Americans' infatuation with jazz in the 1930s presented difficulties for African Americans. In some ways this infatuation resembled whites' embrace and commercial exploitation of black musical styles since the days of minstrelsy. White "jazz" bands, many of which rarely played improvised instrumental blues, regularly received higher pay and longer engagements than their black counterparts. In the 1920s the "sweet" bandleader Paul Whiteman, at the pinnacle of his success, claimed the title "King of Jazz," and a decade later white promoters marketed the bandleader Benny Goodman as the "King of Swing." Many African Americans were also disappointed by the critical praise that the white composer George Gershwin received for his jazz-influenced "Negro folk opera" *Porgy and Bess*, which premiered in 1935. Unlike black musicians, touring white band members could stay in good hotels and walk through the front doors of the clubs and halls in which they performed. Furthermore, the Frenchmen who wrote the first histories of jazz embraced the primitivist notion that the music owed a strong debt to the aboriginal music of Africa and New World slave plantations. Most disturbing to some younger African Americans, some older black jazz musicians, especially Louis Armstrong, consented to appearing on stage and in Hollywood films as happy-go-lucky clowns, mangling their grammar and exaggerating their facial expressions in ways that evoked 1800s blackface minstrelsy.

In other ways, though, the interracial encounter in jazz raised the social position of African Americans. Technology changed the profile of the black musician. Although race record labels employed racial stereotypes in their advertising, they usually presented African American musicians playing and singing the way they wanted to, free of caricature, for an appreciative mass audience that included many nonblacks. Pioneering black recording entrepreneurs also appeared. George W. Broome formed a phonograph company in Massachusetts in 1919, and the next year Harry Pace, a former business partner of W. C. Handy, created the highly successful Black Swan Records. Like many business efforts growing out of the Great Migration, Broome and Black Swan Records struggled, and both declared bankruptcy in 1923. But Pace sold the latter company to Paramount Records, and its rich legacy of recordings inspired future efforts to record black musicians. Entrepreneurs such as Handy, Perry Bradford, and Mayo Williams enlarged the black presence in music publishing and show contracting. Meanwhile, with the assistance of white promoters, bandleaders such as Ellington and Basie made substantial incomes and gained international fame.

By the late 1930s, thoughtful white musicians and jazz fans were broadcasting an unprecedented appreciation of African American music. While some of their praise of black jazz was condescending or lacked keen perception, it mostly enhanced the stature of black performers and their music. *Down Beat*'s annual polls regularly placed performers of both races at comparable popularity. Some critics were uneasy about the greater celebrity and higher earnings of white bandleaders and publicly questioned whether white musicians could "really" play jazz. In the 1940s, some white critics fell into a heated debate about the value of early New Orleans jazz. One result of this conflict was that champions of this music revived the careers of neglected black New Orleans jazz pioneers such as Sidney Bechet and cornetist Bunk Johnson. Perhaps the most important white advocate of black jazz was John Hammond. A wealthy young New Yorker, Hammond was a civil rights activist, producer of jazz concerts at Carnegie Hall, and a self-styled talent scout who helped to guide the careers of Count Basie and Billie Holiday. Partly at the urging of John Hammond, Benny Goodman hired Teddy Wilson and the vibraphonist Lionel Hampton to racially integrate his famed big band. Later Goodman created his celebrated quartet, which united Wilson and Hampton with Goodman and the white drummer Gene Krupa in a highly visible symbol

Photo 4.2.   Composer and bandleader Edward Kennedy "Duke" Ellington performing in the early 1940s. Source: Prints and Photographs Division, Library of Congress.

of biracial jazz. Other progressive-minded white leaders, such as Artie Shaw and Charlie Barnet, followed Goodman's lead.

The label "the Swing Era" pertained to the years during which big-band jazz ruled as the most popular music in the United States. The Benny Goodman orchestra's sudden rise to fame in 1935 signaled the embrace by white America of swinging rhythm, polished ensemble work, and extroverted solo jazz improvisation. Along with John Hammond, the pioneering black bandleader Fletcher Henderson, who became Goodman's chief arranger, was central to the band's success. In addition to Henderson, African American arrangers such as his brother Horace, Don Redman, Eddie Durham, and Sy Oliver successfully embedded swinging blues improvisation in written big band arrangements. In the late 1930s Duke Ellington, with the assistance of a young black arranger named Billy Strayhorn, reached new creative heights. Extraordinary new band members such as the saxophonist Ben Webster and the bassist Jimmy Blanton inspired Ellington and Strayhorn to create some of the most innovative short pieces in jazz. "Ko-Ko," "Cottontail," "Jack the Bear," and other numbers experimented with new structures, used novel instrumentation, and introduced more dissonance and unusual harmonies.

There were numerous major African American musicians in the swing era. The drummer Chick Webb's physical growth had been stunted in childhood by tuberculosis. Webb led a celebrated and hard-swinging band at Harlem's Savoy Ballroom, where black swing dancing reached its zenith. The lead vocalist at the Savoy, Ella Fitzgerald, became celebrated, and she led Webb's band after his death in 1939. Jimmie Lunceford headed the most heralded black "show" band, which melded musical excellence with entertaining physical flourishes in highly successful national tours.

Billie Holiday, a musician's daughter whose childhood was afflicted by poverty and abuse, was brought to public attention by John Hammond. In the 1930s, Holiday toured with Count Basie's and Artie Shaw's bands. Much in the style of her friend and collaborator, the Basie saxophonist Lester Young, Holiday projected a quiet, smoky-sounding, and introspective voice that was limited in its range of notes but deeply expressive. She uniquely and hauntingly adapted the blues style to the Tin Pan Alley songbooks of the day. Holiday and Young would significantly influence jazz and black music in general, in the decades to come. In the late 1930s, though, as popular entertainment rebounded from the darkest times of the Depression, they were merely two of the many black jazz instrumentalists and vocalists who prospered in the big band era. These musicians made sophisticated swing and improvisation—as well as the moves, the fashion, and the "jive" slang that went with the music—into a potent statement of the younger, mostly urban, black generation's style and substance.

BLACK JAZZ GOES TO WAR

After 1940, world events had a profound effect on African Americans and their music. In the late 1930s, Italy's invasion of Ethiopia had caused concern in black communities, and some African Americans became involved in the left-wing antifascist Popular Front, but most blacks remained focused on problems at home. As the 1940s began, the Great Depression lingered, and African Americans continued to see little improvement in their lives and social status. At first, World War II did not seem to herald any change for the better, but by 1941, it was clear that the U.S.'s military mobilization was expanding jobs and training. African Americans mounted concerted efforts for equal employment and the integration of the armed forces. A prospective war against worldwide racism and genocide, leaders of these efforts wagered, would require black participation and would revive the campaign for civil rights and equality in America.

After the Japanese attack on Pearl Harbor and the United States entry into the war in December 1941, African Americans were discouraged by developments at home that were reminiscent of their experience in World War I. The armed forces remained segregated; blacks in uniform were denied privileges that were accorded even to German prisoners of war; Congress did not award the Medal of Honor to any African American soldiers; war jobs given to blacks were disproportionately low paying and dangerous; and deadly race riots struck Detroit and Harlem. Still, one million African Americans served in the war, many in visibly heroic roles. Millions more gained factory jobs and technical training, and wages for black workers nearly doubled. With guarded optimism, civil rights lawyers, black newspaper publishers, and veterans hoped that these contributions and gains would translate into a brighter future for black America.

Like other segments of American society, jazz was transformed by the U.S. war effort. Changes on the home front severely disrupted the swing music business. Big bands had to deal with high personnel turnover, rapidly increasing travel costs, and a two-year long ban on recording imposed by the musician's union during a bitter dispute with companies over royalties. Many African American musicians entered military service, but few of them were able to display their talents while in uniform. All-white service bands were heavily promoted in the U.S. mass media, and they obscured the more skilled jazz improvisers confined to segregated units. The most famous white jazz musician, Army Air Force Orchestra leader Glenn Miller, epitomized the bland and mechanical bigband style that gained the greatest popularity in the years before his death, while on duty, in 1944. However, military service in World War II exposed a large number of talented black American musicians to cultures overseas that inspired them artistically and often conveyed a foreigner's greater apparent tolerance for people of color.

The war, ironically, brought the heyday of jazz as a popular music to an end. The 1920s and 1930s were decades of daring modern behavior, in which the social tolerance and brash innovations of city culture were embraced by many Americans. The rapid tempo, sophisticated rhythms and harmonies, and instrumental virtuosity of jazz symbolized the new prevalence of modernity in American culture. The unprecedented prominence of African American jazz musicians in mass entertainment made it evident that many whites and blacks were adopting a similar urban, modernist mentality. Jazz especially was typical of African Americans' embrace of life in northern cities, away from the stagnation of the rural South, in a new environment in which their skills, education, and initiative might receive greater reward. Black jazz musicians were among the most unusually proficient—and highly paid—skilled workers in their communities, where they served as stylistic trendsetters and leaders of public opinion. World War II caused upheaval across America, but it especially transformed African American society and music in dramatic ways. As a result, jazz would evolve rapidly away from its roots in prewar New Orleans, Harlem, and Chicago.

NOTES

1. During this period Armstrong switched from the cornet to trumpet, as did his imitators.
2. William Francis Allen, Charles Pickard Ware, and Lucy McKim Garrison, *Slave Songs of the United States* (1867; repr., New York: Arno Press, 1971), v.

5

Jazz at the Philharmonic

The Jazz Avant-Garde and Black Classical Expression

On January 23, 1943, jazz fans in New York City flocked to Carnegie Hall to witness what they considered a historic event. The Duke Ellington Orchestra was making its first appearance in the hall, the home of elite musical artistry for half a century. Ellington marked the occasion with the first performance of his longest composition to date, *Black, Brown and Beige*. The bandleader called the forty-five minute work "a tone parallel to the history of the American Negro," tracing the African American odyssey from Africa to slavery, from freedom to the promise of the Great Migration. The work received respectful applause but was lambasted by jazz and classical critics alike. Ellington was shocked, and he withdrew the complete *Black, Brown and Beige* from his band's repertoire. Nevertheless, he continued to create extended works for the rest of his life. The dream of achieving a reputation as a major concert composer never deserted Duke Ellington.

The aura of the classical music stage lured and motivated many talented individuals in the history of African American music, just as it has affected American musicians of all ethnicities. They were attracted in part by classical music's removal from the hurly-burly of popular performance that gave composers the freedom to follow their own artistic wishes and musicians the ability to perform before audiences that listened with quiet attentiveness. Before 1800, musicians and singers (even in aristocratic courts) mostly performed within arm's reach of listeners and dancers, but in the nineteenth century they increasingly appeared on stages, at a physical remove from audiences. This was especially true of the symphony orchestra, which became a prestigious fixture of the concert stage.

In addition, on both sides of the Atlantic leading intellectuals endowed classical music with an aura of moral and cultural uplift. Eighteenth-century American Protestants had condemned theater performances as sinful, but their Victorian descendants found a spiritual importance in classical music that transformed concerts into the equivalent of a religious service. In the United States, the white journalist John Sullivan Dwight led the movement for the enshrinement of classical music, and William M. Trotter's *Music and Some Highly Musical People* echoed many of Dwight's arguments. Trotter, as we have seen, placed African American musicians within this genteel classical tradition. Beginning in Trotter's day, members of the African American middle class embraced classical music as an expression of racial culture and uplift. Prominent black soloists of the late nineteenth century, such as Thomas Wiggins and Sisieretta Jones, benefitted from the middle class's efforts to locate black artists in the revered classical tradition. Scott Joplin attempted to make the ragtime opera a new art form. James Reese Europe's Clef Club concerts at Carnegie Hall beginning in 1912 brought spirituals and ragtime to a performance space that, since its opening in 1891, had become a shrine for prestigious music in New York City. In the 1930s and 1940s, the mystique of classical music in America reached new heights. Promoters such as Arthur Judson and Sol Hurok used radio, the phonograph, and motion pictures to make leading conductors and soloists such as Arturo Toscanini and Jascha Heifetz into celebrities and to portray their musical gifts as mysterious, spiritual, and intellectual powers.

In the twentieth century, the African American impulse to make music in the concert hall created two distinct traditions. The first of these was the more conventional tradition of composers and performers who worked within the classical music sphere. These men and women were the heirs of Thomas Wiggins and Sisieretta Jones. They pursued the formal training and professional opportunities—such as choral conducting, university teaching, and concert touring—that white classical musicians pursued as well. In part due to the excitement caused by Antonin Dvořák's prediction in 1892 that black music would form the basis of America's national music, numerous African American composers throughout the twentieth century created works in classical genres, such as chamber music, symphonies, and operas. Some of them, in addition, used black musical traditions to transform the sound and form of the European models that dominated classical music. Similarly, while African American vocalists and instrumentalists who entered classical careers mostly performed works from the European repertoire, the brilliant success of musicians such as Marian Anderson, Leontyne Price, André Watts, and Jessye Norman was partly due to their ethnic heritage. In diverse ways they blended vital aspects of black musical expressiveness into their classical performances.

The second tradition had been anticipated by Scott Joplin, and initiated by Duke Ellington that evening in Carnegie Hall: the tradition of black jazz concert music. Jazz musicians from middle-class backgrounds such as Ellington had been encouraged by parents and teachers to seek prestige on the concert stage. In addition, Ellington and jazz composers such as John Lewis, George Russell, and Ornette Coleman also were reacting to the mass popularity of jazz and the blues. In part to gain greater respect for this black popular music, but also to free themselves somewhat from the constraints and pressures of the commercial music business, these composers wrote longer works and sought to associate jazz, to some extent, with classical music. Like classical composers in the United States, jazz composers often found professional refuge in university music departments.

A third artistic tradition helped to shape attitudes among black classical and, especially, black jazz composers. This was the tradition of the avant-garde. Europe's circles of avant-garde or modernist composers, artists, and writers grew out of bohemian groups of the nineteenth century that had rejected conventional society to follow their creative urges. Avant-garde creators shunned both the commercial and classical realms and pursued their own artistic standards; they self-consciously considered themselves at the "cutting edge" of their fields. By the 1930s, critics and intellectuals considered modernists such as Igor Stravinsky, Pablo Picasso, and James Joyce to be the most significant artistic voices of that time. Their American counterparts, such as Charles Ives, Alfred Stieglitz, and Gertrude Stein, had gained attention, too, so a U.S. avant-garde tradition had also begun.

After 1940, some young black jazz musicians in Harlem rejected the popular standards of big band swing and pursued an independent new artistic identity. Some observers considered bebop, as their new music came to be called, to be the arrival in jazz of an avant-garde mentality, of a new desire to create innovatively with little regard for the general public's reaction. In later decades, major figures in the bebop tradition such as Charles Mingus, John Coltrane, and Ornette Coleman created a tradition of extended and complex works that could be called a jazz-classical avant-garde. Since their works emerged during the time of struggles for civil rights and Black Power, they also passionately explored black identity and consciousness in musical terms.

Since 1940, African American composers in the classical field and in the jazz avant-garde have constituted two branches of an important stream in black music. Their symphonies, operas, and other works reflect a wide array of intellectual and artistic influences, but they also explore and enshrine core elements of vernacular African American music. In the process they have helped to revive interest in the African and Caribbean roots of black music and won new respect for that music from critics, academics, and other intellectuals. Due to the efforts of black jazz composers, jazz moved increasingly into the conservatory, the university, and the concert hall, where today, like classical music, it is championed mostly by a small and musically sophisticated multiracial (and international) audience. While classical music contrasts strongly with African American popular styles that seek out and attempt to satisfy the grass-roots musical preferences of the mass audience, it remains a very important element of black musical expression.

CLASSICAL PERFORMERS AND COMPOSERS

As chapter 2 showed, classically trained African American composers and performers first appeared in the mid-1800s. Thomas "Blind Tom" Wiggins, Sisieretta Jones, and others made successful tours. By 1900, the popular vogue for black classical performers had passed, and Antonin Dvořák's former students Harry T. Burleigh and Will Marion Cook were forced to find work in churches and in the popular theater, respectively. But the mystique of the concert hall and the appeal of harmonic techniques that allowed composers to write compelling large-scale works continued to entice black musicians to the classical tradition.

Few examples are as illustrative as that of Roland Hayes, the most celebrated African American classical vocalist of the early twentieth century. Born in 1887 to former slaves who sharecropped in rural Georgia, Hayes was raised in circumstances that appeared most likely to make him a blues singer. When Hayes was eleven, his widowed mother moved her large family to Chattanooga, Tennessee, where economic woes forced him to leave school and work in a factory. In his teens Hayes sang in a church choir and quartet, but exposure to an early recording by Enrico Caruso, he recalled later, overwhelmed him. Determined to become a classical singer, he attended Fisk University and toured with the Jubilee Singers. In 1911, Hayes relocated to Boston.

The tenor struggled to win recognition in the North. Despite the achievements of earlier black performers and Dvořák's famous proclamation about the importance of African American music—or, in part, because of them—most white classical musicians remained racist. Concert halls and record companies refused to employ Hayes, but he persisted, arranging his own recitals and paying for his own recordings. A self-arranged tour of Europe in the early 1920s proved triumphant. Hayes returned to America to hire the manager of the Boston Symphony Orchestra, a man who had refused to book him years before, as his agent. During the rest of the 1920s, Hayes became perhaps the most celebrated black musician in America, a wealthy, handsome fixture on concert stages and the toast of Renaissance-era Harlem. Hayes triumphantly revived the recital format that the Fisk Jubilee Singers had pioneered in the early 1870s, presenting classical songs and singing spirituals only as encores. An occasional composer and teacher, a fixture on radio through World War II, and a vivid musical presence in Harlem until his death in 1977, Roland Hayes ranks with Louis Armstrong as one of the great self-made figures in the history of African American music.

The contralto Marian Anderson became an even more celebrated artist and symbol of African American achievement in classical music. Anderson was a native of Philadelphia who enjoyed the support of a middle-class black community that underwrote her education and early recital appearances. In the 1920s she traveled to Europe, where she was tutored by leading classical singers and scored her first major concert successes. Critics and listeners praised the rare magnificence of Anderson's voice and interpretations, but when she returned to America she confronted racial prejudice that kept her out of the mainstream symphonic repertoire, recitals, and opera. While touring the Northeast in the late 1920s Anderson met Roland Hayes, who became an important mentor.

Hayes's and Anderson's careers became dramatically linked in 1931. That year Hayes gave a recital at Constitution Hall, a new venue in Washington, D.C., operated by the Daughters of the American Revolution (DAR). Hayes's insistence on desegregating his audience, in defiance of municipal segregation codes, led the DAR to institute a policy of booking only white performers in the future. Eight years later, Marian Anderson attempted to book a concert at Constitution Hall and was refused. Now managed by Sol Hurok, the leading classical impresario, Anderson had become one of the most successful classical performers in the country. The DAR's denial thus made newspaper headlines. In response, Harold Ickes, the racially progressive secretary of the interior, with the support of First Lady Eleanor Roosevelt, arranged for Anderson to perform on the steps of the Lincoln Memorial.

Overlooking the western end of the two-mile-long National Mall, with a magnificent view of the Washington Monument and the Capitol building, the Lincoln Memorial was perhaps the grandest concert stage an American singer could hope for. In 1922 this monument to the Great Emancipator had been dedicated before a racially segregated audience. On Easter Sunday, April 9, 1939, though, Marian Anderson sang before 75,000 black and white spectators. Millions more heard the concert on their radios. Her performance helped to make the Lincoln Memorial an unambiguous symbol of black aspirations and struggle in the "land of the free," and it increased the visibility of dignified African Americans in the national media. In later years Anderson's reputation as a performer continued to grow. In 1955, as the civil rights movement was being born, New York City's Metropolitan Opera finally ended its seventy year-long ban on nonwhite singers. Although Marian Anderson was now past her vocal

Photo 5.1. Contralto Marian Anderson, circa 1940. Source: Prints and Photographs Division, Library of Congress.

prime, the company paid tribute to her stature by selecting her to break the color barrier, in a role in a production of Verdi's *Un Ballo in Maschera*.

Hayes's and Anderson's successes, like those of the Fisk Jubilee Singers and their imitators, underscored the special richness of African American vocal traditions, and how, if given proper exposure, multiracial audiences might embrace black performers. In countless and elusive ways, African American singers' timbres, phrasing, and other vocal inflections endowed the classical repertoire with elements of the black musical tradition and gave them fresh and vibrant new meaning. Marian Anderson's success at the Met opened the way for generations of younger operatic soloists, including Robert McFadden, George Shirley, Martina Arroyo, Shirley Verrett, Grace Bumbry, and William Warfield. The most prominent career belonged to Leontyne Price, a native of Mississippi who came north in the 1940s to study classical singing. For a time she was married to Warfield, an important baritone soloist. In the 1950s, while working in Europe, Price became one of the world's most celebrated operatic sopranos. The alto Jessye Norman, a Georgia native ten years Price's junior, followed a similar trajectory to international fame, and gained particular praise for a richness in her voice that seemed alien to singers of European descent.

Among the great African American concert singers of the twentieth century, Paul Robeson probably had the least formal training and the most narrowly focused repertory, but his extraordinary and diverse life gave him a special prominence. The son of a former slave, Robeson excelled in athletics and academics as a youth in New Jersey, and at Rutgers University he was one of the greatest college football players of his era. After graduating from Columbia University's law school and working briefly as an attorney, he decided to become a professional actor and singer. Perhaps more than anyone else, the young Robeson embodied the "renaissance" spirit of 1920s Harlem. As an actor Robeson appeared in landmark roles written for him by Eugene O'Neill and conquered the London stage in Shakespeare's *Othello*. Endowed with a rich baritone and a towering physical presence, Robeson in 1925 gave a recital consisting entirely of spirituals—possibly the first of its kind—in Carnegie Hall. A film star in the 1930s, he received the widest fame in the role of Joe in the 1935 version of Jerome Kern's musical *Show Boat*. Robeson, who had also appeared in the show onstage, made a point of rewriting Oscar Hammerstein's racially derogatory lyrics for "Old Man River," which the baritone had made popular.

This act reflected Robeson's deep commitment to civil rights and racial justice, which was evidenced in his political activism in Europe and Africa, as well as the United States. A prominent participant in the left-wing Popular Front campaign against fascism in the 1930s, Robeson sang "The Ballad for Americans" for national radio audiences as war clouds gathered, interpreting the coming struggle as a global crusade against bigotry. The war, along with Robeson's fervent championing of the Soviet Union's social structure, eclipsed his acting and singing careers, and in the post–World War II era he was vilified by anticommunist crusaders as a "disloyal" American. Years of limited professional opportunity due to blacklisting and exile in Europe took a toll on Robeson's health, and after his return to the United States in 1963 he only occasionally performed. By the time of his death in 1976 at the age of 77, Paul Robeson epitomized the promise of the Great Migration and the perils of political radicalism during the Cold War. His magnificent voice, though, had given major testimony about the centrality of musical expression to black social activism.

Black classical instrumentalists also benefitted from the gradual relaxation of discrimination in American concert halls in the twentieth century. Since the time of Beethoven (whose best-known violin sonata was first performed by a Black English virtuoso), classical instrumentalists of African descent have earned recognition. Thomas "Blind Tom" Wiggins's successors on twentieth-century U.S. concert stages include the pianists Philippa Duke Schuyler (a famed child prodigy), André Watts, Natalie Hinderas, and Awadagin Pratt. Important African American conductors have included Dean Dixon, Paul Freeman, Calvin Simmons, Henry Lewis, and Marian Anderson's nephew, James De Priest. Today, symphony orchestras in major U.S. cities employ dozens of African American instrumental virtuosos; many of them assist the orchestras' efforts to build relationships with schoolchildren and other residents of the inner cities.

In the early decades of the twentieth century, at the same time that black concert performers struggled to achieve prominence, composers in the United States began to accept the challenge that Antonin Dvořák had issued in 1892: to create an American classical music out of African American materials. White composers dominated the field, so it was not surprising that those among them who respected African American music made the most publicized early attempts to realize Dvořák's vision. Two of the Czech composer's white students in New York, William Arms Fisher and Rubin Goldmark, tried to use African American harmonies and rhythms in concert works, as did Henry F. Gilbert (in *The Dance at the Place Congo*, which evoked old New Orleans) and John Powell (in *Rhapsodie Nègre*). In the 1920s, jazz influenced the work of the white American composers John Alden Carpenter, Daniel Gregory Mason, and George Gershwin, as well as Europeans such as Darius Milhaud and Ernst Krenek.

George Gershwin's opera, *Porgy and Bess,* based on a novel by the white South Carolinian DuBose Heyward, appeared in 1935 with the publicity that befitted the young composer's celebrity. The last major work Gershwin completed before his premature death in 1937, *Porgy* was the culmination of his lifelong absorption of black ragtime and jazz. The opera, though, brought the issue of white composers' advocacy of black music to a sort of crisis. Many African Americans (as well as some whites) attacked what Duke Ellington called "Gershwin's lampblack Negroisms," his reliance on caricature in depicting poor, uneducated, razor-wielding, and drug-consuming black people. Critics and musicologists noted that Gershwin's melodies relied on simplistic notions of ragtime and the blues, and rarely demonstrated the subtlety and sophistication of recent jazz and blues music. Decades afterward some African American singers still refused to appear in the work. Despite this criticism, the undeniable vitality of Gershwin's Tin Pan Alley–style inventiveness has made *Porgy and Bess* into a worldwide favorite and a classic of the American musical theater.

Nevertheless, the controversy it created virtually halted all efforts by white composers to represent black music and culture in their works.

From 1900 to 1940, while white composers explored black music in their work, an important group of classically trained African American composers also emerged. They answered the call of Dvořák, as well as that of Scott Joplin, who had hoped that *Treemonisha* would initiate a tradition of ragtime opera. Dvořák's most notable students did not follow in his classical footsteps. Harry Burleigh worked as a song composer, publisher, and performer, while Will Marion Cook found his fortunes in the popular musical theater. After the turn of the century, though, more inspiration arrived from abroad. Samuel Coleridge-Taylor, a young British composer of African descent, made a highly successful tour of the United States in 1904. Coleridge-Taylor encouraged black Americans to write classical music and to form concert choirs. Residents of Washington, D.C. responded by founding the Samuel Coleridge-Taylor Choral Society. Among the earliest of the young composers to answer this call was R. Nathaniel Dett, the Canadian-born son of genteel musical parents. After attending Oberlin College in Ohio, Dett became the longtime director of music at the Hampton Institute in Virginia. A composer especially of choral works and piano suites, Dett also was active in the National Association of Negro Musicians (NANM). Founded in Chicago in 1919, NANM was the first and most important organization to encourage African American composition and performance. Dett nevertheless refused to consider himself an exponent of black musical traditions. In the 1930s, he led a chorus on network radio, toured with his own ensemble, and worked with the military performing organization, the USO, during World War II before his death in 1943.

William Grant Still also worked in radio, but in contrast to Dett he incorporated African American musical traditions into his compositions, and during his long career he successfully bridged the worlds of classical and popular music. Born in Mississippi in 1895, Still grew up in Little Rock, Arkansas, and was educated at Wilberforce University in Ohio. An oboist and a skilled arranger, he was an important fixture in Broadway musical revues of the 1920s and a creator of big band charts in the 1930s and 1940s. Simultaneously, though, Still created an array of symphonic, chamber, and vocal works that effectively fit black music into classical forms. These included the *Afro-American Symphony* and the operas *Blue Steel* and *Troubled Island*, the latter set in revolutionary Haiti with a libretto by Langston Hughes. In 1935, Still conducted a concert of his own music at the Hollywood Bowl; *Troubled Island* became the first opera by a black composer to be premiered by a major American company; and in 1955, Still became the first African American to conduct a major symphony orchestra in the Jim Crow South, in New Orleans. Still's productivity and enthusiastic example inspired generations of younger black composers, but his music proved controversial for a significant reason. Critics often argued that Still's compositions showed the inadequacy of classical forms (such as sonata, rondo, or variations) as frames for African American musical expression. Like *Porgy and Bess*, the critics claimed, Still's works diluted the special harmonic, polyphonic, and timbral qualities of black vernacular and popular music by mating them with classical forms and conservatory-trained performers. Meanwhile, they noted, popular music such as jazz and the blues were providing far more hospitable homes for black musical traditions.

The criticism directed at Still exposed a central dilemma for black composers. Since the 1930s they have tried to adapt classical forms more fully to the special qualities of the African American musical heritage. As the historian Eileen Southern has argued, for composers born after 1910, the urge to write "nationalistic" works in an African American flavor has been replaced by "experimentation," often radical efforts to bend European harmony, rhythm, and forms to black aesthetics.[1] These experiments took place at the same time that composers of European descent also struggled to transcend traditional harmony with **atonality**, complex rhythmic schemes, the use of chance or East Asian musical techniques, and other avant-garde strategies.

One notable African American experimentalist was Howard Swanson, who toiled in government jobs to support his work as a composer, which included celebrated settings of the poems of Langston Hughes. Margaret Bonds, the most significant black female classical composer of the mid-twentieth century, also befriended Hughes and wrote settings of his poetry. Hale Smith, a native of Washington, D.C., especially experimented with the twelve-tone or serial method popular among avant-garde composers after World War II. Ulysses Kay, the Arizona-born nephew of the jazz pioneer Joe "King" Oliver, worked for decades for the songwriters' organization Broadcast Music, Inc. (BMI) to support his production of a large body of concert and chamber works, crowned by his final opera, *Frederick Douglass*. Swanson, Smith, and Kay all received appointments to university professorships late in life.

For African American composers, like experimentalists of all ethnicities, the university became the most dependable place of employment. Unlike the most charismatic or skilled performers of the traditional vocal, symphonic, or operatic repertoire, classical modernists could not rely on a large audience to support their music or their careers. Beginning with Duke Ellington in the 1940s, though, some successful jazz musicians also supplemented their performing careers with ambitions for the concert stage. Their efforts bridged the worlds of subsidized (or nonprofit) and commercial music, and the intellectual and expressive richness of their work ensured that jazz composition for the concert hall would become important "classical music" in its own right.

Photo 5.2. Classical composer William Grant Still in the 1930s. Source: Prints and Photographs Division, Library of Congress.

JAZZ IN THE CONCERT HALL

In the three decades after *Black, Brown and Beige*'s unfortunate debut in 1943, Duke Ellington's ambitions never ebbed. He composed a long series of extended suites for his orchestra, ballets, and film scores and in his last years he produced his most ambitious and lengthy works, the three *Sacred Concerts*.

Other ambitious jazz composers followed Ellington's lead. Mary Lou Williams, a major pianist and arranger in 1930s Kansas City, dedicated much of her later career to the composition and performance of sophisticated and challenging concert works. The pianist John Lewis, a member of Dizzy Gillespie's big band in the mid-1940s, applied his conservatory training to works that brilliantly recast contemporary jazz into classical forms. In the 1950s, Lewis created the first "jazz conservatory," a summer institute for jazz composition in Lenox, Massachusetts, and organized the Modern Jazz Quartet—an experimental combo that presented itself in tuxedos, in the style of a classical ensemble. George Russell, another jazz pianist of Lewis's generation, made it his mission to uncover the harmonic foundations of the innovative "bebop" style. His 1953 text, *The Lydian Chromatic Concept of Tonal Organization*, was a landmark treatise that incorporated jazz into the academic realm of music theory and instruction. Russell's extended compositions, such as *New York, New York*, and his decades of teaching at the New England Conservatory of Music further helped to integrate jazz and classical music.

Younger African American composers such as Arthur Cunningham and Thomas Anderson followed in the wake of Russell and Lewis. Olly Wilson, a beneficiary of St. Louis's rich musical heritage and extensive academic training, made pioneering experiments with electronic music and became a leading university educator. More than any of his contemporaries, Wilson has thoughtfully attempted to describe the legacy of African American music and its relevance to the concert composer of the late twentieth and early twenty-first centuries. Dorothy Rudd Moore, a longtime resident and teacher in Harlem, has created many large-scale works, including her own operatic treatment of the story of Frederick Douglass. Tania León, a native of Havana, is one of the leading concert composers to bring Afro-Cuban characteristics to opera and chamber music in the United States. David Baker, a product of Indianapolis's rich black music scene, became the most influential jazz pedagogue when he took the helm of the jazz studies program at Indiana University, where he has also written a series of compositions that integrate jazz and classical forms.

Some younger black jazz musicians of the 1950s and 1960s delayed their entry into the concert halls and universities for ideological reasons. In those years, they believed that the civil rights movement, followed by the

Black Arts movement of the late 1960s, required them to put jazz in the service of the African American social struggle. The bassist Charles Mingus, only twenty years Ellington's junior, was the first jazz composer to combine works of symphonic complexity and scale with a crusade against American racism. Mingus's most extended composition, *Epitaph*, was not arranged and performed until after his death in 1979, though. Partly as a retreat from discriminatory hiring practices on the nightclub scene, Ornette Coleman, the boldest saxophone improviser of the early 1960s, gravitated within a few years to studying with classical composers and writing works for symphony orchestra. Younger "free jazz" experimenters of the 1960s such as Anthony Braxton, Roscoe Mitchell, and Anthony Davis adopted forms of classical composition and performance in African American musical expressions while working in university settings. Anthony Davis's opera *X*, about the life of Malcolm X, represented a culmination of this generation's work, which generally fused jazz and the European avant-garde into a dynamic and often dissonant new concert music.

For decades now, new "classical" music by composers of all ethnicities has existed on the margins of America's musical life. The mystique of the European art-music tradition, nurtured in the early twentieth century by promoters of star conductors and soloists, has been overwhelmed by the cachet and star-making machinery of the popular music industries, and "music appreciation" has lost its place in the standard academic curriculum. For classical African American composers, as well as others in their field, the amount of financial support for commissioned works and the opportunities for performance and recording by skilled professional groups available is unprecedented, and the diversity and quality of their work is astonishing. Still, supporters of their music need to make much more of an effort before their audience will grow beyond the present small minority of the national listening public. Unfortunately, the status of these composers today shows that Will Marion Cook was right, and Antonin Dvořák and Scott Joplin were wrong, in predicting the trajectory of African American music in the twentieth century. Its dominance in American music was won not in concert halls or opera houses, but in theaters, dance halls, and cabarets.

THE JAZZ AVANT-GARDE

Most black jazz musicians after World War II did not follow Duke Ellington into the concert hall. In the 1940s, Ellington was probably the only African American jazz composer who could present extended works in Carnegie Hall. The other composers—even famed bandleaders—had their hands full struggling against racial discrimination, exploitation by the music business, restrictions imposed by the musicians' union, and the disruptions of wartime.

Rebellion against these restrictions was part of the impetus behind the bebop revolution, which transported jazz to new levels of introspection, creative intensity, and complexity. In some ways, bebop and its proponents remained rooted in the commercial world that had spawned swing music, but in others, it represented the first major, politically informed avant-garde statement by African American jazz musicians. Until the 1960s, when universities and classical concert halls began to woo and attract some modern jazz leaders, the self-consciously artistic labors of bebop, hard bop, "cool," and "progressive" musicians took place in nightclubs and recording studios. Nonblack musicians participated in the revolution as well, but its core aesthetic was African American, and its intellectual energy was drawn from the postwar struggles for civil rights at home and colonial independence abroad.

By the 1940s, Harlem had lost much of the "renaissance" luster that white visitors had perceived two decades earlier. Despite the artistic achievements of African American residents and the presence of considerable black affluence, the majority of the population remained poor. The Great Depression and the 1935 race riot had swept away most illusions about the district's socioeconomic condition. Another riot in Harlem in 1943 reiterated the anger of the community, which by now was absorbing a large Puerto Rican migration at its eastern border. These problems contrasted with the full wartime employment and dramatic increase in income that occurred elsewhere in the nation, especially among whites. Economic disparities would only deepen in the postwar era and cause deeper resentment in Harlem and other African American ghettoes.

In part due to this tension, Harlem in the 1940s played host to a revolution in jazz. During the Depression the music business had become increasingly centralized in Manhattan, and younger African American musicians made Harlem their base. (Louis Armstrong and Count Basie had moved from Manhattan to Corona, Queens, making it a residential center for older jazz stars.) Musicians laid off by big bands during the economic upheavals of the war era welcomed the job opportunities and sense of community that the Harlem scene offered. Minton's Playhouse and Monroe's Uptown House, especially, became the gathering places for young big band musicians eager to shed the clichés of swing jazz and experiment musically. Thelonious Monk, a pianist from North Carolina, was the pioneer, working regularly at Minton's beginning in 1939.

While older band stars such as the trumpeter Roy Eldridge also visited and played at Minton's and Monroe's, it was the younger core players—including Monk, the pianist Bud Powell, trumpeter John "Dizzy" Gillespie, and drummer Kenny Clarke—who were the key experimenters. Inspired somewhat by Count Basie and Art Tatum, Monk and Powell developed a style that was much sparer than the usual swing piano playing.

They often avoided playing a steady boogie-woogie-style beat in the left hand, made greater use of dissonant extra notes in chords (so-called ninths and elevenths) and often substituted alternate chords for the standard ones used in a song. Their new playing provided impressionistic, often quirky accompaniments to the solo instruments (a practice called "comping"), which players such as Powell embellished with dazzlingly rapid runs along the keyboard. Kenny Clarke and Max Roach developed a similar light and diversified use of drums and cymbals.

Dizzy Gillespie became the unofficial leader of this group of Harlem musicians. Gillespie was a native of South Carolina who had grown up in Philadelphia. His youthful hot temper got him fired from Cab Calloway's orchestra, but in Harlem his rapid and high-flying trumpet playing set new standards for bebop solos. In addition, as the most enterprising member of the group, he brought musicians together and encouraged a separate identity for the young rebels. Collectively, they set higher standards for the already-brutal "cutting contests," the after-hours competitions between jazz instrumentalists, and notably accelerated the tempos of standard numbers. Like bluegrass—an analogous wartime innovation in country and western music, based in Nashville—what jazz critics came to call "bebop" reflected the faster pace of life and more highly mechanized working world of the 1940s.

But bebop also reflected much more. This was apparent in the slow but steady incorporation of the alto saxophonist Charlie Parker into the Harlem jazz avant-garde. Parker was a native of Kansas City, Missouri. Nicknamed "Yardbird" as a child, he absorbed the rich and vibrant blues and jazz activity of that city throughout his youth. In his teens, Parker was a competent swing saxophonist who flourished locally, and in 1939, he made a visit to New York that extended into the next year. Returning to Kansas City, he toured with Jay McShann's fine regional orchestra. Parker later recalled that during this time he discovered the ability to improvise on the higher chord degrees in standard swing tunes, successfully blending them with his strong blues feeling and increasingly rapid finger work. Frequent returns to Harlem steadily increased his reputation among local musicians. Parker worked for a time in Earl Hines's big band, which also featured Gillespie and the vocalist Sarah Vaughan. In 1944 these three musicians, among others, left Hines to join singer Billy Eckstine's orchestra, which became an incubator for experimental jazz. Most important, it solidified the bond between Parker and Gillespie, who worked together in a series of combos from 1945 to 1946 that recorded the most influential early classics in bebop. Often joining the two men were Max Roach and a young trumpeter from St. Louis named Miles Davis.

In 1945, Gillespie, ever the entrepreneur, formed a short-lived big band and then a series of combos that often featured Parker, as well as Sarah

Vaughan, Max Roach, the drummer Sid Catlett, the bassist Slam Stewart, the pianist Al Haig, and others. Dexter Gordon, a young saxophonist from Los Angeles, also recorded with Gillespie. Charlie Parker, meanwhile, fronted ensembles that featured some of the same players, as well as Miles Davis frequently substituting at trumpet for Gillespie. Al Haig was white, as were some of the other performers who were active contributors to the birth of bebop, such as the trombonist Kai Winding and the trumpeter Red Rodney. White fans such as Leonard Feather, Ross Russell (later a bebop historian) and Dean DeBenedetti (who made valuable wire recordings of early jam sessions) also figured in the promotion of this new style. Another white promoter, Norman Granz, began his long-lived "Jazz at the Philharmonic" concert and recording series in 1945, employing groups fronted by Gillespie, Parker, and others at the Philharmonic Auditorium in Los Angeles and later taking them on tour.

Parker's stay in Los Angeles, beginning late in 1945, lasted more than a year due to the saxophonist's worsening addiction to heroin. By this time, jazz insiders had come to celebrate Parker's extraordinary command of the blues idiom, his tightly focused and completely unsentimental tone, and his fleet, highly disciplined, and harmonically revelatory improvisations. Offstage, though, the saxophonist's life was marked by an extreme lack of self-discipline. Parker ate too much and led a chaotic sexual existence, but he suffered most from his abuse of alcohol and drugs, especially heroin. Arrested in July 1946, after setting his hotel room on fire, he served a six-month sentence in a state hospital. During the remaining decade of his life, Parker repeatedly reached peak form in concerts and in recordings. In the tradition of Joplin and Ellington he became interested in classical music, evidenced first in an unusual recording project with a string orchestra and then in a short-lived effort to study with the composer Edgard Varèse. These musical peaks, though, masked Parker's inexorable physical decline due to self-abuse.

Charlie Parker's death in 1955 at the age of thirty-four was one of the greatest premature losses in the history of African American music. Disturbingly, the cult of "Bird" also encouraged young black and white disciples of his music to emulate his use of narcotics. Drug use had been encouraged by avant-garde modernists in various arts as a relaxant and as a creative trigger, but in urban African American communities municipal governments also encouraged such consumption by tolerating the diversion of organized crime activity (including drug trafficking) into the ghettoes. Residents of inner cities were drawn to narcotics use because poverty and lack of economic and social opportunities had brought them to a point of despair.

Despite the menace of drug abuse, a tremendous diversification of jazz music beyond the hot and swing traditions took place in the decade after 1945. Bebop combo playing, with its harmonic sophistication, sensitivity to the blues, quick tempos, and subtle rhythmic pulses, flourished especially in New York and Los Angeles, the two major centers of the postwar music business. Besides the musicians discussed previously, influential African American bebop innovators included the trumpeters Fats Navarro, Howard McGhee, and Clifford Brown, the drummer Philly Joe Jones, and the saxophonists Sonny Stitt and Don Byas, as well as the older swing legend Coleman Hawkins. Thelonious Monk, present at the creation of bebop at Minton's, remained obscure before 1955, but his fame would increase in the following years.

A fascinating tension developed within bebop. Most major black innovators did not hesitate to perform and record with white musicians who demonstrated skill in the new music. A list of such musicians would be headed by the saxophonist Stan Getz, the trombonist Kai Winding, and the drummer Buddy Rich. At the same time, though, African American bebop innovators invested their music with social significance. De facto segregation in northern neighborhoods, hotels, and restaurants, along with southern Jim Crow and unequal hiring in the music business, persisted in the postwar era. In reaction to these conditions, bebop performers disdained the high-style attire of swing-band musicians and pointedly refused to pander to audiences. Bebop music was introspective and impossible to dance to. Some players, notably Miles Davis, made a show of ignoring his listeners or holding them in contempt, while others, such as Kenny Clarke, left America to live in Europe. Dizzy Gillespie associated bebop with the growing movements for black civil rights in America and for freedom from colonialism in Africa and the Caribbean. Gillespie also hired the Afro-Cuban percussionist Chano Pozo in 1947 to supplement his new big band's sound with Caribbean rhythms and melodies. The popularity of Cuban-American bands headed by Mario Bauza, Tito Puente, and others also helped to bring multiracial Caribbean musical styles to prominence. Musicians, like other African Americans, were at a historical crossroads where they reconsidered their every interaction with white America, and decided whether to conform to the old racial hierarchy or to protest and challenge inequality.

At first, innovative postwar jazz featured very little overt political content. In 1949 and 1950, Miles Davis recorded the *Birth of the Cool* sessions with a racially mixed ensemble of arrangers and eight other musicians. Featuring arrangements by John Lewis, Jerry Mulligan, John Carisi, and Gil Evans—who also conducted on occasion—the nonet performed, as Davis put it, like a unified choir, creating harmonically sophisticated and largely subtle sound pictures which some critics likened to French Impressionism.

To an extent, the sessions indicated Davis's break with the mainstream of bebop. The son of a wealthy dentist in the St. Louis region, Davis brought a sensibility all his own—ironic, soft-spoken, but sharp-edged— to his playing and to his dealings with others. He preferred to play the trumpet in a limited range of volume and notes, investing his solos with brilliantly effective shadings of timbre and harmony. From the start he was determined to work as an equal with white musicians and move in their circles, forming early associations with Mulligan, a baritone saxophonist, and Evans, a pianist and former arranger in Claude Thornhill's orchestra. (The Thornhill and Woody Herman bands were among the leading white big bands to absorb the bebop style.) The so-called cool jazz style emerged in the 1950s on the West Coast, largely among white musicians, years after the *Birth of the Cool* recordings, while Davis himself was battling drug addiction. John Lewis's Modern Jazz Quartet excelled much more at swinging and the blues than at classical formalism, largely due to the rhythmic drive of its vibraphonist, Milt Jackson, but some jazz historians also include this group in the "cool jazz" tradition.

On the East Coast in the 1950s, African American jazz musicians expressed themselves more assertively. The energetic solo improvisations of Parker, Powell, Gillespie, and others were models for younger new stars. By middecade, younger saxophonists such as Sonny Rollins, John Coltrane, and Julian "Cannonball" Adderley were building upon Parker's legacy, moving seamlessly from blues ballads to rapid and highly complex improvisation. These years also witnessed the emergence of Thelonious Monk as a major voice in jazz. An eccentric, private man, Monk had endured neglect from the jazz critics as well as drug addiction. A conviction for narcotics possession kept Monk from performing in New York City clubs for years. Monk refined his highly individual piano playing and wrote a large catalog of tunes that distilled the harmonic revolution of bebop into classic statements. Monk's reputation grew through gigs in other cities, and in 1957, when a city court allowed him to perform once again in New York, he became the toast of jazz circles.

Around this time, styles that transformed jazz beyond bebop also emerged. Gospel music began to influence black jazz musicians, especially in cities such as Detroit and Philadelphia with many Sanctified or "holy rollers" churches (discussed in the next chapter). In what came to be called the "hard bop" style, ensembles led by black musicians such as the pianist Horace Silver, the brothers Hank, Elvin, and Thad Jones, and another set of brothers, Julian and Nat Adderley, adopted gospel chord progressions and inflections, a simpler and heavier beat, and a greater use of the vocal timbres found in gospel singing. Charles Mingus, a leading bassist and former band member for Louis Armstrong, Duke Ellington, and many others, similarly incorporated gospel elements into colorful and powerful compositions he wrote for his own large orchestra.

In 1957, the same year Thelonious Monk returned to New York nightclub stages, the alto saxophonist John Coltrane emerged from a long struggle with heroin, spiritually transformed and dedicated to a musical mission. Like his mid-1950s collaborator Miles Davis, Coltrane became fascinated with the ancient modes that spaced the seven notes of the scale differently than the traditional major or minor keys. Davis, who had conquered his own drug addiction a few years earlier, pursued modal playing in a series of big band albums beautifully arranged by Gil Evans, and in the landmark 1959 combo album *Kind of Blue* (which also featured Coltrane). Coltrane took modal playing in a far more intense direction, launching a spiritually charged improvisatory style that exhausted combinations within modes and then modulated to others, playing relentless streams of fast notes that the critic Ira Gitler called "sheets of sound." The saxophonist's new style, announced in a series of major albums, especially *Giant Steps*, offered a prelude to the explosive diversity and inventiveness of 1960s jazz.

At the beginning of the 1960s, though, critical attention was directed not at Coltrane but at another avant-garde saxophone innovator. Ornette Coleman grew up in Fort Worth, Texas, where he was influenced by local blues and gospel singing and country western bands. His playing was unusual, not the least because he preferred a plastic toy saxophone to the standard brass instrument. Coleman's rough-hewn, unique blending of bebop with his homegrown influences was both praised and ridiculed by listeners in the Los Angeles nightclubs he visited in the late 1950s. The City of Angels had a deep-rooted African American community, which had exploded in size since World War II, and a long jazz history dating back to Kid Ory's pioneering black jazz recordings in 1921. A succession of swing bands and bebop soloists and combos had emerged from South Central Los Angeles, and the relocation of much of the record business to the city made it a major jazz center. Ornette Coleman's sound was perplexingly new, though, and it made an equally striking impression in New York City in 1959, when the saxophonist, accompanied by the trumpeter Don Cherry, the white bassist Charlie Haden, and the drummer Billy Higgins, made his debut there. His 1960 album, *Free Jazz*, featuring completely unarranged and frequently atonal improvisation between two quartets, announced the arrival of the avant-garde rule breaking at the heart of mainstream jazz. While Coleman soon dropped from public view and would later revise his ensemble's sound and approach, in line with a developing music philosophy he called "harmelodics," the shock he applied to the jazz system set the tone for the loosely defined "free jazz" movement of the late 1960s.

Jazz in the 1960s was also shaped by the cresting movement for African American civil rights and equality in the United States. While jazz was not on the front lines of the battles for equality in the Jim Crow South—as the following chapter shows, "freedom songs" in the gospel and protest traditions held those posts—that battle made a deep impression on improvisers in the northern jazz centers. Max Roach and his wife, the vocalist Abbey Lincoln, joined forces for the *We Insist! Freedom Now Suite*, while Charles Mingus penned savage parodies of white segregationists such as "Fables of Faubus" and celebrations of faith-inspired Freedom Riders. In 1963, as the civil rights movement reached its peak, the African American poet Amiri Baraka (then known as LeRoi Jones) published *Blues People*, an ambitious attempt to place the entire tradition of black music in the context of U.S. history. The first study of its kind, *Blues People* scathingly attacked the impact of the genteel black middle class on musicians through the decades, and celebrated what Baraka perceived as the core of working-class blues culture in the most potent and effective modern jazz, which, for Baraka, continued to epitomize recent African American music.

Black jazz musicians in the North became increasingly angry and activist as they became swept up in the growing urban movements against persistent racism and inequality. As early as the 1940s, during the heady first days of global colonial revolt, African American musicians became attracted to Islam as a source of racial pride and spiritual solace. The drummer and bandleader Art Blakey, the pianists Ahmad Jamal and Muhal Richard Abrams, and others became converts to Islam in the postwar era. In the decade after World War II, the homegrown Nation of Islam became a strong advocate for black separatism and protest. John Coltrane and his loyal bandmates, especially the multi-instrumental and short-lived prodigy Eric Dolphy, delved into a cosmopolitan form of eastern spirituality. Coltrane's death in 1967 at the age of forty intensified the quasi-religious dedication of his most fervent followers. Meanwhile, the pianist and composer Sun Ra, an Alabama native who (as Herman Blount) had been one of the last major big band arrangers of the 1940s, built a science fiction–influenced community around his group, the Arkestra. Sun Ra launched his own record company and sustained the most enduring free-jazz ensemble of the 1960s and 1970s.

Jazz in the 1960s was filled with energy, talent, and ideas, but as in the avant-garde classical music of that era, the deterioration of traditional tonality and meter and the new emphasis on freedom and chance splintered musicians and their listeners into small cliques. The examples of Coltrane and Coleman encouraged brilliant pianists such as Cecil Taylor and McCoy Tyner to unleash torrents of extended and dissonant improvisation. Among saxophonists, Sun Ra's colleagues Pharoah Sanders and Rashaan Roland Kirk, as well as Albert Ayler and others, experimented with honks, squawks, and other unconventional effects (such as Kirk's blowing on three instruments at once) to push back the frontiers of improvisation. Miles Davis, meanwhile, retreated from modality and explored a wide range of strategies to make jazz trumpeting and combo playing more relevant to wild and decidedly "uncool" new times. In the process Davis formed one of the most exciting and talented jazz groups of the decade, featuring new young stars such as the pianist Herbie Hancock and the drummer Tony Williams. Within a generation, it seemed, the big band sound had become a distant memory. Duke Ellington, Count Basie,

Cab Calloway, and others remained active, but their music and their audiences now seemed to be purely nostalgic, the relics of an earlier epoch.

For many black jazz innovators, the deadly urban uprisings of the 1960s provided a new sense of purpose and focus. Beginning in 1964, a rash of riots broke out in largely African American ghettoes on hot summer days and nights. An attempted arrest of a black youth by a white policeman usually provided the spark, which ignited heckling and vandalism against the squad car, a greater police response, and escalation into widespread looting and burning of white-owned businesses and property. Uprisings occurred in Harlem in 1964, in the Watts neighborhood of Los Angeles the following year, and in Detroit and Newark in 1967. Observers of the 1965 Watts conflict estimated that as much as a quarter of the ghetto's black population was involved. National Guard troops shot and killed dozens of suspected looters. Sociologists suggested later that the rioters had tried to "cleanse" black neighborhoods of white-owned businesses and the police.

The rioters' destructiveness expressed their despair about ghetto life and lack of faith in civil rights laws as a solution, but it also demonstrated a new cultural energy that produced a new perception of African American identity. Here, at least, was a call to action that shook off the throes of drug addiction and passivity. In its wake came the Black Power movement, which sought to bury old "Negro" identities and restore African American pride and allow the people to express themselves in an "authentic" manner. The Black Arts movement, led by Amiri Baraka among others, spearheaded this latter initiative.

Musicians in the jazz tradition took active part in the Black Arts movement. In Chicago, Muhal Richard Abrams expanded his earlier attempt to create an artists' collective into the Association for the Advancement of Creative Musicians (AACM), founded in 1965. Roscoe Mitchell, Anthony Braxton, and Henry Threadgill led musical groups affiliated with the AACM. The Art Ensemble of Chicago, including Mitchell, the trumpeter Lester Bowie, the bassist Malachi Favors, and others, was the best known of these ensembles. In performances they utilized a huge array of instruments to recapture some of the myriad musical timbres of the African diaspora, as well as costuming, makeup, and choreography that evoked rituals on both sides of the Atlantic.

Similar organizations arose in other cities. In St. Louis, the Black Artists Group tapped into the historically rich musical traditions of that city—now blighted by a large ghetto—and produced dynamic ensembles such as the St. Louis Saxophone Quartet. Conditions in Los Angeles's Watts district had encouraged the pianist and bandleader Horace Tapscott to found the Union of God's Musicians and Artists Ascension (UGMAA) in 1961. Tapscott, in the spirit of Sun Ra and John Coltrane, conceived his organization to be a vessel of cultural enlightenment and healing, and he was joined in the UGMAA by a vast collection of skilled musicians, including Arthur Blithe,

Linda Hill, Stanley Crouch, and Bobby Bradford (a trumpeter in Ornette Coleman's ensemble). These and other artists' organizations established community music centers to teach musical skills, form ensembles, and use jazz as a vehicle for personal and collective empowerment. Their activities were classic examples of the radical ambition, revisionism, and occasional euphoria that infused cultural experimentation in the 1960s.

The Black Arts initiative has never really ended, but by the early 1970s it was apparent that the white majority and political establishment had suppressed the political and social goals of the Black Power movement. Martin Luther King, Jr. was assassinated in 1968; the Federal Bureau of Investigation (FBI) succeeded in breaking up the Student Nonviolent Coordinating Committee and the Black Panther Party; and white voters elected President Richard M. Nixon and other officeholders who vowed to "get tough" on inner-city radicalism. In the 1970s, African American musical creativity was popular and profitable, but largely in genres besides jazz. The jazz avant-garde's attempts to tie itself to popular "street" culture mostly failed. Many in the jazz community felt that the music faced a crisis. After "free jazz" had thrown out tonality and regular rhythm, they asked, what could come next? The exhaustion of earlier jazz styles from Dixieland to free jazz put black musicians in a classic "postmodern" dilemma: was there anything new left to say?

JAZZ SINCE 1970

The most popular jazz genre of the 1970s featured the "fusion" of traditional improvisation with amplified rock instruments and soul/funk rhythms and chord changes. The always restless Miles Davis launched this style in the late 1960s with his provocative and best-selling albums, *In a Silent Way* and *Bitches Brew*. The participants in Davis's projects were a multiracial collection of leading jazz innovators, such as the African Americans Herbie Hancock and Wayne Shorter and the white performers Chick Corea, John McLaughlin, and Joe Zawinul. All of them participated with Davis in the fusion experiments of the 1970s and later years.

Since 1980, jazz in the United States has led a vital existence in the universities, as leading players and composers have taken professorships and thousands of talented young performers have been nurtured in formal degree programs. Across the world, especially in Japan and in Europe, government subsidies and enthusiastic fans continue to provide support for appearances by leading American jazz performers. In the past quarter-century, the trumpeter and composer Wynton Marsalis has served as the focal point for debate about the future of jazz in America. Marsalis's dazzling technique, which embraces classical and jazz music, earned him fame and wealth when he was still in his early twenties, and led some critics to consider him to be the potential savior of jazz. In 1991, Marsalis assumed the highly visible post of artistic director of Jazz at Lincoln Center (JALC), which has become the most lavishly funded jazz program in the country. In 2004, JALC took up residence in a magnificent new venue in the Time Warner Center, overlooking Central Park in New York City.

Marsalis, a member of an important New Orleans musical family, has been assertive in his defense of what he calls the central jazz tradition, stretching from Louis Armstrong to John Coltrane, and in his attacks on the post-1960 avant-garde and recent black popular music (especially hip hop). The cultural critic Stanley Crouch, a former free jazz drummer, became a prominent champion of Marsalis's vision of jazz, in which well-dressed, well-mannered adherents to tradition would triumph over the allegedly vulgar music and lyrics of embarrassing and unschooled gangbangers. A less prominent debate about the degree of whites' contributions to jazz history has also flared since 1990, joined by Marsalis's partisans on one side and the white jazz historians James Lincoln Collier and Richard Sudhalter on the other. As the final chapters in this volume will show, the jazz debates in which Wynton Marsalis has taken part are episodes in larger controversies of our time about the identity of African Americans in an era of civil equality and economic inequality. Should black people "dress up" and join the white-dominated social establishment, or should they maintain a separate and critical distance from those classes?

In the past six decades, two types of music favored mostly by small audiences of aficionados—classical music and post-bebop jazz—have daringly explored and deconstructed traditional musical styles and forms. African American musicians in these fields have been among the most well-informed and sophisticated performers and composers to rediscover the riches of centuries of black music and explore their relevance to our times. Although popular music styles have eclipsed jazz and classical music for the last fifty years, listeners should not neglect the complex and thoughtful explorations of black composers and performers who have resisted the formulas and genres of the musical mass market.

NOTE

1. Eileen Southern, *The Music of Black Americans*, 3rd ed. (New York: Norton, 1997), 425.

6

Gospel, Freedom Songs, and the Struggle for Equality

The Lincoln Memorial had served as the stage for Marian Anderson's historic concert in 1939. On August 28, 1963, the Memorial was the site of another milestone in the history of African Americans. The March on Washington for Jobs and Freedom brought a quarter of a million people to the Mall, coincidentally on the day after W. E. B. Du Bois died in Ghana at the age of ninety-five. The March was a crossroads in the struggle for black equality, a moment at which years of suffering and conflict seemed to herald a revolution in national legislation regarding race. The formal program on the steps of the Memorial, of course, is best remembered for the Reverend Martin Luther King, Jr.'s ringing vision of equality: "I have a dream."

The Lincoln Memorial program marked a crossroads in the history of African American music as well. Returning to the site of her triumphant concert, Marian Anderson led the crowd in the national anthem. She was followed by A. Philip Randolph, Myrlie Evers, John Lewis, James Farmer, and other civil rights speakers. The Eva Jessye Choir then sang a gospel selection. Eva Jessye's rich life had taken her from a rural Kansas childhood to 1920s Harlem. In later years she composed choral works and conducted choirs for Hollywood studios and for the first production of George Gershwin's *Porgy and Bess*. Following more speeches—and minutes before King's oration—Mahalia Jackson sang the spirituals "How I Got Over" and "I've Been 'Buked and I've Been Scorned."

Mahalia Jackson had been born in poverty in New Orleans, but in Chicago, she became a student of Thomas A. Dorsey, the "father" of modern gospel music, and rose to stardom. By 1963 she was an international celebrity. Two years earlier, at the other end of the Mall, Jackson had sung at the inauguration of President John F. Kennedy. The singer is credited by some with encouraging King to deliver the "I Have a Dream" speech (which she had heard him give a few weeks earlier in Detroit) instead of the new oration he had composed for the event in Washington. Five years after the March, Jackson would appear at the funeral services of the assassinated civil rights leader, rendering Thomas Dorsey's most famous gospel composition, "Take My Hand, Precious Lord."

The convergence of extraordinary individuals on the steps of the Memorial that day—a day poised between the triumphs and tragedies of the civil rights era—helps to introduce several key points about the evolution of African American music in these years. Despite the brilliance and success of ragtime, the blues, jazz, and African American concert music in the twentieth century, it was the music of the church that epitomized the spirit of concern, fellowship, and crusading righteousness that animated the civil rights movement and the more general sense among black Americans that change must occur.

In 1963 as well as today, the term "gospel music" embraced white as well as black Protestant American church singing—two styles that shared many hymn texts and southern roots, but that had been largely segregated from each other for a century and a half. Emerging as a national force in the 1930s, black gospel was the product of the complex evolution of nineteenth-century song styles (especially spirituals) in the Jim Crow era, when persistent poverty and bigotry undercut advancements by African Americans. Black gospel became big business, and some of its performing stars, such as Mahalia Jackson, became celebrities. Nonblack performers and audiences generally co-opted gospel less than other African American musical styles, and it remains at the core of black Protestant churches, where a racially separate culture and community persists. Since the 1930s gospel music, rising from thousands of choirs and congregations, has been the most idiomatic musical expression of African Americans. Having been told repeatedly that they are different from others, they have embraced gospel as the musical essence of a separate identity.

This important music could not be contained in the churches. Gospel became a rich influence on the secular musical life of African Americans as well. Its cultural importance, first apparent during the Great Depression, grew dramatically in the post–World War II decades. Even African American vocalists, instrumentalists, and listeners who did not lead religious lives responded to gospel's powerful wedding of the spirituals tradition with the harmonies, timbres, and performance practices of the blues and jazz. Gospel's influence simplified the beats and the harmonies of jazz and urban rhythm and blues, transforming the latter into a driving, body-shaking dance music that defined black youth culture in the 1950s. As gospel's vocal elements were popularized by best-selling artists—such as secularized vocal quartets and an innovative young performer named Ray Charles—African American popular music gained "soul." In the 1950s, Martin Luther King, Jr. encouraged civil rights activists to "meet . . . physical force with soul force," and he embraced freedom songs as a psychological aid and weapon in the arduous struggle for justice.[1] In the turbulent 1960s, "soul" came to define much of the secular music that was most popular in African American communities, especially among youth. This music—not the avant-garde jazz of more intellectual activists—was a major source of community invigoration, a healing agent in the aftermath of ghetto uprisings, and a cultural force well into the 1970s.

THE RISE OF GOSPEL

Before the 1930s, the spirituals tradition transformed gradually, even imperceptibly at times, into gospel. The first evolution, after Reconstruction, was the most drastic. Eager to refine their parishioners, many black ministers discouraged the exuberant heterophony of slave choirs. Simplified spirituals, such as those found in the published collections of slave songs and the performances of the Fisk Jubilee Singers, dominated singing in AME, Methodist, and, to a lesser extent, Baptist congregations. Especially in the North, ministers and chorus directors discouraged the antebellum practice of "lining out," in which the preacher called out lines of hymns and the congregation sang them in response. Many churches now favored unison singing in the European style. European-American hymns even outnumbered black spirituals in many hymnals published by black churches, while the most prosperous urban parishes often favored classical sacred music. Spirituals were even less evident in numerous African American Roman Catholic parishes, as well as in black Jewish temples, where the European musical heritage also predominated.

In the twentieth century the spiritual adapted further to changing times. The Fisk Jubilee Singers made its first phonograph recordings in 1909, and Harry T. Burleigh, among others, prospered as a publisher of arranged spirituals. Roland Hayes, Marian Anderson, and Paul Robeson pioneered the presentation of spirituals in concert recitals. In the 1920s, Robeson's example especially caused artists and writers of the Harlem Renaissance to extol the heritage of spirituals. Nevertheless, as Langston Hughes's blues poetry and Zora Neale Hurston's studies of black folklore indicated, new expressions were emerging—and even exploding—onto the black musical scene, via race records, nightclub performances, and even in street corner renditions. Black commentators in the 1920s were split over how educated African Americans should express themselves, with genteel traditionalists continuing to favor standard English and innovators such as Hughes and Hurston championing a grassroots black language. Advocates of black vernacular expression gradually persuaded most well-educated African Americans to appreciate the artistic value of the blues, jazz, and spirituals.

In the 1920s, there was plenty of new and exciting black sacred music for these individuals to appreciate. The originators of much of this music were the new African American Pentecostal denominations. From humble roots in the 1890s, these new churches rose to claim millions of congregants by 1930. Pentecostalism grew out of white and black Protestant innovations after the Civil War, filtered through debates within the Methodist church that had their roots in theological controversies dating back to Martin Luther and John Calvin. The Holiness movement, launched at a white parishioners' revival in New Jersey in 1867, emphasized the "sanctification" of the individual through the word of God. Pentecostalism, an allied development, stressed the role of adult baptism in achieving a second birth for individuals, a "filling with grace" that resulted in physical manifestations, such as speaking in tongues and the ability to safely handle poisonous snakes. These practices had deep roots in European pagan belief, as well as slave religion and its African antecedents.

More genteel African American worshipers rejected what they considered the rough and unschooled beliefs and practices of most Penecostal churches. As a result, Pentecostal parishes broke away from the AME and black Baptist organizations in the late 1800s. In 1897 the Baptist minister Charles H. Mason created a new sect, the Church of God in Christ (COGIC). Out of the Methodist fold came William J. Seymour, a Texas-born preacher, tutored by a leading white Pentecostalist, who in 1906 launched the sensational Azusa Street revival in Los Angeles. This raucous event is often called the birth of the modern Pentecostal movement, which spread rapidly across the Southwest and Southeast in the next decade and a half. Biracial revivals testified to the commonality of a profound spiritual experience, undoubtedly intensified by the terrors of World War I, new science and technology, and urban migration (in which rural whites as well as blacks took part). In the mid-1920s, though, prevailing white segregationism forced a schism between white and black Pentecostals.

COGIC and other parishes were ubiquitous in African American communities nationwide. They were housed in urban storefronts and rural shacks, and occasionally in some large city tabernacles. The entire culture of black Pentecostalism disdained the formality and learned pretense of many established Protestant churches. Sacred slave songs were within the living memory of black congregations, and moaning and shouting—the vocal staples of those songs—were accepted in Pentecostalism as the unvarnished manifestations of sanctification, of the holy spirit at work in the congregation. Outsiders labeled such parishes "holy rollers" for their energetic singing and dancing. Pentecostal churches revived line reading and other old-time features of black Protestant services. By the time of the Great Depression, the powerful cultural impact of these churches was beginning to influence worship in many churches in the established black denominations.

By 1930 the new churches had especially welcomed the sounds of the blues into their services. Most of them used the traditional Methodist hymnal, which had provided many of the texts (entire or partial) of 1800s spirituals, but the staid European tunes of tradition gave way to vernacular harmonies closely aligned with secular blues. Some exciting early recordings capture preachers' sermons as they moved from the spoken word to call and response singing with parishioners. Other recordings from the 1920s preserve the singing and playing of Arizona Drane (billed as Arizona Dranes), a blind woman from Texas who combined blues-style shouting with skilled boogie-woogie piano playing in a highly influential early form of solo gospel singing.

Well before 1930, Pentecostal church music began to influence the mainstream black denominations. An interesting transitional figure was the Reverend Charles A. Tindley of Philadelphia. At the turn of the century Tindley kept his parish in the Methodist fold, despite his attraction to the Pentecostal message. Tindley composed and published numerous new hymns that departed from Methodist models, utilizing a modified (sixteen-bar) blues stanza and the cadences of blues song, even before the blues had emerged as a popular style. Tindley's "Stand By Me" remains a popular favorite. Other, less well-known hymn composers, such as "Professor" W. M. Nix, also published blues-inflected hymns in succeeding years. In 1921, the National Baptist Convention (NBC)—the main umbrella organization for black Baptist churches—acknowledged the influence of vernacular hymns by publishing *Gospel Pearls*, its first collection of new hymns. The composer and performer Lucie Campbell, the choral coordinator for the NBC, was central to its publication. *Gospel Pearls'* wide popularity among millions of old-line Baptists helped to bring elements of the Pentecostal hymning style into the black Protestant mainstream, and also popularized the term "gospel" as a designation for newer church songs.

Thomas Andrew Dorsey personified the transition at work in African American church music, as well as the new relationship between the sacred and secular that developed in black culture between the world wars. In the 1920s, Dorsey alternated between work as a blues pianist and composer, performing with Ma Rainey, Bessie Smith, and others, and involvement in the Baptist church, where he performed and published hymns. During the next decade, though, he devoted himself exclusively to the composition and promotion of gospel music, and became one of the most influential figures in the history of African American music.

Born in 1899, Dorsey was the son of a preacher and his devout wife. He grew up first in a small Georgia town and then in Atlanta, where he began to play the piano. His devotion to religion was challenged by diversions in the city, and by the age of fourteen he was playing for money in local brothels, theaters, and rent parties. At one theater he met Ma Rainey and her young protégé, Bessie Smith. Eager to move north to advance his career, he finally settled in Chicago in 1919. Making use of his early familiarity with the blues, Dorsey found work as a pianist in taverns and cabarets. In these years, he later said, he associated blues with being "grievous" and having "a wounded heart."[2] Dorsey published his first blues in 1920, and as an employee of a sheet music company and Paramount Records he made many arrangements of popular blues. As "Georgia Tom," he began touring with Ma Rainey and making his own recordings, often with a partner, "Tampa Red."

In 1921, though, Dorsey attended the National Baptist Convention annual meeting in Chicago and embraced religious song, which (unlike the blues) he believed might heal a wounded heart. In subsequent years he moved between blues recording, touring, and composition and working in the church as a composer and chorus master. His hymns reflected his rich youthful experience of diverse traditions in southern sacred music, including the "shape-note" singing of rural whites. Shape-note hymns were notated on paper in geometric shapes and relayed in performance through hand signals. Dorsey used these signals when he trained choruses.

Dorsey demonstrated an entrepreneurial skill in organizing church choirs, and in the early 1930s his work in gospel music supplanted his blues songwriting and performing. His inclusion of blues harmonies and phrases in his published hymns and their performances earned him the opposition of some denominational ministers. The often savage inter- and intrachurch politics in black Chicago helped to make worship music a cultural battleground. At the same time, though, Dorsey noticed that the moaning and shouting styles of the Pentecostal churches were seeping into Baptist hymnody and increasing the vitality of singing in services. He made the acquaintance of Sallie Martin, a gifted solo church singer who shared his love of the blues and encouraged him to promote blues-inflected gospel hymns.

In 1932, Dorsey and Martin organized the National Convention of Gospel Choirs and Choruses. Within months, Dorsey employed his distinctive brand of showmanship to spread his musical vision throughout black America. During this time, the death of Dorsey's wife and newborn son inspired him to write a heartfelt plea, "Take My Hand, Precious Lord," based on a nineteenth-century hymn melody, which became his most famous composition. By the 1940s, the musician had published hundreds of "Dorseys," as church singers often called his hymns, and his di-

Photo 6.1. Children singing in the glee club of the Ida B. Wells housing project in Chicago, circa 1940. Glee clubs and church choirs maintained African American choral traditions. Source: Prints and Photographs Division, Library of Congress.

rection of gospel workshops across the country made his brand of the gospel blues the dominant music in African American churches. Thanks to Dorsey and Martin, the Sanctified blues hymn won the stylistic war in the mainstream black denominations. Wilson Pickett, a future commercial singing star, was a child gospel singer in Detroit. As he recalled, the blues were the essential material for his music in his neighborhood. "You got no cash for music lessons, arrangers, uniforms, backup bands, guitars. No nothin'. So you look around for a good, solid used chassis. This be your twelve-bar blues."[3]

Aside from Dorsey, almost all of the leading early figures in black gospel music were female. Since the Reconstruction era, women had increasingly dominated African American church congregations. While the posts of power, such as preacher and deacon, continued to be monopolized by men, women made up a large majority of the individuals in the pews and determined the churches' social and emotional life, especially on Sundays. As a result, beginning with Sallie Martin, virtually all of the stars of Thomas Dorsey's "gospel highway" were female. This professional touring circuit bore a resemblance to TOBA and the other secular territorial routes. Dorsey negotiated the thickets of African American church politics and personal feuds to spread the message of gospel music. In the process he helped to make nationally known figures out of singers who otherwise might have pursued careers in blues or jazz singing. Among these women was Willie Mae Ford Smith, a Mississippi native who lived in St. Louis. An ordained minister, Smith refused to record or give commercial concerts and devoted her life to gospel touring and education. Roberta Martin, a migrant to Chicago, was an early associate of Dorsey's who possessed a dazzling high vocal register. Like Smith, Martin shunned a commercial career. She led her own choir in Chicago, and her smaller ensemble, the Roberta Martin Singers, toured nationally.

Two great commercial successes emerged out of Thomas Dorsey's hive of gospel activity. When she was still in her teens, Rosetta Nubin had only brief contact with Dorsey in Chicago. A native of eastern Arkansas, the heart of COGIC territory, Nubin was already a veteran church performer who had accompanied her mother vocally and on the guitar. In the 1930s, she married and moved to New York, where, billed as Sister Rosetta Tharpe, she recorded gospel songs with a jazz band. Tharpe's rapid ascent to stardom in the late 1930s was fueled by the same gospel blues sound that brought Dorsey to prominence, but she rose to greater commercial heights. Appearing in concert halls and nightclubs, Tharpe brought gospel into the glare of the mass spotlight, and anticipated the "crossing over" of future gospel singers into secular venues and repertoire. Tharpe also astounded listeners with her skilled and theatrical guitar playing. Tharpe's boogie-woogie backbeats (which emphasized the second and fourth notes in quadruple-time musical bars) and up-tempo sixteen-bar blues anticipated their use in rock 'n' roll music. Her playing resembled the band music of another pioneer of rock 'n' roll, the saxophonist and bandleader Louis Jordan, who had grown up in the same region of Arkansas. By 1948, Tharpe was overshadowed in the gospel field by new female stars, such as Clara Ward. An exuberant pianist and vocalist from Philadelphia, Ward toiled for years with a family-based choir until she became a success at National Baptist Convention meetings during World War II. In later years her ensemble became highly commercial, and in the 1960s it appeared in Las Vegas nightclubs and at Disneyland.

Photo 6.2.   Publicity photo for the Clara Ward Singers, 1950s. Source: Prints and Photographs Division, Library of Congress.

Dorsey's other protégé was Mahalia Jackson, who became the most successful gospel star of them all. Many strands of African American music and culture united in Jackson's amazing career. She was born in 1912 in New Orleans, in the same neighborhood as Louis Armstrong, and grew up surrounded by both poverty and a rich musical scene. Like Armstrong, Jackson was hindered by family instability, but she received a vital musical education at local Baptist and Pentecostal churches. As a teenager she strove to sing like her idol Bessie Smith, but a spiritual conversion caused her to commit to church music. Moving to Chicago, she met Thomas Dorsey, a man of similar background, and began to sell his hymns on street corners. Her magnificent voice led music teachers and her first husband to recommend classical training. She refused to do so, and even divorced her husband over the issue. Nightclub owners also failed to enlist her talent. Jackson made gospel recordings and gradually gained a following, while she cannily invested her growing earnings in a successful beauty parlor. After World War II, Jackson made more recordings, which led to a triumphant appearance in New York City. Her impact on audiences, particularly nonchurch listeners, was extraordinary. More than any other gospel star, Jackson infused sacred song with the full arsenal of blues vocal inflections. No other performer could match her booming, golden voice or reproduce the ecstatic body movements that accompanied her singing.

In the 1950s, Jackson was one of America's most successful and popular performers, recording for Columbia Records, appearing regularly on television, and hosting a national radio program. She did refuse on religious grounds, though, to perform in Las Vegas. Jackson's unique fame alienated her from members of the African American gospel community, who claimed that she now ignored her roots. In part to overcome this criticism, she became active in politics. Jackson lobbied Democratic politicians from Harry Truman to Lyndon Johnson on behalf of civil rights and anti-lynching legislation; sang at John F. Kennedy's inauguration; consoled Chicagoans on live television after Kennedy's assassination; befriended Chicago's mayor, Richard J. Daley; and participated in the 1963 March on Washington. Health problems in the 1960s, along with a very public divorce battle, weakened her voice and limited her performing, and she died in 1972. Jackson's extraordinary career, like Louis Armstrong's, illustrated how African American music could conquer a diverse national audience—and how such a conquest might cause a superstar to risk losing touch with average black listeners.

Male vocal ensembles rose concurrently with female gospel stars in the late 1930s. African American churchgoers embraced them, and so, to an extent, did a diverse national audience. The ensembles had deep roots in black communities, descending from post–Civil War sacred ensembles,

barbershop quartets, and harmonizing groups found in minstrelsy, vaudeville, and ragtime. As with other genres of modern gospel, male quartets
and other groups emerged gradually after the first recording sessions and
concert tours took place in the 1920s. In 1926, the Soul Stirrers quintet originated in Trinity, Texas, an active center of male group singing. The cres-
cent stretching from the mid-Atlantic to the Deep South proved even more
fertile, launching such notable groups such as the Dixie Hummingbirds
(from South Carolina), the Golden Gate Quartet (from Norfolk, Virginia),
the Kings of Harmony, and the Famous Blue Jays (from Alabama).

The music and the image of the male groups differed markedly from
those of female gospel stars. The singers adopted the fine clothing, styled
hair, and gentlemanly airs of preachers and deacons. However, unlike
moaning and shouting female gospel singers, they rarely emulated the
preachers' ecstatic blend of speech and song. Male gospel groups instead
expressed ecstasy in flawless multipart harmony, a style derived from earlier traditions but which also featured rich new blues inflections. The bass
singer often supplied imitations of drum and double-bass jazz rhythms, the
middle voices filled out the chords, and the tenor sang the melodic leads,
often in a thrilling falsetto. The dedicated artistry of the groups was perceived by many as an expression of their religious faith, but their handsome
profiles and ecstatic harmonizing thrilled the female congregation members in a markedly nonspiritual way. A few male performers outshone their
ensemble mates and became the sex symbols of the gospel highway.

The stories of three men's groups help to describe the rise of this gospel
genre. The Soul Stirrers languished in relative obscurity in Texas, although in the 1930s they were recorded by the folklorists John and Alan
Lomax for the Library of Congress's folk music project. A move to
Chicago in 1937 brought the group into competition with the new rising
stars, the Golden Gate Quartet. This ensemble from Norfolk, Virginia,
which featured Willie Johnson, Henry Owens, and Bill Landford as
soloists, pioneered national fame for male gospel groups. In 1937, the
quartet sang on network radio, and during the next two years they appeared in Carnegie Hall in "From Spirituals to Swing" concerts produced
by John Hammond. The Golden Gate Quartet's inventive "jubilee"
arrangements of old and new gospel standards shared the polished sophistication of Duke Ellington's compositions. Many other groups imi-
tated the singers' ability to mimic bird, train, and other sounds with their
voices, and their gentlemanly bearing helped to attract white middle-class
audiences. For religious reasons the quartet became committed antifas-
cists, allying itself with the left-wing Popular Front and performing at the
Café Society nightclub, where Sister Rosetta Tharpe also appeared.
Eleanor Roosevelt invited the group to the White House, and movie appearances followed as well. Meanwhile, the Dixie Hummingbirds, from

Greenville, South Carolina, led by an exuberant teenager named Ira Tucker, rose slowly to fame, gaining a wide audience in the 1940s. The Hummingbirds used written arrangements, but their style was closer to the emotive spirit of shouting Pentecostal congregations than the restrained delivery of the Golden Gate Quartet.

The success of these pioneering male groups inspired many imitations in the years after World War II. The Soul Stirrers rose to the height of their popularity right after the war, thanks to the addition of a charismatic new lead singer, R. H. Harris. The Swan Silvertones, a spinoff from the Dixie Hummingbirds, also was successful. Two groups that originated in schools for the disabled in the Deep South—Five Blind Boys from Mississippi and the Blind Boys of Alabama—revived the Pentecostal style in quartet singing, although audiences often confused the two groups. The second massive black northern migration during the war, as well as migrants' economic and political hopes, helped to encourage gospel music associations and groups to set their sights higher, push for wider distribution on records and radio, and expand their touring. While performers still faced difficulties along the gospel highway, including white discrimination and outright hostility, their irresistible music continued to bestow an unmatched feeling of spiritual and physical liberation on working-class black people, and churches reverberated with its energy.

FROM R & B TO ROCK 'N' ROLL

But that was not all. In the 1950s, gospel music also decisively changed African American secular or popular music. The success of male gospel ensembles inspired a vogue in the late 1940s for secular groups that sang unaccompanied. Pioneering acts such as the Mills Brothers and the Inkspots had been recording hit singles since the early 1930s, crossing over into the "sweet" big band repertory but maintaining their black vocal timbres. Now the phenomenon of street-corner singing in black communities experienced a revival. Love songs tended to dominate these street performances, but since many of the young performers had first sung in churches, their execution was almost exclusively gospel-inflected. The Ravens rose to fame in New York City, the Orioles began in Baltimore, and other "bird groups" such as the Swallows and the Penguins followed in their wake. Clyde McPhatter, who had grown up in Baptist church choirs, led the Dominoes to popularity, founded the best-selling group the Drifters, and became a solo star. Talking bass solos, falsetto tenor voicings, choral backgrounds, and rhythmic vocal accompaniment in wordless syllables—commonly called "doo-wop" rhythm in later years—typified the sound of these 1950s vocal groups. White impresarios such as Ahmet

Ertegun and Jerry Wexler of Atlantic Records (who signed McPhatter and the Drifters) encouraged these groups to "cross over" by crafting recordings that appealed to nonblack audiences.

The contribution of gospel to post–World War II blues resulted from the complex relationship between the two musical styles. The fact that "classic" pre-1930s blues had given much of modern gospel its energy suggested that sacred and secular black music had never been separate. The fragmentary evidence of the origins of the blues in the late 1800s suggests that this genre was heavily indebted to the religious singing of the time. It was true that secular music was performed outside of the churches' sacred sphere, often in sites rife with behavior that preachers regularly condemned, and was championed and exploited by an incurably greedy popular music industry. Nevertheless, after decades of coexistence, gospel music and the blues invariably influenced each other, and, in artists such as Thomas A. Dorsey and Mahalia Jackson, they coexisted happily. Perhaps it was almost inevitable that the interaction of gospel and the blues would profoundly affect popular music after World War II.

By the 1940s the rural blues, exemplified by male singers such as Charley Patton and women such as Bessie Smith, had moved into new regions of American music and society. In the South, the black and white music touring circuits often intersected, and musicians heard and influenced each other. These meetings allowed the blues to shape the development of country or "hillbilly" music, a largely white popular music that emerged in the 1920s. African American mentors helped to shape the distinctive singing style of Jimmie Rodgers, the first country singing star of the 1930s, and Hank Williams, the most successful country soloist of the late 1940s. For decades the harmonica player DeFord Bailey was the sole black star on Nashville's Grand Ole Opry, the most prominent showcase for country-western music on national radio. Bailey's career prepared the way for Charley Pride, the unique African American country star of the 1960s and 1970s, who sold over 70 million records.

Unamplified, traditional country blues lived on in the South, remaining especially influential in the Delta region around Memphis, Tennessee. In other ways, though, the music changed with the times. Nationally, the Great Depression stifled the vogue of the female blues singer. Bessie Smith struggled to adjust to the swing era before her death in an automobile accident in 1937. Ethel Waters retreated for a time into the church, while Alberta Hunter began a long career as a nurse. It was gospel that helped to revive the ranks of blueswomen. During World War II, a young Mississippi migrant named Ruth Jones, a veteran of Sallie Martin's pioneering gospel choir, found success with big bands. After the war she began to perform under the name Dinah Washington, and became the most prominent new exponent of the female blues tradition.

Among men, by the 1930s the experiments of the first generation of Delta guitarists had produced a solid blues playing tradition, which gave newcomers such as Robert Johnson a foundation on which to build striking individual styles. In the early 1940s, male blues singers finally gained exposure on radio, most notably on the Arkansas-based program *King Biscuit Time*. Simultaneously, guitar electrification (which was first popularized by swing bands) made performers audible in noisy venues and allowed them to sustain, bend, and otherwise transform their notes in new ways.

The electric guitar was a musical symbol of the dramatic modernization that was taking place in the South during World War II. Hydroelectric dams, military bases, large-scale textile manufacturing, mechanized agriculture, wartime industries, and even indoor air conditioning fundamentally changed the economy and way of life of the South, making it more similar to the rest of the nation. African Americans, however, benefitted only in limited ways from these sweeping changes, and often found their situation worsened. The introduction of mechanical cotton harvesters, for example, eliminated the need for sharecroppers on large plantations, and forced many poor black people to migrate north. Participants in the Second Great Migration of the 1940s were lured north by hopes for a better life, but they were also pushed out of the South by changing local conditions.

This migration transformed the blues. The search for war work brought 300,000 African Americans to Chicago, which became a special destination for Delta musicians. The great "Chicago blues" era began after 1947 at the white Chess brothers' new Aristocrat label, which they soon renamed Chess Records. The company released enormously successful single tracks by McKinley Morganfield, a deep-voiced, forceful guitarist from Mississippi who performed under the name of Muddy Waters. Waters's example brought dozens of musicians to Chicago to record for Chess, most notably the bassist Willie Dixon, who became a prolific songwriter and colleague of Waters and the Chesses, and the blues singer Chester Burnett, a burly migrant from Memphis who performed under the name of Howlin' Wolf.

The migration of the blues to Chicago, Los Angeles, Philadelphia, and elsewhere brought the genre closer to the centers of the nation's popular music business. What the white-run major record companies now called "rhythm and blues" (R & B) stuck to a rather limited set of chord progressions, instrumentations, and song topics—especially focused on male-female conflict—and allowed the powerful personalities in front of the microphones to stamp their individuality on the material. Vocalists such as Waters, Wolf, Charles Brown, Koko Taylor, and Bobby "Blue" Bland brought some of the call-and-response ecstasy of gospel music into R & B. In the swiftly changing musical currents of the 1950s and 1960s, this relatively rigid early style of R & B, like big band jazz, lost popularity among younger African Americans and relied on the support of nostalgic, mostly white fans.

The postwar decline of the big bands, the ascent of the electric guitar, and the success of gospel music also encouraged the growth of another new musical style: rock 'n' roll. Ragtime, jazz, and, in its own way, classical music had influenced the use of rhythm in popular music, making it increasingly subtle and sophisticated. Gospel, though—and to a lesser extent, the blues—promoted a return to simple underlying beats. The simplified beat worked its way into jazz, first in boogie-woogie and much later in the gospel-inflected sound of 1950s "hard bop." In the mid-1940s an intermediate style, variously called "jive," "jump blues," or R & B, emerged. Jive groups were reduced swing bands that often emphasized the backbeat, accenting the second and fourth notes of four-quarter note rhythm. Straightforward blues harmonies and the time-honored twelve- and sixteen-bar blues stanzas became standard in jive. Against this hard-driving background, guitarists and saxophonists played heavily blues-laden solos that (unlike in bebop) stuck close to the basic beat. Louis Jordan's Tympani Five, Sister Rosetta Tharpe, and blues soloists such as Arthur Crudup and Big Mama Thornton inspired popular music listeners to dance again. Young southern black blues singers distilled the elements of jive into a rawer new style. Rock 'n' roll historians often point to "Rocket 88," recorded in Memphis in 1950 by Ike Turner and his band, as the song that initiated the new genre. By 1953 the mass media christened the music, "rock 'n' roll," from an African American slang term for sexual relations.

Rock 'n' roll quickly became the most revolutionary new popular music of the 1950s. It was free enough from the trappings of 1930s and 1940s styles to permit young people to consider it their own music. These youths were African American, white, and of other ethnicities. It is well known that the racial identity of early rock 'n' roll is tangled. Bill Haley and His Comets, a white northern band, modeled itself on Louis Jordan well before many black rock 'n' roll pioneers recorded their first hits. "Rockabilly," the blending of white country and western singing with blues progressions and rhythms, was well under way by 1953 as well. Sam Phillips's now-famous Sun Records of Memphis began by recording blues and R & B ensembles as well as country singers. Phillips, along with the white disk jockey Dewey Phillips, helped to publicize many local black and white musicians. In 1954, the nineteen-year-old Elvis Presley, a lover of music who especially cherished black and white gospel, became Sun Records's biggest seller. A product of white Pentecostal churches around Memphis, Presley brought a semblance of quasi-religious spirit possession into his hip-swiveling, arm-gyrating movements and his choked, falsetto-tinged vocal delivery, which took the national youth market by storm.

While Presley dominated the scene, early rock 'n' roll was populated with many exciting African American male presences. Two Chess Records singer-guitarists, Chuck Berry (from St. Louis) and Bo Diddley (born Elias

Bates in Mississippi, home of the "bow diddley" folk instrument) rocketed to fame in 1955 as rock 'n' roll pioneers. Berry, in particular, developed the slashing rhythms and blues-inspired modes that helped to define rock 'n' roll guitar playing.

Two other African American pioneers drew strongly on southern traditions. Antoine "Fats" Domino, a pianist and singer born and bred in New Orleans, contested for the title of first rock 'n' roll performer with his single "The Fat Man," recorded in 1949. Domino's extroverted and genial delivery helped to attract many white listeners to R & B, and his releases on Imperial Records enjoyed steady success throughout the 1950s. Only Elvis Presley sold more recordings during the decade. "Little Richard" Penniman grew up in Macon, Georgia. As a boy he was thrilled by the old-time African American medicine shows that came to town. Pentecostal church music deeply influenced Little Richard's singing, which employed the shrieking and wailing techniques of "hard" gospel. In 1955, after gigs in New Orleans, Little Richard traveled to Los Angeles, where the owners of Specialty Records groomed him for stardom. His first single, "Tutti Frutti," became one of the key style-setters of the early rock 'n' roll era, featuring the highly influential "choo-choo" drum rhythm. Little Richard's flamboyance, ambiguous sexual orientation, and frequent detours into the ministry brought an intriguing diversity to the 1950s rock 'n' roll scene.

SOUL MUSIC

R & B, rock 'n' roll, and other new styles were almost entirely secular in content. They reflected the new affluence of the 1950s, a period that seemed to promise more leisure and "the good life" to all. African Americans saw some improvement in their standard of living and enjoyed the high spirits found in the new popular music.

Nevertheless, discrimination and poverty continued to dominate their lives. In the music industry, persisting inequality was best represented by the phenomenon of the "white cover" recording, in which a Caucasian singer with a clean-cut, middle-class image—such as the highly successful Pat Boone—made a rhythmically and emotionally pale version of a black R & B or rock 'n' roll hit that outsold and outearned the original. Moreover, as Little Richard's occasional returns to the pulpit illustrated, African American musicians and listeners questioned the value of commercial success in a segregated country and sought answers and comfort in religion. Unlike R & B or rock 'n' roll, gospel music continued to urge black audiences to remain concerned about their community's spiritual and social welfare. Male gospel quartets had been a direct musical inspiration for secular vocal groups that rose to fame on the popular charts. Now, in the mid-

1950s, gospel music, as well as its messages of black spirituality and group solidarity, inspired an important new current in black popular music.

Much of the credit for the birth of "soul" music goes to Ray Charles, the man whom Little Richard had considered his main competition during his early days at Specialty Records. Ray Charles Robinson grew up in poverty in Albany, Georgia. He suffered the onset of blindness as a child, but used his keen hearing to master piano blues. His brief stint with a white country and western band instilled in him a lifelong love for this music. After traveling to Seattle to try his luck as a jazz musician, Ray Charles, as he was now billed, began to front bands, and he gained attention in Los Angeles as a vocalist. In 1951, Charles's early recording successes encouraged Atlantic Records, an enterprising New York label specializing in jazz and R & B, to sign him.

A few years into his contract, Charles embraced a full gospel sound in his single "I Got a Woman," the first of a series of songs that reworked popular hymns. He pared down his piano ornamentations and incorporated the repetitious riffs and vocal moans and shouts of gospel into his numbers. His addition of the Raelettes, a female vocal trio, accentuated the gospel flavor of late-1950s songs such as "What Kind of Man Are You." "What'd I Say?" from 1959 translated church moans into unmistakable allusions to sexual ecstasy, opening the door to a new frankness in popular music. Many devout African Americans had been concerned about the sexuality of rock 'n' roll, but Charles's co-opting of broad swaths of the gospel sound for suggestive songs provoked an even sharper initial outrage. Nevertheless, the transfer of "soul" from strictly religious music and settings to nightclubs and concert halls indicated the arrival of deeper emotions and a more provocative social relevance in African American music. Soul spoke to black demands for "freedom and equality now," but also to the liberation of the individual and community spirit.

Singers nurtured within the gospel cocoon followed Ray Charles into secular soul music. Sam Cooke, the slim son of a Mississippi preacher who brought his family to Chicago, joined the venerable Soul Stirrers in 1950 at the age of nineteen. When R. H. Harris retired from the group, Cooke—who was gradually discovering his own style—became its star. His good looks, impassioned physicality, and soaring tenor shouts laid bare the sexual attraction of male gospel quartets to largely female congregations. Cooke's move to secular popular singing in 1957 was inevitable.

After a prostitute fatally shot Sam Cooke in a seedy Los Angeles hotel in 1964, some gospel adherents blamed his death on his decision to abandon the church for commercial fame. Cooke's fans insist that the circumstances surrounding his death did not fit the singer's character, and even today they suggest that his murder was plotted by musical rivals.

Whether or not the singer's death can be blamed on his decision to pursue a secular career, it cannot be denied that low pay and miserable travel conditions encouraged many gospel performers besides Cooke to enter mainstream popular music. For African Americans raised in the church, the temptations of wealth and material comforts always tested their spiritual moorings. This tension, in fact, helped nurture some of the most exciting music of the soul era. At its root, soul music addressed the twin basic needs of African American audiences. It validated their religious foundations and also encouraged them to pursue wealth and physical pleasure. In the face of persistent discrimination, soul offered a reachable, black-defined vision of the American dream.

No soul pioneer exhibited the thirst for success as vividly as James Brown. This South Carolina native, abandoned as a child by his parents and raised in a brothel, graduated to petty crimes and a lifetime of difficulties with the law. In Augusta, Georgia, young James learned guitar from Tampa Red (Thomas A. Dorsey's old blues partner), emulated the showmanship of the bandleader Louis Jordan, and soaked up the local gospel scene. After a three-year stint in juvenile hall, Brown dabbled in semi-pro sports and began a singing career under his local mentor, Bobby Byrd, just as Byrd made the transition from gospel to R & B. In 1955, Brown's group, the Flames, recorded "Please Please Please," for King Records in Cincinnati and made the national sales charts. Years of struggle followed, though, during which Brown played countless concert dates, especially in the South, and perfected a highly energetic and flamboyant persona.

Brown's star rose almost simultaneously with the fortunes of the civil rights movement, and in 1963, the year of the Birmingham campaign, the March on Washington, and the Kennedy civil rights bill, he reached permanent fame with his album *Live at the Apollo Theater*. As civil rights triumphs gave way to urban riots, Brown's explosive shouting and innovative backup band virtually defined the extroverted and hyper-masculine energy of the Black Power movement, as he produced hit singles such as "Papa's Got a Brand-New Bag" and "Say It Loud—I'm Black and I'm Proud." These sentiments were echoed by Curtis Mayfield, a keyboardist, singer, and composer with deep roots in the Pentecostal church, who performed songs such as "Keep on Pushing" and "People Get Ready" with his group, the Impressions.

Female singers also helped to define the new soul sound. Etta James was a teenaged gospel singer who ran away from home to sing professionally in Los Angeles, where she was discovered by Johnny Otis, a white bandleader who had integrated into the local black music scene. James burst onto the record charts in 1960 as an innovative and passionate balladeer. The arrival of Aretha Franklin as the "First Lady of Soul" was delayed until 1967, when her new label, Atlantic Records, finally freed her from the jazz and pop album concepts that had constrained her at Columbia Records. Franklin's roots in gospel were deep, and her stardom had been predicted for a decade by many of her listeners. Her father was C. L. Franklin, perhaps the most famous black Baptist minister in the North. Reverend Franklin was a spellbinding performer in his own right, a sermonizer who shouted, sang, wailed, and persuaded in the grand tradition and attracted huge crowds at his Detroit church and on national tours. He brought gospel stars to his church and home, and from childhood young Aretha received tutelage from Mahalia Jackson and others. Father and daughter both embodied the ambivalences in African American culture. The preacher was a serial womanizer whose business dealings were constantly under government scrutiny, while Aretha was a tempestuous young woman who gave birth to two children while in her teens. No one doubted her magnificent alto voice, though, and her talent allowed her to master virtually every vocal style. As her career took flight in the 1960s, her father continued his friendship with Martin Luther King, Jr. and his close association with the civil rights movement.

FREEDOM SINGERS

The movement for black equality produced a rich musical legacy itself. This legacy, also, was inseparable from the African American sacred music tradition. The early stage of the civil rights battle occurred in courtrooms, leading to the landmark *Brown* decision, which mandated the desegregation of public schools, and to countless local integration orders. Legislatures and executive branches of government, in the states and in Washington, D.C., were also fronts in the battle. The emotional core, however, was the struggle within hundreds of black communities across the South, by citizens who mobilized to boycott stores, march in silent protest, demand the vote and a voice in government, and hold the federal government to its constitutional commitments.

From the beginning, the grassroots civil rights movement used music to foster community, solidarity, and fortitude. Nonviolent protesters faced the prospect of arrest, mistreatment in the courts and jails, and attacks by racist mobs. In 1955, during the bus boycott in Alabama that launched the movement, the Montgomery Improvement Association led by the Reverend Martin Luther King, Jr. organized a chorus to spread the message and instill morale throughout the city's large black community. Their songs were recorded by journalists, as were the hymns and gospel songs sung at the church meetings where King mobilized the boycotters. Later in the 1950s, when King began to develop his techniques for training communities in nonviolent resistance, his assistants in the Southern Christian Leadership Conference (SCLC) made "freedom songs" a key tool for building solidarity and instilling courage in the activists.

In the 1960s, the Student Nonviolent Coordinating Committee (SNCC), a new organization of young activists, encouraged the use of music. Important ensembles of the movement included the Nashville Quartet, consisting of the SCLC activist James Bevel and three other young graduates of the American Baptist Theological Seminary, which supplied many SNCC leaders. The Quartet composed and performed political songs in the gospel mode such as "You Better Leave Segregation Alone" and "Your Dog Loves My Dog." In 1962, during Martin Luther King, Jr.'s ultimately unsuccessful campaign to desegregate Albany, Georgia, Cordell Reagon, a local activist, was encouraged by SNCC leader James Forman and folksinger Pete Seeger to form a vocal quartet. The SNCC Freedom Singers spread news of the campaign, organized other communities, and raised money. Among their members was Bernice Johnson, the daughter of an Albany minister, who later married Reagon. Another important group emerged in Birmingham, Alabama in 1963, during the longest and most violently opposed campaign of King's career. The Birmingham Movement Singers mobilized black congregations and school populations and contributed to one of the most important victories of the civil rights movement.

For the remainder of the struggle, Albany, Georgia's SNCC Freedom Singers spread musical messages throughout the South. They toured African American communities at considerable risk to their safety to encourage local resistance. In Mississippi, the Singers made the acquaintance of Fannie Lou Hamer, a civil rights activist in the KKK-infested Delta region with an imposing presence and rich singing voice, who gained national fame in 1964 by seeking delegate status at the Democratic National Convention. By this time the Freedom Singers had become an all-male quartet, and Bernice Johnson Reagon was more active as a fundraiser in the North. In 1966, she and Hamer made a celebrated appearance at the Newport (Rhode Island) Folk Festival. Reagon went on to earn a doctorate in music, found the vocal ensemble Sweet Honey in the Rock, and become a leading scholar of African American music.

During the height of the struggle in the early 1960s, one song became the anthem of the civil rights movement. The history of "We Shall Overcome," though, indicates how sources besides the African American church nourished the movement and its music. The labor and antifascist struggles of the biracial American Left of the 1930s—in which black performers such as Paul Robeson, Teddy Wilson, and Josh White took part—had nurtured a rich tradition of protest songs, many of which derived from the Anglo-American ballad tradition and concerned mostly non-black workers, such as textile operators in the South and longshoremen on the West coast. In the 1930s and 1940s most African American workers overcame their traditional mistrust of established unions and played a major role in the labor struggle.

One such struggle was the tobacco workers' strike of 1946 in South Carolina, in which a black worker named Lucille Simmons sang a song titled "We'll Overcome." Scholars suggest that her song derived from a gospel song featuring the phrase "I'll overcome someday," which itself may have come from an older composition by Charles Tindley. Simmons's song was transcribed by Zilphia Horton, a white woman who later cofounded the Highlander Folk School, a grassroots activist training center in rural Tennessee. Highlander featured a music program headed by Guy Carawan and assisted on occasion by Pete Seeger, the well-known folksinger and activist. Carawan and Seeger, possibly with assistance from African American Highlander participants, crafted and copyrighted the song "We Shall Overcome," which Seeger popularized at SNCC gatherings beginning in 1960. Thus it was largely through the efforts of white participants in the labor and civil rights struggle that the song—which was of black gospel and labor origins—gained pride of place in the musical history of the movement. President Lyndon B. Johnson even quoted the song's title in 1965, when he proposed the Voting Rights Act in a televised speech to Congress.

Just as the civil rights movement inspired other movements for greater rights—among other people of color, women, and homosexuals, to name a few—the protest music of African Americans served as an inspiration for the wide cultural ferment of the 1960s. The "Old Left" of Depression-era labor activism had benefitted from black musicians such as Leadbelly, Josh White, and Billie Holiday, who sang "message songs" at fund-raising events and other political gatherings. The New Left, emerging in the 1950s from the shadow of McCarthyism, was invigorated by veterans of the earlier struggle (such as Woody Guthrie and Pete Seeger), and by new troubadours as well. Among African Americans, Harry Belafonte, an established star of stage and screen, lent his voice and his fund-raising skills to diverse causes. Odetta Holmes, a veteran actress, became a mainstay of folk-revival festivals, which became major arenas of left-wing expression. Singing a blend of gospel, blues, ballads, and protest songs, Odetta, as she was billed, inspired Bob Dylan, Janis Joplin, and other major white rock performers. Until about 1965, it at least seemed possible to many in the New Left, as well as other Americans, especially in the white middle class, that new civil rights laws would bring about racial integration, and that the crossover popularity of black performers and music indicated possible cultural integration as well.

CONCLUSION

These hopes for integration would be dashed. Race riots in the late 1960s, a white backlash against the demands of the Black Power movement, Martin Luther King, Jr.'s murder, and a lack of progress in closing the gaps in wealth and opportunity between blacks and whites—coupled with political disasters ranging from the Vietnam War to the assassination of Robert Kennedy—soured the mood of virtually every racial optimist. There are other reasons, though, why cultural integration became a dim possibility. The milieu of black gospel music indicates how separate the feelings and communities of most African Americans were from those of whites. Gospel's popularity showed average black people not weakening, but strengthening their identification with the rich musical (and cultural) traditions that virtually defined their difference from Americans of European stock.

In addition, in the decade after 1965, in the face of the smoldering wreckage in the ghettoes and the deepening political frustration, African American music continued to flourish within communities, separate from the mainstream, with tremendous energy and vitality. Gospel music kept producing important new talent, such as the prolific Los Angeles composers and chorus leaders Andrae Crouch and James Cleveland. The gospel workshop network founded by Cleveland marked him as the new generation's answer to Thomas A. Dorsey, who in 1970 was still going strong. The instrumental innovations of soul music and its stepchild, funk—electronic keyboards, front-beat rhythms, and showy riffs—rebounded back onto gospel. In addition, a recording by a COGIC choir in Berkeley, California of Edwin Hawkins's "Oh Happy Day"—a surprise national best-seller in 1969—sealed the arrival of rock and pop-style rhythms and melodies in the new gospel.

Gospel music had emerged from the spirituals tradition and the new Pentecostal churches of the early twentieth century. At the same time that secular music such as ragtime and jazz were conquering popular music, gospel music revived passionate African American religious traditions that dated back to before the Civil War. It provided a new context for collective singing that made full use of the vocal effects and individual improvisation that have persisted in black musical traditions on both sides of the Atlantic. Gospel's huge success in the 1930s and 1940s led to help reshape popular music, as the music's irresistible musical qualities and message of black salvation were adopted, sometime obliquely, by rhythm and blues and rock 'n' roll. In the 1950s, though, gospel more directly influenced the freedom songs of the civil rights movement and the energetic soul music of the inner cities. As African Americans made the uneasy transition from segregation to integration in the 1960s and demanded more equal conditions in all aspects of their lives, the dynamic expression associated with the gospel tradition would continue to shape black music and express a community's strongest emotions.

NOTES

1. *A Testament of Hope: The Essential Writings and Speeches of Martin Luther King, Jr.*, ed. James Melvin Washington (New York: HarperCollins, 1990), 17.

2. Michael W. Harris, *The Rise of Gospel Blues: The Music of Thomas Andrew Dorsey in the Urban Church* (New York: Oxford University Press, 1992), 53.

3. Quoted in Elizabeth A. Wheeler, "'Most of My Heroes Don't Appear on No Stamps': The Dialogics of Rap Music," *Black Music Research Journal* 11 (1991), 198–99.

7

Black Popular Music as Big Business

S ince 1970, some African Americans in popular music have achieved unprecedented fame, wealth, and cultural influence. At the same time, though, their achievements have contrasted strongly with persistent economic, social, and racial struggles of black communities in the post–Jim Crow era. To perceive how recent popular music fits into African American history since 1970, it is helpful to begin in the middle of the story, with the facts surrounding the best-selling recording of all time.

In December 1982, Epic Records released Michael Jackson's new album, *Thriller*. Jackson was a proven star, so it was not surprising that *Thriller*, containing tracks such as "Wanna Be Startin' Somethin'," "Billie Jean," "Beat It," and the title song, quickly reached the top of the sales charts. Unexpectedly, though, the album remained a top ten best-seller in the United States for the next eighteen months. American listeners purchased more than 30 million copies of *Thriller*, and 70 million more units sold overseas. It became the most commercially successful record album ever released, and it put Jackson on course to join Bing Crosby, Elvis Presley, and the Beatles as one of the biggest-selling musicians in history. That final fact may have been important to Jackson, the only African American member of that elite group. In later years he would buy the rights to all of the Beatles' songs and marry Presley's daughter.

Thriller earned a share of its success, and a great deal of its historical significance, from its position at the intersection of important trends in African American music. Jackson was twenty-five years old when *Thriller* was released. As a child, he had been the youngest member of the family ensemble the Jackson 5, which had enjoyed commercial success since the

149

late 1960s. Motown Records, the group's record label for most of those years, had established itself in the 1960s as the most successful black-owned music company ever, and the Jackson brothers' sound was representative of Motown's brand of commercially crafted soul music.

Styles that predated even Motown's found their way into *Thriller*, as well as into the Jackson albums that bracketed it, *Off the Wall*, released in 1979 and *Bad*, released in 1987. This was largely due to the influence of their producer, Quincy Jones. Jones, born in 1933, had roots in African American popular music going back to the swing era. His rich career encompassed jazz (as a trumpeter in the Lionel Hampton band), classical music (including study in Paris with Nadia Boulanger, a famed teacher of composers), band arranging (for Count Basie, Frank Sinatra, and many others), and film scoring, as well as producing albums (on some of which he performed). Few individuals rivaled Jones's smooth and highly lucrative movement through the highest echelons of the popular music business, which made him an icon of post–Jim Crow racial integration.

At the same time *Thriller* referenced earlier styles, it also heralded emerging new trends in African American culture and popular music. Jackson and Jones drew cannily on music and dance trends of the late 1970s and early 1980s, most prominently funk, disco, salsa, "glam" rock, and rap. In performances after the release of *Thriller* Jackson pushed the last two elements into the foreground, flaunting glittering, fantastic costumes and a highly stylized, even eccentric persona. *Thriller*'s huge success persuaded Music Television (MTV) in 1983, tardily, to make Jackson the first African American performer ever to appear on the popular cable channel (in the video of "Billie Jean"), nineteen months into its run. This development was both a testament to the persistence of racism in the post–Jim Crow United States and the music business, and a confirmation of the new centrality of videos in the popularization of new songs and albums.

Videos of songs from *Thriller*, such as the title tune and "Beat It," surprised many white viewers. They included vignettes of resentment and violence, in which Jackson appeared as a gang member, a werewolf, and a zombie. In videos derived from later albums, Jackson's anger at his media coverage and depictions of violent behavior were even more vehement. These developments reflected new strains of pessimism and angry social criticism in black music of the 1980s. "Post-soul" music, percolating out of resentful young urban black communities, also influenced the entertainer. Jackson's adoption of the backslide or "moonwalk" dance step paid homage to Cab Calloway and James Brown, who made similar moves on stage, but it also popularized current urban African American dance styles. Like the gang imagery in the "Beat It" video, the moonwalk paid heed to the emergence of hip hop culture in a decade of new black inner-city unrest. Jackson exhibited a different kind of social concern when he and Quincy Jones produced "We Are the World" in 1985, a song and video project featuring a menagerie of music stars, which raised funds to fight famine in East Africa and rejuvenated social activism in the popular music mainstream.

In later years Michael Jackson was beset by controversy. The self-styled "King of Pop" became increasingly reclusive and eccentric, and startlingly altered his appearance, seemingly by means of plastic surgery and skin bleaching. Allegations that he molested children dogged him for a decade, and in a trial in 2005 threatened to end his career, although he was acquitted of criminal charges.

The story of how Michael Jackson's explosive creativity in the *Thriller* era was sapped in later years by personal confusion and crises is an extreme example of the general tensions that faced African American music at the end of the twentieth century. Massive profitability and exposure established, once and for all, the centrality of black music in American tastes, but its success in the white-majority market still created pressures, tensions, and public images that were disturbing to African American artists and communities. The continuing economic pain and social inequality suffered by many blacks contrasted sharply with the success of a relative few, and forced musicians and others to declare their allegiances either to "the neighborhood" or to the new affluence of the black middle class. In the decades after the release of *Thriller*, rap music and hip hop culture powerfully expressed many concerns that were latent in Jackson's persona and music: male-female conflict, gender confusion, violent resolution of disputes, and mistrust of the nonblack listening audience. At the same time, though, like *Thriller*, hip hop and the broad universe of contemporary African American musical expression also exhibit a healthy vitality, mining a great and diverse musical heritage, new technology, and global music to respond to the personal and social needs of black people and of a wider audience as well.

BLACK ENTERPRISE IN MUSIC: MOTOWN RECORDS

The roots both of prosperity and of cultural dilemmas in African American music today lie in the history of the music business after World War II. The flourishing of gospel, urban blues, rhythm and blues, bebop, and, later, soul music from about 1945 to 1955 was accompanied by a renewal of the black musical entrepreneurialism that had been evident in the 1920s. African American war veterans could use some of their government benefits as seed money for business ventures. Many of these entrepreneurs turned to popular music. After the bankruptcies and consolidations of the Depression era, the late 1940s and the 1950s saw a rebirth of independent record labels. White-owned companies such as Chess, Specialty, Sun, Atlantic, and King were vital to launching the recording careers of many important new black performers, and in the 1960s such new recording venues as FAME Studios, based in Alabama, also publicized artists.

Some African American performers also established new labels. The avant-garde jazz bandleader Sun Ra founded Saturn Records in the 1950s, mainly to record his own group's music; the rock 'n' roll singer Lloyd Price created Double L Records in 1962; and the jazz vocalist Betty Carter began Bet-Car Records in 1970 and maintained it for nearly thirty years. Don Robey built Duke-Peacock Records into one of Houston's most successful African American businesses, while Red Robin Records, begun in Harlem by the record store owner Bobby Robinson, failed to live up to the talent on its rich artist roster.

In the 1950s and early 1960s, no other black-owned company matched the diverse and pioneering achievements of Vee-Jay Records. Founded in Gary, Indiana in 1953 by Vivian Carter, her husband, James Bracken, and her brother, Calvin, the company brought a blues singer from Detroit named John Lee Hooker, the soul singers Jerry Butler and Betty Everett, the Swan Silvertones and other gospel groups, old-time jazz bands, and numerous little-known acts into their studios in nearby Chicago. Some of their recordings sold well. The white doo-wop quartet the Four Seasons got its first major exposure through Vee-Jay, and Little Richard mounted his first musical comeback with the label. In 1963, a successful new British band sent tapes to Vee-Jay and contracted with them to release its first album in the United States. Due to a big backlog in pending releases, though, Calvin Carter delayed the pressing of *Introducing the Beatles* for a few months. After this album took Vee-Jay's earnings to new heights, the company fell prey to its own success. In 1966, Vee-Jay's inability to manage its explosive growth led the company to declare bankruptcy.

Radio stations were far more expensive to start up and maintain, and thus African American ownership remained minimal until the 1960s. Nevertheless, radio's ability to dispense advertising to entire black urban communities enticed white station owners to reach out to them. The radio program, *King Biscuit Time* out of Helena, Arkansas, pioneered this approach, and by 1950 stations in Jackson, Mississippi, and St. Louis were presenting black disk jockeys and live performers. In the South, though, none matched the influence of WDIA in Memphis, a powerful AM station that was within range of 10 percent of the nation's African American population. Nat D. Williams became perhaps the best-known black "DJ" in America, and proved to be instrumental in the early careers of the blues guitarist B. B. King, the soul composer and performer Isaac Hayes, and many other notable Memphis artists. R & B and soul radio faced fierce competition and was tainted by widespread "payola," or illegal bribes paid by record companies to DJs. Companies that recorded black music also received disproportionately low fees and earnings compared to those that specialized in white performers. But DJs on black-oriented stations in the South and North became spokesmen, truth-tellers, town criers, talent scouts, and all-purpose community resources, and they tailored their distinctive vocal deliveries to match their celebrity. Many of them were as well regarded as the star musicians they helped to popularize.

Nonetheless, unlike radio stations, record companies offered African American entrepreneurs both the advantages of ownership and the potential for scoring national successes. In addition, recording allowed them to create and own the rights to music singles and albums. Berry Gordy, Jr. of Detroit perceived some of these advantages in the late 1950s. An army veteran, former boxer, and automobile factory worker, Gordy wrote some successful songs, notably for Detroit's Jackie Wilson, whose flamboyant movements and soaring vocals made him rock 'n' roll's "Mr. Excitement" in the late 1950s. In 1958, Gordy and some partners founded Tamla Records, which they later renamed Motown. One assistant was a skilled producer named William Robinson, who also headlined his own quintet, Smokey Robinson and the Miracles. Robinson's group recorded Motown Records' breakout hit, "Shop Around," which became a million-seller in 1961.

Gordy and Robinson's exacting standards in the studio and the mixing room paid dividends. They carefully calibrated every vocal inflection, treble and bass setting, and instrumental arrangement in Motown's recording sessions to elicit a maximum response from their target audience, American teenagers. Gordy strove from the beginning to capture the black *and* white youth markets. The "Motown sound" was undeniably soul music with R & B elements, but it was unusually sunny and optimistic, and featured clean melodies, rhythms, and orchestrations, sharp treble and bass definitions, and effective use of the electronic echo effect. Gospel-style shouting was virtually absent from Motown's catalog of number one hits. Eddie Holland Jr., an early colleague of Gordy's, soon joined with his brother Brian and Lamont Dozier to become the central songwriting team during Motown's glory years. In the background, Motown's house band, the Funk Brothers, provided skilled accompaniment to dozens of hit records.

"Hitsville, U.S.A.," as Gordy dubbed Motown Records, put carefully groomed star performers in the foreground. Smokey Robinson and the Miracles' "Shop Around" had been preceded at the top of the national charts in 1961 by "Please, Mr. Postman," recorded for Gordy by a high school female quintet called the Marvelettes. Gordy soon recruited Mary Wells, the Four Tops, the Temptations, and Marvin Gaye, carefully groomed their wardrobe, stage manner, and public personas, and presented them in concerts as well as on records. An unusual new recruit was

Stevland Morris, a twelve-year-old harmonica virtuoso, pianist, and song-writer, blind from birth, whom Motown signed and marketed as Little Stevie Wonder. Wonder's sensational performance at a Motown revue, released in 1963 as "Fingertips Part 2," initiated his long career as one of popular music's most inspired and influential composers and performers.

The Supremes, an experienced female trio from Detroit, gained its first national exposure in 1964. This group became Motown's greatest success and the prime product of Berry Gordy's star-making laboratory. The Supremes' vocals were the lightest and most rhythmically lithe of any Motown group, and won the biggest following among white record buyers. Gordy soon focused his attention on developing Diana Ross—who had begun as the equal of her fellow Supremes Florence Ballard and Mary Wilson—into Motown's iconic singing (and, later, motion picture) star. By the late 1960s, as rock music expanded the youth market exponentially, Gordy worked even harder to make Motown Records, in his words, "the Sound of Young America." The Jackson 5 signed with Motown in 1969. Joseph Jackson, a strong-willed and ambitious father of nine children, groomed his five eldest sons to become a dynamic dancing and vocal group. The Jackson 5 gained popularity in the Great Lakes region, and their recordings with Motown brought them nationwide success in the early 1970s. From the age of seven, young Michael Jackson was the group's lead vocalist and its most exuberant dancer.

Berry Gordy's and Motown's relationship with their home city of Detroit was complex. African American migrants dominated Detroit like no other major industrial city after World War II. They constituted half of the population, and rather than being confined to a discrete ghetto, they occupied wide swaths of its territory. The Nation of Islam had been founded in Detroit in the 1930s, and at least since the 1920s the automobile industry had provided black southern migrants with their most dependable source of well-paying unskilled labor. The black prominence in Detroit, though, was also a product of one of the most debilitating "white flights" in the nation, emptying entire neighborhoods of their European immigrant populations and depressing the city's economy. The city government long denied African Americans decent city services, parks, and schools. Against this background, in 1967, Detroit exploded in the most destructive urban uprising of the era, which left forty-three people dead.

The Detroit riot, as well as the Black Power movement and campaigns for black self-sufficiency and cultural separatism, caught Gordy largely by surprise and challenged Motown's strategy of appealing to young listeners of all races. The producer was a close friend of the Reverend C. L. Franklin and an acquaintance of leaders of the civil rights movement, but locally Motown had mostly become involved with white-dominated charities. However, during the urban uprisings of the late 1960s, Motown "party songs" such as Mary Wells' "Dancing in the Street" unexpectedly became anthems of resistance. After the Detroit riot, Gordy tried to recast Motown's community activism into a racially focused, Black Arts-style effort. The company's spoken-word label, Black Forum Records, issued the poetry of Langston Hughes and the speeches of Martin Luther King, Jr. The death of King in 1968 caused more violence in Detroit's streets and increased the isolation and despair of its African American residents. That year black autoworkers formed their own union and staged a strike.

Motown Records evolved as the times grew gloomy. The songwriting team of Holland-Dozier-Holland had left angrily in a dispute with Gordy over royalties, and performers agitated over the same issue. While Gordy focused his plans on launching a motion picture production company and making Diana Ross a film star, artists such as the Temptations and Marvin Gaye recorded songs that commented directly on the pessimism and despair that rose from the flames of Detroit. Gaye's album *What's Going On?*, released in 1971 over Gordy's objections, was both Motown's first concept album—the company had always been focused on creating hit singles—and its first passionate political statement. Lamenting the despair and partial destruction of black Detroit, growing male-female tensions, and pollution of the environment, Gaye temporarily involved Motown in the protest soul music of the early 1970s. Similarly, Stevie Wonder noted that "we as a people are not interested in 'baby, baby' songs anymore."[1] Berry Gordy, however, resisted political statements. In 1972, he moved Motown to Los Angeles, where it profited from Diana Ross's unlikely but Oscar-nominated portrayal of Billie Holiday in *Lady Sings the Blues* and the popularity of the Jackson 5 and other fresh acts. The Jackson 5, however, broke with Gordy in 1975 after a long battle over royalties.

SOUL MUSIC AS BIG BUSINESS

Few cities were dominated by one African American musical entity as Detroit was by Motown. Chicago's black population was larger than Detroit's, but its influence as a center of musical innovation waned in the 1960s. Vee-Jay Records matched Motown's roster of talent, but not its thirst for national success and willingness to dilute the sounds of soul. The main legacy of 1960s Chicago soul was the powerful and socially relevant work of Curtis Mayfield, who composed the best-selling soundtrack score to the film *Superfly* and continued to be productive in the 1970s. Elsewhere, some African American–run record companies embraced the Black Power movement more decisively than Motown, but most of them were not as well-run and often ended in failure. Two notable exceptions, though, were Stax Records of Memphis and Philadelphia International Records.

Stax had been founded in 1957 by a white brother and sister, Jim Stewart and Estelle Axton (who combined their last names to christen the label). Their low-cost operation quickly moved from country music to R & B to exploit Memphis's rich black music scene. The singers Rufus Thomas and Wilson Pickett and the pianists Isaac Hayes and Booker T. Jones, allied with his "Memphis Group" the MGs, provided Stax with songs that took African American record stores by storm. By the time the vocal duo Sam & Dave recorded the iconic single "Soul Man" for Stax in 1967, the label had signed a national distribution deal with Atlantic Records. It had also found its biggest star: Otis Redding, a dynamic young Mississippian who became James Brown's only rival as a shouting soul innovator. Redding's call for "Respect" encapsulated Memphis soul's role in the Black Power ferment of the late 1960s. His recordings were representative of Stax's primitive recording methods and unvarnished roster of artists who were steeped in gospel and the Delta blues. Stax's studio sound also popularized gospel-derived flourishes on the electric organ, a key component of the sound of soul music.

Otis Redding's death in an airplane crash in 1967 began a long era of turbulence for the label. A falling-out with Atlantic Records led Jim Stewart to sell Stax to Gulf & Western, an oil company that had diversified into a massive corporate conglomerate. The label flourished for half a decade, in part because Stewart yielded creative control to Al Bell and other African American producers. Bell upgraded Stax's recording equipment and nurtured a roster of leading soul musicians. Isaac Hayes, a composer, keyboardist, and singer whose towering height and bald head cut a new image for black performers, topped the charts with two albums. In 1972, Hayes became the first black songwriter to win an Academy Award, for the "Theme from *Shaft*." Bell committed Stax fully to the message of African American self-help and cultural pride. The climax of his efforts was the Wattstax concert of 1972 at the Los Angeles Coliseum, a day-long "black Woodstock" designed to raise money for a community music program, the Watts Summer Festival. The documentary film of the event shows the Reverend Jesse Jackson, the self-styled heir to Martin Luther King, Jr. and a close ally of Bell's, leading 100,000 attendees in repetition of the slogan, "I *am* somebody!" Within a few years, though, despite Stax's continuing artistic success, its distribution partner, Columbia Records, abandoned the company, and Stax declared bankruptcy in 1976.

Stax's decline was mirrored by the ascendency of recordings produced by two Philadelphians, the musician Kenny Gamble and the DJ Leon Huff. Philadelphia after World War II was home to an African American community proportionately larger than New York City's. The city's black music scene arguably was more innovative as well. By the 1960s Philadelphia outshone New York City as a gospel center, and it was the home of

John Coltrane, Sun Ra, and other major jazz innovators. The emergence of Italian-American rock 'n' roll stars in Philadelphia, publicized by Dick Clark on his local television program *American Bandstand*, encouraged the growth of first-rate recording studios. Performers from Philadelphia often left town for New York or Los Angeles in the 1950s and 1960s, but new local talent kept emerging. Kenny Gamble was a pianist and singer who led a successful group called the Romeos. In 1965, Gamble, in partnership with local radio DJs and a pianist from nearby Camden, New Jersey, named Leon Huff, launched Excel (later called Gamble) Records.

The "Philly soul" style was in part a repudiation of the smooth Motown sound. Like Stax's releases, Gamble's derived their energy from the gospel training of the performers. While some of the earliest hits featured "blue-eyed," or white, soul performers such as the Soul Survivors and Laura Nyro, Gamble built his signature style around passionate performers such as Billy Paul; Jerry Butler; Harold Melvin and the Blue Notes; the female ensemble Labelle (led by Patti LaBelle); and a male quartet from Ohio called the O'Jays. Gamble and Huff wrote hundreds of powerful songs that blended romantic themes with commentary on racial strife, urban decay, the Vietnam War, and, in the O'Jays' "Love Train," even the Arab-Israeli conflict. They used multitrack recording techniques to capture outstanding session ensembles, which gave the recordings a symphonic richness.

In 1971, Columbia Records, the most profitable record label in the world, commissioned the Harvard Business School to produce an analysis of the music business. The resulting study advised the company to pursue the lucrative African American market. In response, Columbia signed Gamble and Huff to a distribution deal. Under this deal, Philadelphia International Records, as Gamble Records now was called, produced a stream of powerful hits, adding the Alabama-born shouter Wilson Pickett, who had roamed from Stax and other labels; Teddy Pendergrass, the new lead singer for the Blue Notes; and other new stars. Also in the 1970s, Thom Bell, a producer from Philadelphia who worked for a number of major labels, produced a series of similar hit records. In addition to overseeing albums by Johnny Mathis—the best-selling African American ballad singer of all time—and others, Bell shaped records featuring the Spinners and the Stylistics, who were mainstays of the Philadelphia soul sound.

FUNK MUSIC

Philadelphia International's success throughout the 1970s indicated that African American communities were continuing to produce an astonishing array of talent. Young composers and singers had been nurtured by R & B and gospel, but their music expressed both the optimism of the civil rights era and the difficult realities of late 1960s urban life. The last major product of this musical scene was a style called funk. The word "funk" originated centuries earlier in West Africa and persisted in the Caribbean and the American South. It referred to the natural odor of bodies, and, by extension, to anything else that was genuine or unadorned. For decades black musicians and listeners had praised music that sounded raw and unschooled as being "funky."

Funk drew some of its inspiration from Jimi Hendrix and Sly Stone, the two major African American figures in late 1960s rock music. Hendrix and Stone both became rock legends after they appeared at the 1969 Woodstock Festival, but as black musicians they were anomalies. The "British invasion" of 1964 that reinvigorated rock 'n' roll in the United States took the classic twelve-bar blues as its model, and enthroned modal guitar improvisation as the center of its performances. Bands such as the Rolling Stones, Cream, the Kinks, Led Zeppelin, and even the Beatles drew their basic sound from older blues musicians such as T-Bone Walker and Howlin' Wolf. Similarly, the leading blues singer on the American rock scene was a white vocalist, Janis Joplin, who grew up listening to the recordings of Bessie Smith and Big Mama Thornton. Old blues harmonies and elaborate guitar solos held little interest, though, for young African Americans in the 1960s, who generally embraced soul music and turned away from the electric guitar as an inspiration.

Jimi Hendrix, who had played in R & B bands after serving as an Army paratrooper, primarily developed his incendiary guitar playing while living for two years among blues fans in London. In his spectacular short career as a rock star, Hendrix originated the use of electronic feedback, cavorted wildly on stage, even destroying his guitars, and brought the psychedelic "heavy metal" solo to prominence. The guitarist won an immense following among young white listeners before his death from a drug overdose in 1970. Sly Stone, born Sylvester Stewart, was a guitarist and disk jockey in San Francisco who embraced that city's famed counterculture and created the Family Stone, an interracial commune and musical ensemble. Sly and the Family Stone's early albums provided catchy psychedelic anthems that were accessible to a broad youth audience, primarily through a simple, heavy beat and sing-along choruses that demanded little command of the soul singer's repertory of skills.

The funk style might be defined as the simplification, as well as the amplification, of soul music. James Brown's powerful performances of the late 1960s set the tone for later funk performances. His influential band, driven mostly by drummer Clyde Stubblefield, heavily emphasized the front beat and played catchy and endlessly repeated rhythms. Like the Family Stone, Brown's band used brass and saxophones to provide brief melodic punctuations that almost became a new form of percussion.

Brown cultivated a hard-working, sweaty image on stage, and used his seemingly inexhaustible voice and physical energy to lead crowds in chants from soul anthems. He also made extravagant clothing, hairstyles, and theatricality into hallmarks of funk. Brown was largely responsible for pulling soul away from its generally introspective and romantic orientation. Veteran R & B and soul bands blended with newcomers to create successful new groups. The communal nature of the Family Stone influenced bands such as Kool and the Gang and Earth, Wind, and Fire, although the latter group smoothed many edges off of its funk sound. The composer and keyboardist George Clinton's Parliament-Funkadelic orchestra, a Sun Ra-style collective which set the standard for stage theatricality, popularized a "p-funk" style that boosted the amplified beat and the flamboyant racial separatism of James Brown. The Ohio Players, a recalibrated soul band, also became a leading funk ensemble.

Nonblack performers, such as the aptly named The Average White Band, inevitably released "cover" recordings of soul songs. The main cultural impact of funk music, though, was to solidify a sense of African American urban separatism, a "chocolate city" consciousness (in George Clinton's phrase) that was closed to nonblack influences. This separatist message offered a challenge to white Americans. After passage of the civil rights laws, African Americans were waiting to find out if whites would permit them to gain social and economic equality. The message of funk was that urban black people were prepared to reject integration if it denied them equal opportunities, earnings, and power. The arrival in the 1970s of the boom box, the portable radio/cassette amplifier, carried the throbbing beat of funk through city streets.

Like previous generations of African American musicians, funk performers risked being misconstrued by the white audience. In their case, in the wake of civil rights laws and the widespread assumption that racial integration would take place, the music business integrated 1970s black musicians into broadcasting and publicity far more fully than it had in the past. However, most of these musicians dressed, sounded, and acted in the culturally separatist manner that had been bred by the Black Power movement. The result was that white audiences saw many more black performers than before but often misunderstood them, and since whites tended to fear or at least resent black separatism, they would denigrate the musicians and not take them seriously. This gave rise, for example, to the common reference by whites to portable radios used by blacks as "ghetto blasters." The attitude was evident in publicity campaigns for 1970s soul musicians launched by Columbia Records, the industry giant, which employed few black executives. The company's marketing division exaggerated the "ghetto styling" of the performers' hair and clothing, and offered encouragement to artists who were willing to present themselves in the most outlandish manner. The effect was to create a caricature of funk music and African American expressiveness. It was the same dynamic that reduced the promise of African American cinema in the 1970s, in the shape of Motown's *Lady Sings the Blues* and Gordon Parks' *Shaft*, to the corrosive stereotypes of "blaxploitation" crime movies. Adding injury to insult, at the end of the decade Columbia Records decided that it could not effectively develop its large roster of black performers and terminated most of their contracts.

INTO THE 1980s

The late 1970s was an era of painful transition in popular music, in which many of the dreams of the 1960s—expressed in folk and rock music, as well as soul—evaporated in a time of economic struggle, profit-mindedness, and diluted musical styles. The prevalence of trends such as "smooth soul" and "crossover" suggested the music industry's and the mass publics indifference to bold new expression and resistance to music with a social conscience.

In these years, the main innovations in African American music came from abroad. The late 1970s brought the international arrival of reggae, the new rock music of black Jamaicans. A longtime British colony, Jamaica had nurtured Afro-Caribbean music and dance for centuries, and after 1930 bred its own reactions to jazz and the blues. The "ska" and "rock steady" styles of the 1960s mated with Rastafarianism, the Pan-African spiritualistic movement of the island, to create reggae ("raggedy") music. Employing a loping backbeat, chant-like singing, and rich Jamaican inflections and slang, Bob Marley and the Wailers, Jimmy Cliff, and Peter Tosh helped to fill the void left by the decline of straightforward soul in U.S. popular music and gained a biracial following.

Disco, by contrast, derived largely from Europe, where discotheques (dance clubs featuring recorded, not live, music) had been popular for decades. Producers in West Germany and France applied electronically synthesized dance beats to rock and soul numbers, and soon the chanting, heavily orchestrated sounds of funk were absorbed into the emerging disco style. Georgio Morodor, a producer and musician based in Munich, recorded the African American singer Donna Summer, whose "Love to Love You Baby" set sexually suggestive lyrics against a pulsating electronic beat. The song was released in the United States by producer Neil Bogart's Casablanca Records, which refashioned black soul groups such as Chic into best-selling disco performers. The most publicized artists, however, were a reworked white Australian rock ensemble, the Bee Gees, guided to fame by producer Robert Stigwood on the soundtrack recording to the disco-themed film *Saturday Night Fever*.

Although disco in part became another black musical style co-opted by white performers, during its heyday in the late 1970s it played an important role in shaping future African American popular music. The genre re-popularized dancing in tightly packed clubs and promoted moves, such as the hustle, which had been neglected even in the black inner-city dance halls where they had originated. Disco also enabled funk bands to maintain their viability, and it increased black performers' and producers' understanding of the potential of computerized distortion and mixing in the shaping of recorded music.

While discotheques such as New York's Studio 54 were highly publicized nightlife locales for white celebrities and elites, clubs in black and Latino neighborhoods encouraged new grassroots musical activity. Among African Americans, the fancy-speaking, record-spinning master of ceremonies or "MC" brought the vocal artistry of the radio DJ into nightclubs. Donna Summer, Gloria Gaynor, Grace Jones, and other African American disco stars enabled women to share some of the limelight of the mostly male headliners in soul and funk music. Female stars especially enjoyed the adulation of the gay male fans of all races, who made disco music the anthem of their campaign for visibility, acceptance, and civil rights. Outsiders often ridiculed disco fans' dressing up in campy versions of high fashion, but the practice reflected many listeners' eagerness to shed the blue-jeans casualness of the rock era. The stylishness of disco struck a chord with African Americans, who for generations had shown particular approval for well-dressed musical performers. Soul musicians such as the singer Barry White and his Love Unlimited Orchestra also helped to revive elegant attire in late 1970s popular culture.

Even more than funk, disco suffered unusual hostility from its detractors. Some of the mostly white rock fans who sneered at disco's relative lack of melody, improvisation, and "authenticity" also resented its identity as the music of assertive African Americans. The historian Bruce Schulman has argued that the antidisco movement was part of a general white backlash against black social integration, as well as against gay rights. Disco's decline in the early 1980s came about in part because of this hostility, but also because of the rapid flourishing of new musical ideas which were germinating in urban African American clubs and which were exploited in recording studios.

DIVERSITY IN 1980s POP MUSIC

Artists such as Michael Jackson plunged into the confusion of musical styles that prevailed in the early 1980s, producing albums that mixed recent musical influences into potent new songs that defined "pop" music (for want of a better term) for the next two decades. Tina Turner, a veteran

soul performer who had long fronted the band led by her one-time husband, the R & B and rock pioneer Ike Turner, refashioned herself into a
postdisco diva. Her 1984 album *Private Dancer* succeeded Jackson's *Thriller*
as one of the great eclectic pop successes of the decade. The white British
musicians Phil Collins and Peter Gabriel, both indebted to R & B and early
rock, also released best-selling 1980s albums that featured diverse stylistic influences and meticulous studio production. Tina Turner's persona as
a strong female performer paved the way for later major stars in the pop
mold such as Whitney Houston, who had strong family roots in gospel
and R & B, and Mariah Carey.

Most striking, though, was the emergence of a slight, mysterious guitarist and composer from Minneapolis, Minnesota—not generally considered a center for black music—whose idiosyncratic reworking of recent
popular music stands as the most original of the decade. Prince Rogers
Nelson, in fact, never left Minneapolis, where a small tradition of blues
and R & B gave him all of the inspiration he needed. Capturing a major
record deal in his early twenties, Prince spent months in the recording studio with an entourage of musicians and singers, some of whom he would
spin off into new bands. Prince and the Revolution released the landmark
album *Purple Rain*, as well as an accompanying film, in 1984. The explicit
sexual frankness of "Darling Nikki" gained the most attention, but fans of
African American music also noted Prince's evocation of Jimi Hendrix's
rock guitar mastery, gospel chord progressions, jazz and soul improvisation and voicings, diverse instrumentation, and postdisco electronic effects. Prince's eccentric ways and messianic pretenses led many to liken
him to Michael Jackson—a collaboration between the two was planned
but did not take place—but his reinvention of black genres and his prodi-
gious output, including hundreds of songs that he withheld from release
for decades, marked him as a special talent whose career and influence
seem to have outshone Jackson's.

THE HIP HOP YEARS

In the meantime, rap—the most recent major innovation in African American popular music—burst onto the scene. Rap was both an aggressively
different form of expression and the core of a new urban black youth culture, generally called hip hop by the late 1980s, which both reshuffled traditions of African American expression and rather rudely challenged the
behavioral, social, and aesthetic norms of the black and white middle class.

It is generally agreed that rap originated in New York City, specifically
in the South Bronx, in the late 1970s. After President Jimmy Carter toured
the South Bronx, full of blocks of crumbling, smoldering, and abandoned
housing that served as havens for drug deals and gang warfare, the dis-

trict became burdened with the reputation as the most blighted failure in contemporary urban America. Many white suburbanites considered the South Bronx to be the best reason to ignore pleas for assistance coming from the inner cities. Yet the South Bronx and similar heavily African American neighborhoods in New York City still simmered with rich musical and other cultural legacies. Deindustrialization and crime did reduce the quality of life in many ways, and inevitably it deprived new generations of young people of the stable music education and instrumental and vocal apprenticeships that their parents and grandparents often enjoyed. Strong musical traditions and newfound uses for technology, though, led young urbanites to discover genres of creative expression.

In basement parties in the South Bronx, record spinners or DJs manipulated the turntables and made scratches a part of the dance beat, while masters of ceremony (MCs) let loose with streams of informal poetry, a spoken complement to the shouting, moaning, and other diverse qualities of funk and disco vocalists' deliveries. On street corners, basketball courts, and in block parties, the blend of spoken rap with soul, funk, and disco on boom boxes melded with slam-dunk contests, "tagging" (graffiti writing with spray paint), and new dance moves—"popping," "breaking," "spinning," and other elements that revolved bodies around multiple axes and caused joints to splay, dislocate, and relocate in jagged synch with percussion rhythm. For these pioneers in the Bronx, rap was becoming as intense a generational music as jazz had been for young black New Orleanians in the 1910s or R & B for Chicagoans in the 1940s. The boasting, the contests, the occasional fights that surrounded the music—none of those, in themselves, were original to rap.

What did distinguish rap from previous black popular musical styles, of course, was its emphasis on nonmelodic but highly rhythmic speech. As these pages have suggested, African, Afro-Caribbean, and African American oral traditions evolved in ways that were roughly similar to how black music was shaped. In the United States, slavery and second-class citizenship in freedom had forced conversationalists, preachers, and others to mask their meanings, to "signify" creatively to convey and to disguise their messages. Humor, featuring artful insults and intentional absurdity, remained a rich element of oral culture from Africa to the New World. In the twentieth century, the northern migration helped to urbanize African American oral traditions. Soapbox orators, Pentecostal preachers, and Islamic and Rastafarian exhorters all applied oratorical techniques to the issues and passions of city life; poets, comedians, and radio personalities strove to put their stylistic stamps on their deliveries; and schoolchildren practiced "the dozens" (insult games, usually targeting mothers), delivered "toasts" (proto-rap orations), and talked their way cleverly out of the perilous situations that were endemic to ghetto life.

Music and verbal dexterity coexisted for decades before rap music emerged. The earliest blues and jazz recordings featured spoken introductions and interludes by vocalists, while nightclubs and dance halls often mixed verbal and musical performers together on their playbills. Male gospel ensembles included preacher-like exhortations in their numbers, and song-speech in jazz, R & B, and soul became widely accepted. In the 1960s, the Black Arts movement encouraged the mixing of music and poetry, and these years saw the conscious exploitation of black verbal richness in various forms of multimedia performance art. Some music historians consider Gil Scott-Heron to be an early originator of rap music. The son of a Jamaican immigrant, Scott-Heron recited his socially conscious poetry to the accompaniment of jazz ensembles in the early 1970s.

The West Indian connection was important. Early rap music generally shared something of reggae's ability to describe everyday life in frank terms. Important early MCs such as Grandmaster Flash (Joseph Saddler) and Kool Herc (Clive Campbell) were immigrants to New York from the West Indies. Their colorful stage names were part of the special "flash" that audiences demanded in the postdisco era, an attention to brash style that became central to hip hop. A prominent Bronx DJ, Afrika Bambaataa (Kevin Donovan), echoed Pan-Africanism in his stage name and the name of his early rap collective, the Zulu Group, founded in 1973. Harlem played host to D. J. Hollywood, whose rapping in clubs drew young performers from across the city. MCs, DJs, and collectives would be central to the growth of rap in city after city in later decades.

In 1979, a New Jersey-based trio, the Sugarhill Gang, recorded "Rapper's Delight" for Sugar Hill Records. Owned by Sylvia Robinson, a veteran soul singer, and her husband Joe, Sugar Hill Records symbolized the wave in black-owned record companies that came to maturity in the hip hop era. "Rapper's Delight" used a bass line from a song by Chic as its musical motif; the disco group quickly sued for copyright infringement, initiating the endless stream of litigation over "sampling" in rap. The song nevertheless became a national best-seller. Also in 1979, Harlem's Kurtis Blow (Curtis Walker) became the first rapper to sign a contract with a major record company. Two years later his satirical song "Rapper's Christmas" became a crossover hit—a sign of things to come in the white reception of rap music.

Meanwhile, Grandmaster Flash, a pioneering record spinner and mixer, scored success in 1982 with a much different number, "The Message," an impassioned critique of degraded living conditions in an inner-city housing project. "The Message" foreshadowed the general tone of rap music as it developed during the rest of the 1980s. At first, the spectacular mainstream success of Michael Jackson, Prince, and Tina Turner still eclipsed the occasional high-selling rap song, but the musical culture of hip hop was taking shape. Def Jam Records was founded in 1984 by two young men from New York: Russell Simmons, who was black, and Rick Rubin, who was white. Both of them would become major figures in popular music production. Def Jam's favorite group, Run-DMC, which featured Simmons's brother, Joseph "Run," became the first consistent national rap success. Run-DMC's glory days, while now regarded as part of rap's "old school" style, encapsulated the subsequent history of hip hop: angry social messages cloaked in exuberant fashion, humor, and profanity, staged in huge concert halls filled with black and white faces, and featured on popular MTV videos, in one instance with the established white heavy metal band Aerosmith.

By 1985, the casual observer might have expected rap to become a bankrupt fad. The music business was expert in turning African American creativity into highly profitable, inoffensive fodder for a largely white mass audience—a process that made a few black artists wealthy, and record executives far wealthier, while it exploited the music into a state of decay. In fact, though, the prophecy of Grandmaster Flash's "The Message" was that the plight of working-class black people would not improve soon, and that the hip hop expression it inspired would persist as well. It was a prediction that would be proven correct in the years to follow.

The 1970s and 1980s were a time of dramatic contrast for African Americans. The black middle class grew more rapidly than ever before, and the black poverty rate decreased by almost half. The 1970s became the first decade in American history in which more African Americans moved to the former segregationist South than moved out of it, as the old Confederacy became a site of black economic opportunity and political leadership. African Americans became mayors of Atlanta, Los Angeles, Cleveland, and other major cities. It was no longer a novelty for African American performers to regularly star in popular music, the movies, and other entertainment venues. Few artifacts summarized this spirit of successful integration as nicely as the most popular network television program of the 1980s, *The Cosby Show*, which featured Bill Cosby, long a favorite of white audiences, as the head of a young urban professional family. Cosby portrayed a genteel, prosperous physician with an attorney wife and a brood of well-behaved children.

Simultaneously, however, working-class African Americans confronted a new and devastating series of crises. Social programs and other innovations of the 1960s had improved the general standard of living, but the basic economic foundation of the inner cities was being eradicated. From 1960 to 1985 some 100,000 manufacturing jobs in Los Angeles alone were transported to Mexico and other countries or eliminated by automation. The South Bronx was only one of many mostly black and Latino neighborhoods that found itself almost devoid of jobs and small businesses and invisible to financial lenders and investors. In these neighborhoods garbage piled up, paint peeled, schools became dilapidated, and rats and vermin spread. No hopefulness about civil rights could alleviate this situation; that revolution was won, but conditions were still deteriorating. Homelessness became a staple of 1980s cities. For young women, relationships and babies gave some hope of meaning and love; the result, though, was a sharp increase in the number of underage and unwed mothers and of young children living in unhealthful and hazardous environments. The Reagan administration then removed much of the social "safety net" and put these vulnerable citizens at greater risk.

For inner-city youth without high scholastic aptitude, street gangs were the time-honored way of spending free time and ordering existence. These cliques were poisoned by the intrusion in the cities of the international narcotics business, which recruited many gang members as couriers and dealers of their illegal wares. In the 1980s, inner-city gangs became heavily armed protectors of turf. In these circumstances drug addiction became more widespread, and addicts compounded burglaries and other local crime rates. The introduction of cheap and highly addictive crystal or "crack" cocaine in the late 1980s and early 1990s increased the plague exponentially.

The political mainstream declared a "war on drugs" which took young ghetto residents as prisoners. In the 1970s, states had begun to punish drug users with long prison terms, and in the 1980s, in a much more conservative political climate, laws regulating drug possession and use of firearms in crimes became far tougher. The incarceration of vast numbers of inner-city youth became a major legacy of the 1980s and 1990s, as the U.S. prison population quadrupled. One-third of all young African American males became caught up in a general police dragnet, which included widespread racial "profiling" that made any prosperous-looking black man into a potential drug suspect. To many, the general backlash against Black Power revived many of the worst features of antiblack racism. Indeed, some state governments allowed prisoners to become low-paid industrial labor and deprived parolees of the right to vote. Critics charged that forms of slavery and disfranchisement were returning to post–Jim Crow America.

These disturbing developments brought a new potency and bluntness to rap music in the late 1980s. The Long Island-based group Public Enemy broke loose with two powerful albums of social criticism. From South Central Los Angeles came a new brand of best-selling rap music from Ice-T (Tracy Marrow) and NWA (Niggaz With Attitude), flavored by the drawling accents of artists with roots in Texas and Louisiana and punctuated by furiously profane, antipolice diatribes.

The creations of West Coast "gangsta" rappers such as Ice-T, Ice Cube (O'Shea Jackson), Dr. Dre (André Young), and later "West Coast" stars such as 2Pac (Tupac Shakur) and Snoop Dogg (Calvin Broadus) also featured insults against women and sexual boasting. The African American battle of the sexes had been brewing for decades over the flames of career and economic disparities, the lure of interracial relationships, and other issues, and it had found its way into generations of popular music. Now, male-dominated hip hop culture seemed to dispense entirely with the romantic sentiments found in soul music, not to mention the strict morality of the gospel tradition. Antihomosexual rhetoric also was rampant in "new-school" rap, despite—or likely because of—the frequency of homosexual acts in the jails in which many rap artists had once resided. Time behind bars encouraged these performers to profess callousness about sex of all kinds.[2]

Gangsta rap soon became the target of intense criticism from many whites, as well as some blacks, and stimulated cries for censorship and record ratings. The rise of gangsta rap made it difficult for many to discern the dividing line between rap's social criticism and its loud proclamations in favor of violence, misogyny, homophobia, and other kinds of hostility. Performers protested that, like black and other performers dating back to the days of minstrelsy, they were presenting stage personas that enabled listeners to escape temporarily into fantasy worlds, which offered both adolescent wish fulfillment and analysis of real-world problems.

It did not help the performers' reputations, though, that by 1993 a loud and occasionally violent feud had erupted between West Coast rap stars (the roster of Death Row Records, the latter founded by Dr. Dre and Marion "Suge" Knight) and East Coast artists (largely in the stable of Def Jam and Bad Boy Records, the latter founded by Russell Simmons's protégé, Sean "Puffy" Combs). The fighting cost the lives of the New Yorker Christopher Smalls ("Biggie Smalls" or "the Notorious B.I.G.") and Los Angeles's Tupac Shakur. Shakur, born into an extended Harlem family that was enmeshed in the activism of the Black Power era, carried a deep interest in social issues into his early rap career in California, and in his last years his frequent troubles with the law contrasted with his thoughtful writings, inspired film acting, and potential as an expressive artist. Numerous other rivalries, violent and otherwise, carried the traditional competitiveness of male African American musicians to new heights, and they received considerable publicity. Boasts in rap about material wealth commenced in the "new jack" era of the late 1980s and reached new heights after 1999 in beefs about "bling." Feuds and boasts displayed both the high stakes of success in hip hop music and the "street" backgrounds of many artists, but the occasional rites of public peacemaking between rival groups showed the civility and fraternity that existed in hip hop as well.

As fans of rap are quick to point out, gangsta lyrics and antifemale rhetoric are only part of the music. Gangsta rap's prominence within hip hop was exaggerated by both the male teenage listening public, which embraced the gangster persona as an escapist role model, and by "concerned" politicians who exploited proposals to censor rap lyrics. The attitudes of these two largely white groups recapitulate in some ways whites' distorted visions of 1920s blues and 1950s rock 'n' roll music. An analysis of hip hop's diverse legacy gives a more complex portrayal of the music. Early rap included many relatively tame variants, such as "house music," a Chicago brand of DJing that perpetuated the upbeat spirit of disco to an equally synthesized beat. Critics, also, tended to ignore the musical creativity in hip hop. The art of sampling, even in gangsta rap, was at least as crucial as lyric creation to the aesthetic development of hip hop. Countless licks and "grooves" from R & B, soul, and funk were reworked into rap numbers, with the powerful innovations of James Brown's band leading the way, and with Brown himself as a supreme model for strutting male showmanship. Love and even spirituality have been explored in hip hop music and lyrics, albeit with the style's trademark sharp-edged realism.

Hip hop music and culture now display great diversity. The first major female rap performers emerged in the early 1990s, including Queen Latifah (Dana Owens), now a film actress; the hybrid R & B and rap trio TLC, which sold millions in the early 1990s; and Da Brat (Shawtae Harris). They paved the way for a score of women stars in later years, such as Lil' Kim (Kimberly Jones); the award-winning Lauryn Hill, an American member of the largely Haitian ensemble the Fugees; and Missy Elliott, also a former singer, now the best-selling female rapper of all time. Regional variations in hip hop have diversified the lyrics, syntax, mixing, and even the rhythms of the music, as strong collectives and studio scenes arose in Houston, Oakland, Detroit, Memphis, Atlanta, and many other cities. Atlanta's Ludacris (Chris Bridges), OutKast, and Lil Jon (Jonathan Smith) have helped to make Martin Luther King, Jr.'s hometown the capital of the "southern rap" scene.

By the 2000s, hip hop had insinuated itself thoroughly into the fabric of American popular culture. Russell Simmons, Sean Combs, and Jay-Z (Shawn Carter, the best-selling African American rap soloist since 1998) have used their earnings from record producing to become entrepreneurs in politics, fashion design, and major-league team ownership. Hip hop remains controversial because of its association with inner cities and misbehavior, but it has become the most vital and profitable venue for African Americans in the history of their music. Rap's devaluation of sustained melody has put it in disfavor with older listeners, but R & B and soul remain vital, especially through the talents of performers such as Luther Vandross, R. Kelley, Usher, Anita Baker, Macy Gray, Alicia Keys, and Beyoncé Knowles, and recorded interactions with rap have provided rethinking and remixing of recent popular African American music. In 2007, even Wynton Marsalis, the jazz icon who had long criticized rap, released a hip hop album, in part, he said, to try to appeal to his own son's tastes.

Inevitably white rappers appeared on the scene. The Beastie Boys, a talented New York City group promoted in the 1980s by Russell Simmons, and an exploitation act called Vanilla Ice were polarized examples of the forms that blue-eyed rap might take. After 2000, the unprecedented success of the Detroit rapper Eminem (Marshall Mathers), whose occasionally hate-filled lyrics and turbulent personal life have overshadowed his creative gifts, threatened to retell the story of white co-optation of black genres, seen in the past in the stories of Paul Whiteman, Benny Goodman, Elvis Presley, and others. But such co-optation has not taken place. Nor have rap collectives in nations around the globe dislodged the centrality of African Americans to the hip hop movement.

CONCLUSION

Into the twenty-first century, African Americans' centrality in popular music and position at the money-earning portal of the music business seem assured. Jazz, the blues, soul, funk, and disco persist as niche music, while gospel retains its status as a sacred music industry unto itself, thriving in thousands of black churches. Recent technological developments such as file-sharing and the Internet have accelerated the decentralization of music broadcasting, and through them even "pop" music, as represented in the recent past by Michael Jackson, and hip hop have become fragmented. In 2007, Prince made headlines by making his latest album available to listeners at no cost. Thousands of performers can now solicit listeners from thousands of different taste groups.

Musical diversity today is matched by a new awareness of the diversity of black identity. Government reports after the 2000 U.S. Census indicate that as many as five million persons of African descent (one-sixth of the total) describe themselves as being of "mixed race." This designation reflects, and celebrates, old and recent trends in intermarriage in a new way. These self-reporting individuals, in addition, may be only a fraction of the actual mixed-race population in America. Their collective self-definition calls into question the basic solidity of African American identity, although blackness, as a construct, still serves insiders and outsiders in many ways.

African American music provides a soundtrack to the major themes of the black past. Although slavery, segregation, and civil rights legislation all have attempted to strictly define the relationship between the races, social and cultural intermixing has taken place since the beginning of the

African slave trade. The earliest evidence we possess of slave music indicates the mixing of African, European, and Native American influences. In the 1800s, blackface minstrelsy and "coon" songs plainly expressed the racism and white supremacy of the era, but they also showed a white fascination with black music and provided professional opportunity to the first generations of commercial black musicians.

In the twentieth century, African Americans migrated north and increased their agitation for legal and social equality. Musicians were highly visible pioneers in black cultural leadership in the United States, even before black people could hope to become political or social leaders. Scott Joplin, Louis Armstrong, Charlie Parker, and others, including classical and popular musicians, helped to make music a statement for black recognition in American society at large. The passion of African American gospel music inspired the civil rights movement and shaped soul, the popular music of the Black Power movement. While white co-optation of black music persists, it remains a key indicator of black cultural identity, which African Americans cherish and guard even as they seek to gain access to the opportunities offered by American society at large.

An inquiry into the musical expression of African Americans, past and present, shows black musicians and audiences constantly redefining the sonic terrain. Black music reflects the intermarriage of continental music and the constant interaction of black and nonblack cultures. At all times, though, especially in the present, African American music also reveals continuity. The history of black music tells of a heritage preserved across the span of oceans, generations, and centuries. Throughout that history, voices that lift, console, celebrate, and critique will continue to resonate, along the long and hard path to freedom and equality.

NOTES

1. Quoted in Guthrie P. Ramsey, Jr., *Race Music: Black Cultures From Bebop to Hip-Hop* (Berkeley: University of California Press, 2003), 2.
2. See for example Nelson George, *Hip Hop America*, 2nd ed. (New York: Viking, 2005), 44.

Documents

*T*hree excerpts from memoirs of Africa follow. The first is by Olaudah Equiano, an African man kidnapped into slavery, who survived to write his extraordinary life story. The second is by the British physician Mungo Park, who traveled equatorial Africa extensively in the 1790s. The final account is a summary of the experiences of Robert Adams, a British sailor shipwrecked off the coast of Africa, as related by other travelers, Richard and John Lander. Describing different areas of West Africa, these accounts allow us to compare music in these regions.

What was the role of music in the societies described in these excerpts?
How has Islam influenced music and society in these cultures?
How reliable do you think each of these observers are? Why?

*   *   *

Olaudah Equiano

[In Benen] The [wedding] ceremony being now ended the festival begins, which is celebrated with bonfires, and loud acclamations of joy, accompanied with music and dancing.

We are almost a nation of dancers, musicians, and poets. Thus every great event, such as a triumphant return from battle, or other cause of public rejoicing is celebrated in public dances, which are accompanied with songs and music suited to the occasion. The assembly is separated into four divisions, which dance either apart or in succession, and each with a character peculiar to itself. The first division contains the married men, who in their dances frequently exhibit feats of arms, and the representation of a battle. To these succeed the married women, who dance in the second division. The young men occupy the third; and the maidens the fourth. Each represents some interesting scene of real life, such as a great achievement, domestic employment, a pathetic story, or some rural sport; and as the subject is generally founded on some recent event, it is therefore ever new. This gives our dances a spirit and variety which I have scarcely seen elsewhere. We have many musical instruments, particularly drums of different kinds, a piece of music which resembles a guitar, and another much like a stickado. These last are chiefly used by betrothed virgins, who play on them on all grand festivals.

*   *   *

Mungo Park

In the evening the *tabala*, or large drum, was beat to announce a wedding, which was held at one of the neighboring tents. A great number of people of both sexes assembled, but without that mirth and hilarity which take place at a negro wedding. Here was neither singing nor dancing, nor any other amusement that I could perceive. A woman was beating the drum, and the other women joining at times like a chorus, by setting up a shrill scream, and at the same time moving their tongues from one side of the mouth to the other with great celerity. I was soon tired, and had returned into my hut, where I was sitting almost asleep, when an old woman entered with a wooden bowl in her hand, and signified that she had brought me a present from the bride. Before I could recover from the surprise which this message created, the woman discharged the contents of the bowl full in my face. Finding that it was the same sort of holy water with which, among the Hottentots, a priest is said to sprinkle a newly-married couple, I began to suspect that the old lady was actuated by mischief or malice; but she gave me seriously to understand that it was a nuptial benediction from the bride's own person, and which, on such occasions, is always received by the young unmarried Moors as a mark of distinguished favor. This being the case, I wiped my face, and sent my acknowledgments to the lady. The wedding drum continued to beat, and the women to sing, or rather whistle, all night. . . .

Of their music and dances some account has incidentally been given in different parts of my journal. On the first of these heads I have now to add a list of their musical instruments, the principal of which are—the *koonting,* a sort of guitar with three strings; the *korro,* a large harp with eighteen strings; the *simbing,* a small harp with seven strings; the *balafou,* an instrument composed of twenty pieces of hard wood of different lengths, with the shells of gourds hung underneath to increase the sound; the *tangtang,* a drum open at the lower end; and, lastly, the *tabala,* a large drum, commonly used to spread an alarm through the country. Besides these, they make use of small flutes, bow-strings, elephants' teeth and bells; and at all their dances and concerts *clapping of hands* appears to constitute a necessary part of the chorus.

With the love of music is naturally connected a taste for poetry; and fortunately for the poets of Africa they are in a great measure exempted from that neglect and indigence which in more polished countries commonly attend the votaries of the Muses. They consist of two classes; the most numerous are the *singing men,* called *jilli kea,* mentioned in a former part of my narrative. One or more of these may be found in every town. They sing extempore songs in honor of their chief men, or any other persons who are willing to give "solid pudding for empty praise." But a nobler part of their office is to recite the historical events of their country; hence in war they accompany the soldiers to the field, in order, by reciting the great actions of their ancestors, to awaken in them a spirit of glorious emulation. The other class are devotees of the Mohammedan faith, who travel about the country singing devout hymns and performing religious ceremonies, to conciliate the favor of the Almighty, either in averting calamity or insuring success to any enterprise. Both descriptions of these itinerant bards are much employed and respected by the people, and very liberal contributions are made for them.

*   *   *

Robert Adams

Dancing is the principal and favorite amusement of the natives of Timbuctoo; it takes place about once a week in the town, when a hundred dancers or more assemble, men, women, and children, but the greater number are men. Whilst they are engaged in the dance, they sing extremely loud to the music of the tambourine, fife, and bandera,* so that the noise they make, may be heard all over the town; they dance in a circle, and when this amusement continues till the night, generally

---

*The bandera is made of several cocoa-nut shells, tied together with thongs of goat-skin, and covered with the same material; a hole at the top of the instrument is covered with strings of leather, or tendons, drawn tightly across it, on which the performer plays with the fingers, in the manner of a guitar.

round a fire. Their usual time of beginning is about two hours before sunset, and the dance not unfrequently lasts all night. The men have the most of the exercise in these sports while daylight lasts, the women continuing nearly in one spot, and the men dancing to and from them. During this time, the dance is conducted with some decency, but when night approaches, and the women take a more active part in the amusement, their thin and short dresses, and the agility of their actions are little calculated to admit of the preservation of any decorum. The following was the nature of the dance; six or seven men joining hands, surrounded one in the center of the ring, who was dressed in a ludicrous manner, wearing a large black wig stuck full of cowries. This man at intervals repeated verses, which, from the astonishment and admiration expressed at them by those in the ring, appeared to be extempore. Two performers played on the outside of the ring, one on a large drum, the other on the bandera. The singer in the ring was not interrupted during his recitations, but at the end of every verse, the instruments struck up, and the whole party joined in loud chorus, dancing round the man in the circle, stooping to the ground, and throwing up their legs alternately. Toward the end of the dance, the man in the middle of the ring was released from his enclosure, and danced alone, occasionally reciting verses, whilst the other dancers begged money from the bystanders.

The Interesting Narrative of the Life of Olaudah Equiano, Or Gustavus Vassa, The African, Written by Himself (London: published by author 1789), chapter 1; Mungo Park, *Travels in the Interior of Africa* (London: W. Bulmer, 1799), chapters 10 and 21; Robert Huish ed., *Travels of Richard and John Lander into the Interior of Africa* (London: John Saunders, 1836), chapter 10. All selections in the public domain.

THE OLD PLANTATION (CIRCA 1790)

This famous watercolor from South Carolina is the only surviving image of African American music making in the United States created before 1800. The artist is unknown.
   Questions to consider:

   Based on your reading of chapter 1, how African does the music and dance seem, and why?
   What social function(s) does the music and dance in this scene seem to perform?
   How accurate or inaccurate would you say this painting is? Why?

Photo A.1. *The Old Plantation*

Anonymous, *The Old Plantation* (circa 1790). The Abby Aldrich Rockefeller Folk Art Museum, The Colonial Williamsburg Foundation, Williamsburg, Va. Reprinted by permission.

MISSISSIPPI SLAVE NARRATIVES

In the 1930s, the Works Progress Administration, a New Deal agency, financed an oral history project to collect the memories of surviving former slaves. The narratives are problematic as historical sources. The speakers were often cautious or nostalgic (Mississippi, of course, was still profoundly segregated in the 1930s), and the transcripts rendered black speech in caricatured written dialect.

These excerpts from interviews in Mississippi are rewritten in standard spelling. Except in one song title, "nigger" is replaced with "Negro" (the former invariably was used in the Mississippi transcripts). Readers may see the original full transcripts at the Library of Congress's American Memory digital library at memory.loc.gov.

What variety of musical experiences in slavery and freedom are displayed here? What was the function of specific music, lyrics, and dance in these excerpts? How reliable are these interviews and transcripts as a record of the history of slavery?

Jim Allen: We had a neighborhood church and both black and white went to it. There was a white preacher and sometimes a Negro preacher would sit in the pulpit with him. The slaves sat on one side of the aisle and white folks on the other. I always liked preacher Williams Odem, and his brother Daniel, the "[back]sliding Elder." . . . They come from Ohio. Marse Bob Allen was head steward. I remember lots of my favorite songs. Some of them was, "Am I Born to Die," "Alas and Did My Savior Bleed," and "Must I to the Judgment Be Brought." The preacher would say "Pull down the line and let the spirit be a witness, working for faith in the future from on high." . . . A song we used to sing [at funerals] was: "Come on Chariot and Take Her Home, Take Her Home, / Here Come Chariot, let's ride, / Come on let's ride, Come on let's ride."

Dora Franks: Since then it's the hardest thing in the world for me to remember the songs us used to dance by. I do remember a few like "Shoo, Fly," "Old Dan Tucker," and "Run, Nigger, Run, the Patroller Catch You." I don't remember much of the words. I does remember a little of "Old Dan Tucker." It went this way: "Old Dan Tucker was a mighty mean man, / He beat his wife with a frying pan. / She hollered and she cried, 'I'm going to go, / They's plenty of men, won't beat me so.' / Get out of the way, Old Dan Tucker, / You come too late to get your supper. / Old Dan Tucker, he got drunk, / Fell in the fire, kicked up a chunk, / Red hot coal got down his shoe / Oh, Great Lord, how the ashes flew. . . . "

Prince Johnson: Nobody worked after dinner on Saturday. Us took that time to scrub up and clean the houses so as to be ready for inspection Sunday morning. Some Saturday nights us had dances. The same old fiddler player for us that played for the white folks. And he sure could play. When he got that old fiddle out you couldn't keep your foots still.

James Lucas: Slaves didn't know what to expect from freedom, but a lot of them hoped they would be fed and kept by the government. They all had different ways of thinking about it. Mostly though they was just like me, they didn't know just exactly what it meant. It was just something that the white folks and slaves all the time talk about. That's all. Folks that ain't never been free don't know the *feel* of being free. They don't know the meaning of it. Slaves like us, what was owned by quality-folks, was satisfied and didn't sing none of them freedom songs. I recollect one song that us could sing. It went like this: "Drinking of the wine, drinking of the wine, / Ought-a been in heaven three thousand years / A-drinking of that wine, a-drinking of that wine." Us could shout that one.

Charlie Moses: Lincoln was the man that set us free. He was a big general in the war.

I remember a song we sung, then. It went kind of like this: "Free at last, / Free at last, / Thank God Almighty, / I'm free at last."

Susan Snow: I got more whuppings than any other Negro on the place, because I was mean like my mammy. Always a-fighting and scratching with white and black. I was so bad Marster made me go look at the Negroes they hung to see what they done to a Negro that harm a white man.

I'm going to tell this story on myself. The white children was a-singing this song: "Jeff Davis, long and slim, / Whupped old Abe with a hickory limb. / Jeff Davis is a wise man, Lincoln is a fool, / Jeff Davis rides a gray, and Lincoln rides a mule." I was mad anyway, so I hopped up and sung this one: "Old General Pope had a shot gun, / Filled it full of gum, / Killed them as they come. / Called a Union band, / Make the Rebels understand, / To leave the land, / Submit to Abraham."

Old Miss was a-standing right behind me. She grabbed up the broom and laid it on me. She made *me* submit. I caught the feathers, don't you forget it.

I didn't know it was wrong. I'd heard the Negroes sing it and I didn't know they was a-singing in they sleeves. . . .

Isaac Stier: Us slaves mostly sung hymns and psalms. But I remember one song about a frog pond and one about "Jump, Mr. Toad." I'm too wordless to sing them now, but they was funny. Us danced plenty, too. Some of the men clogged and pigeoned, but when us had dances they was real cotillions, like the white folks had. They was always a fiddler and, on Christmas and other holidays, the slaves was allowed to invite they sweethearts from other plantations. I used to call out the figures: "Ladies, sashay. Gents to the left, now all swing." Everybody liked my calls and the dancers sure moved smooth and pretty. Long after the war was over the white folks would engage me to come around with the band and call the figures at all the big dances. They always paid me well.

Molly Williams: Miss Margerite [wife of the white master] had a piano, an accordion, a flute, and a fiddle. She could play a fiddle good as a man. Lord, I heard many as three fiddles going in that house many a time. And I can just see her little old fair hands now, playing just as fast as lightning a tune. . . . All us children begged [her?] to play that and we all sing and dance—*great goodness*!

One song I remember mammy singing: "Let me nigh, by my cry, / Give me Jesus. / You may have all this world, / But give me Jesus."

Singing and shouting, she had religion all right. She belonged to Old Farrett back in Missouri. . . .

There was plenty dancing amongst darkies on Marse George's place and on one nearby. They danced reels and like in the moonlight: "Mamma's got the whooping cough, / Daddy's got the measles, / That's where the money goes, / Pop goes the weasel." "Buffalo gals, can't you come out tonight, / Come out tonight, and dance by the light of the moon?" "Gennie, put the kettle on, / Sallie, boil the water strong, / Gennie, put the kettle on / And let's have tea!" "Run tell Coleman, / Run tell everybody / That the Negroes is arising! / Run Negro run, the patterrollers catch you— / Run Negro run, for it's almost day, / The Negro run; the Negro flew; the Negro lose / His big old shoe."

Clara Young: [After the war] the Yankees tried to get some of the men to vote, too, but not many did because they was scared of the Ku Kluxers. They would come at night all dressed up like ghosts and scare us all. We didn't like Yankees anyway. They weren't good to us; when they left we would always sing that little song what go like this: "Old Mister Yankee, think he is so grand, / With his blue coat tail a-draggin' on the ground!"

Excerpts from *Born in Slavery: Slave Narratives from the Federal Writers' Project, 1936–1938. American Memory*, Library of Congress, memory.loc.gov. In the public domain.

FREDERICK DOUGLASS ON SLAVE SINGING

This famous brief passage from the young escaped slave's Narrative, *published in 1845, recounts his memories of slave singing from his boyhood on a plantation in Maryland. More than a half century later, it would inspire W. E. B. Du Bois to write one of the most poignant chapters of his classic work* The Souls of Black Folk.

> *Do Douglass's memories of slave music making seem to confirm or refute the recollections of former slaves in the previous document? Why?*
>
> *According to Douglass, how did the agonies of bondage influence slaves' music making?*
>
> *Why did Douglass feel that he had to correct northerners' impressions about slaves' singing?*

The slaves selected to go to the Great House Farm, for the monthly allowance for themselves and their fellow-slaves, were peculiarly enthusiastic. While on their way, they would make the dense old woods, for miles around, reverberate with their wild songs, revealing at once the highest joy and the deepest sadness. They would compose and sing as they went along, consulting neither time nor tune. The thought that came up, came out—if not in the word, in the sound—and as frequently in the one as in the other. They would sometimes sing the most pathetic sentiment in the most rapturous tone, and the most rapturous sentiment in the most pathetic tone. Into all of their songs they would manage to weave something of the Great House Farm. Especially would they do this, when leaving home. They would then sing most exultingly the following words:

> "I am going away to the Great House Farm!
> O, yea! O, yea! O!"

This they would sing, as a chorus, to words which to many would seem unmeaning jargon, but which, nevertheless, were full of meaning to themselves. I have sometimes thought that the mere hearing of those songs would do more to impress some minds with the horrible character of slavery, than the reading of whole volumes of philosophy on the subject could do.

I did not, when a slave, understand the deep meaning of those rude and apparently incoherent songs. I was myself within the circle; so that I neither saw nor heard as those without might see and hear. They told a tale of woe which was then altogether beyond my feeble comprehension; they were tones loud, long, and deep; they breathed the prayer and complaint of souls boiling over with the bitterest anguish. Every tone was a testimony against slavery, and a prayer to God for deliverance from chains. The hearing of those wild notes always depressed my spirit, and filled me with ineffable sadness. I have frequently found myself in tears while hearing them. The mere recurrence to those songs, even now, afflicts me; and while I am writing these lines, an expression of feeling has already found its way down my cheek. To those songs I trace my first glimmering conception of the dehumanizing character of slavery. I can never get rid of that conception. Those songs still follow me, to deepen my hatred of slavery, and quicken my sympathies for my brethren in bonds. If any one wishes to be impressed with the soul-killing effects of slavery, let him go to Colonel Lloyd's plantation, and, on allowance-day, place himself in the deep pine woods, and there let him, in silence, analyze the sounds that shall pass through the chambers of his soul, and if he is not thus impressed, it will only be because "there is no flesh in his obdurate heart."

I have often been utterly astonished, since I came to the north, to find persons who could speak of the singing, among slaves, as evidence of their contentment and happiness. It is impossible to conceive of a greater mistake. Slaves sing most when they are most unhappy. The songs of the slave represent the sorrows of his heart; and he is relieved by them, only as an aching heart is relieved by its tears. At least, such is my experience. I have often sung to drown my sorrow, but seldom to express my happiness. Crying for joy, and singing for joy, were alike uncommon to me while in the jaws of slavery. The singing of a man cast away upon a desolate island might be as appropriately considered as evidence of contentment and happiness, as the singing of a slave; the songs of the one and of the other are prompted by the same emotion.

Narrative of the Life of Frederick Douglass, An American Slave (1845; New York: Barnes & Noble, 2005), chapter 2.

THOMAS WENTWORTH HIGGINSON: "NEGRO SPIRITUALS"

Higginson, a Boston abolitionist, became a Union colonel during the Civil War and raised the first unit of freed slaves in South Carolina. He was one of a number of educated northerners who collected the lore and songs of the freed people in the occupied coastal areas of the Carolinas and Georgia. Soon after the war ended, Higginson published an article describing black sacred song in the Atlantic Monthly.

> *How do you think Higginson's background and education shaped his perception of former slaves and their music?*
>
> *Do you agree with Higginson's interpretations of the spirituals' texts? Would you add anything to his analyses?*

Do you think it was a good thing that Higginson publicized the spirituals like this? Why or why not?

The war brought to some of us, besides its direct experiences, many a strange fulfilment of dreams of other days. For instance, the present writer has been a faithful student of the Scottish ballads, and had always envied Sir Walter [Scott] the delight of tracing them out amid their own heather, and of writing them down piecemeal from the lips of aged crones. It was a strange enjoyment, therefore, to be suddenly brought into the midst of a kindred world of unwritten songs, as simple and indigenous as the Border Minstrelsy, more uniformly plaintive, almost always more quaint, and often as essentially poetic.

This interest was rather increased by the fact that I had for many years heard of this class of songs under the name of "Negro Spirituals," and had even heard some of them sung by friends from South Carolina. I could now gather on their own soil these strange plants, which I had before seen as in museums alone. True, the individual songs rarely coincided; there was a line here, a chorus there—just enough to fix the class, but this was unmistakable. It was not strange that they differed, for the range seemed almost endless, and South Carolina, Georgia, and Florida seemed to have nothing but the generic character in common, until all were mingled in the united stock of camp-melodies.

Often in the starlit evening I have returned from some lonely ride by the swift river, or on the plover-haunted barrens, and, entering the camp, have silently approached some glimmering Ore, round which the dusky figures moved in the rhythmical barbaric dance the negroes call a "shout," chanting, often harshly, but always in the most perfect time, some monotonous refrain. Writing down in the darkness, as I best could—perhaps with my hand in the safe covert of my pocket—the words of the song, I have afterwards carried it to my tent, like some captured bird or insect, and then, after examination, put it by. Or, summoning one of the men at some period of leisure, Corporal Robert Sutton, for instance, whose iron memory held all the details of a song as if it were a ford or a forest, I have completed the new specimen by supplying the absent parts. The music I could only retain by ear, and though the more common strains were repeated often enough to fix their impression, there were others that occurred only once or twice.

The words will be here given, as nearly as possible, in the original dialect; and if the spelling seems sometimes inconsistent, or the misspelling insufficient, it is because I could get no nearer. . . .

The favorite song in camp was the following, sung with no accompaniment but the measured clapping of hands and the clatter of many feet. It was sung perhaps twice as often as any other. This was partly due to the fact that it properly consisted of a chorus alone, with which the verses of other songs might be combined at random. . . .

"Hold your light, Brudder Robert,
Hold your light,
Hold your light on Canaan's shore."
"What make ole Satan for follow me so?
Satan ain't got notin' for do wid me.
Hold your light,
Hold your light,
Hold your light on Canaan's shore."

This would be sung for half an hour at a time, perhaps, each person present being named in turn. It seemed the simplest primitive type of "spiritual." The next in popularity was almost as elementary, and, like this, named successively each one of the circle. It was, however, much more resounding and convivial in its music.

"Jordan River, I'm bound to go,
Bound to go, bound to go,
Jordan River, I'm bound to go,
And bid 'em fare ye well."
"My Brudder Robert, I'm bound to go,
Bound to go," &c.
"My Sister Lucy, I'm bound to go,
Bound to go," &c."

Sometimes it was tink 'em " (think them) "fare ye well." The *ye* was so detached, that I thought at first it was "very" or "vary well."

Another picturesque song, which seemed immensely popular, was at first very bewildering to me. I could not make out the first words of the chorus, and called it the "Romandàr," being reminded of some Romaic song which I had formerly heard. That association quite fell in with the Orientalism of the new tent-life. . . .

*　　*　　*

Room in There

"O, my mudder is gone! my mudder is gone!
My mudder is gone into heaven, my Lord!
I can't stay behind!
Dere's room in dar, room in dar,
Room in dar, in de heaven, my Lord!
I can't stay behind,"
Can't stay behind, my dear,
I can't stay behind!"
"O, my fader is gone!" &c.

"O, de angels are gone!" &c.
"O, I'se been on de road! I'se been on de road!
I'se been on de road into heaven, my Lord!
I can't stay behind!
O, room in dar, room in dar,
Room in dar, in de heaven, my Lord!
I can't stay behind!"

By this time every man within hearing, from oldest to youngest, would be wriggling and shuffling, as if through some magic piper's bewitchment; for even those who at first affected contemptuous indifference would be drawn into the vortex ere long.

Next to these in popularity ranked a class of songs belonging emphatically to the Church Militant, and available for camp purposes with very little strain upon their symbolism. This, for instance, had a true companion-in-arms heartiness about it, not impaired by the feminine invocation at the end. . . .

*　　*　　*

Hail Mary

"One more valiant soldier here,
One more valiant soldier here,
One more valiant soldier here,
To help me bear de cross.
O hail, Mary, hail!
Hail!, Mary, hail!
Hail!, Mary, hail!
To help me bear de cross."

I fancied that the original reading might have been "soul," instead of "soldier," with some other syllable inserted, to fill out the metre, and that the "Hail, Mary," might denote a Roman Catholic origin, as I had several men from St. Augustine who held in a dim way to that faith. It was a very ringing song, though not so grandly jubilant as the next, which was really impressive as the singers pealed it out, when marching or rowing or embarking. . . .

*　　*　　*

My Army Cross Over

"My army cross over,
My army cross over.
O, Pharaoh's army drownded!
My army cross over."
"We'll cross de mighty river,

My army cross over;
We'll cross de river Jordan,
My army cross over;
We'll cross de danger water,
My army cross over;
We'll cross de mighty Myo,
My army cross over. (*Thrice.*)
O, Pharaoh's army drownded!
My army cross over."

I could get no explanation of the "mighty Myo," except that one of the old men thought it meant the river of death. Perhaps it is an African Word. In the Cameroon dialect, "Mawa" signifies "to die."

Thomas Wentworth Higginson, "Negro Spirituals," *Atlantic Monthly* (June 1867). In the public domain.

JAMES M. TROTTER, *MUSIC AND SOME HIGHLY MUSICAL PEOPLE*

James M. Trotter's book was the first published history of music in the United States. Trotter was an escaped slave and former Union soldier who became a writer and civil servant in Boston. His book offers valuable data on African American music in the mid-1800s and expresses the values of the black middle class in the decades after emancipation.

How do Trotter's opinions reflect the recent turbulent history of African Americans?

Does Trotter entirely share the views of white middle-class music lovers, or not?

How optimistic is Trotter about the future for African American musicians?

While grouping, as has here been done, the musical celebrities of a single race; while gathering from near and far these many fragments of musical history, and recording them in one book, the writer yet earnestly disavows all motives of a distinctively clannish nature. But the haze of complexional prejudice has so much obscured the vision of many persons, that they cannot see (at least, there are many who affect not to see) that musical faculties, and power for their *artistic* development, are not in the exclusive possession of the fairer-skinned race, but are alike the beneficent gifts of the Creator to all of his children. Besides, there are some well-meaning persons who have formed, for lack of the information that is here afforded, erroneous and unfavorable estimates of the art-capabilities of the colored race. In the hope, then, of contributing to the formation of a more just opinion, of inducing a cheerful admission of its existence, and of aiding to establish between both races relations of mutual respect and good feeling; of inspiring the people most concerned (if that be necessary) with a greater pride in their own achievements, and confidence in their own resources, as a basis for other and even greater acquirements, as a landmark, a partial guide, for a future and better chronicler; and, finally, as a sincere tribute to the winning power, the noble beauty, of music, a contemplation of whose own divine harmony should ever serve to promote harmony between man and man, with these purposes in view, this humble volume is hopefully issued.

. . . . The colored people of New Orleans have long been remarked for their love of and proficiency in music and other of the elegant arts. Forty years ago "The New Orleans Picayune" testified to their superior taste for and appreciation of the drama, especially Shak[e]speare's plays. A certain portion of these people, never having been subjected to the depressing cruelties of *abject* servitude, although, of course, suffering much from the caste spirit that followed and presented great obstacles to even such as they, were *allowed* to acquire the means for defraying the expenses of private instruction, or for sending their children to Northern or European schools. . . . [T]here was another portion of this same race, who, in the circumstances of their situation, were far less fortunate than even those of whom I have just been speaking: I mean those who were directly under the "iron heel of oppression." Nevertheless, many of these were so moved by a spirit of art-love, and were so ardent and determined, as to have acquired a scientific knowledge of music, and to have even excelled, strange to say, in its creation and performance, in spite of all difficulties. . . .

. . . . How much, how very much, has been lost to art in this country through that fell spirit which for more than two hundred years has animated the majority of its people against a struggling and an unoffending minority—a spirit which ever sought to crush out talent, to quench the sacred fire of genius, and to crowd down all noble aspirations, whenever these evidences of a high manhood were shown by those whose skins were black! Ah! we may never know how much of grandeur of achievement, the results of which the country might now be enjoying, had not those restless, aspiring minds been fettered by all that was the echo of a terrible voice, which, putting to an ignoble use the holy words of Divinity, cried up and down the land unceasingly, *"Hitherto shalt thou come, but no farther!"* For to judge as to what "might have been," and what yet may be, despite the cruelties of the past, . . . we have only to look at what is.

James M. Trotter, *Music and Some Highly Musical People* (Boston: Lee & Shepard, 1878), pp. 4, 335–36.

JAMES BLAND, "GREAT ETHIOPIAN SONGS," SHEET MUSIC COVER

James Bland was one of the most successful African American performers and songwriters of his generation. His song "Carry Me Back to Old Virginny" was one of the most enduring songs published in America in the 1870s.

What status is Bland accorded on this cover of a collection of his songs?
What images of African Americans and of slavery are presented in the artwork?
How do you think the songs and the artwork would be received by future generations of African Americans (in, say, 1920 or 1960)?

Photo A.2.   James Bland, *Ethiopian Melodies*

James Bland, "Great Ethiopian Songs," sheet music cover (1880). *African-American Sheet Music, 1850–1920. American Memory,* Library of Congress, memory.loc.gov. In the public domain.

ANTONIN DVOŘÁK ON AFRICAN AMERICAN MUSIC

In chapter 2 we noted the famed Czech composer Antonin Dvořák's influential endorsement of African American music. The first excerpt below, from an interview the composer conducted with the New York Herald, *contains that endorsement. The second selection is from an article, "Music in America," that Dvořák wrote for* Harper's Weekly *magazine in 1895, near the end of his stay in the United States. This article offers a more complicated portrait of the place of African American music in the national culture.*

> *Who, in Dvořák's view, should be able to use African American music to create future classical music in the United States? To whom do you think folk music "belongs"?*
>
> *Why, in an era of segregation and racial violence, was Dvořák so optimistic about the future of African American music in the United States?*
>
> *To what extent did American music evolve after the 1890s as Dvořák predicted that it would?*

* * *

New York Herald (1893)

I am now satisfied that the future music of this country must be founded upon what are called the negro melodies. This must be the real foundation of any serious and original school of composition to be developed in the United States. . . . [Negro melodies] are the folk songs of America and your composers must turn to them. . . . In the negro melodies of America I discover all that is needed for a great and noble school of music. . . . I did not come to America to interpret Beethoven or Wagner for the public. . . . I came to discover what young Americans had in them and to help them to express it.

* * *

"Music in America" (1895)

A while ago I suggested that inspiration for truly national music might be derived from the Negro melodies or Indian chants. I was led to take this view partly by the fact that the so-called plantation songs are indeed the most striking and appealing melodies that have yet been found on this side of the water, but largely by the observation that this seems to be recognized, though often unconsciously, by most Americans. All races have their distinctively national songs, which they at once recognize as their own, even if they have never heard them before. When a Tcech [sic], a Pole, or a Magyar in this country suddenly hears one of his folk-songs or dances, no matter if it is for the first time in his life, his eyes light up at once, and his heart within him responds, and claims that music as his own. So it is with those of Teutonic or Celtic blood, or any other men, indeed, whose first lullaby mayhap [perhaps] was a song wrung from the heart of the people.

It is a proper question to ask, what songs, then, belong to the American and appeal more strongly to him than any others? What melody could stop him on the street if he were in a strange land and make the home feeling well up within him, no matter how hardened he might be or how wretchedly the tune were played? Their number, to be sure, seems to be limited. The most potent as well as the most beautiful among them, according to my estimation, are certain of the so-called plantation melodies and slave songs, all of which are distinguished by unusual and subtle harmonies, the like of which I have found in no other songs but those of old Scotland and Ireland. The point has been urged that many of these touching songs, like those of Foster, have not been composed by the Negroes themselves, but are the work of white men, while others did not originate on the plantations, but were imported from Africa. It seems to me that this matters but little. One might as well condemn the *Hungarian Rhapsody* because Liszt could not speak Hungarian. The important thing is that the inspiration for such music should come from the right source, and that the music itself should be a true expression of the people's real feelings. To read the right meaning the composer need not necessarily be of the same blood, though that, of course, makes it easier for him. Schubert was a thorough German, but when he wrote Hungarian music, as in the second movement of the *C-Major Symphony*, or in some of his piano pieces, like the *Hungarian Divertissement*, he struck the true Magyar note, to which all Magyar hearts, and with them our own, must forever respond. This is not a tour de force, but only an instance of how music can be comprehended by a sympathetic genius. The white composers who wrote the touching Negro songs which dimmed Thackeray's spectacles so that he exclaimed, "Behold, a vagabond with a corked face and banjo sings a little song, strikes a wild note, which sets the whole heart thrilling with happy pity!" had a similarly sympathetic comprehension of the deep pathos of slave life. If, as I have been informed they were, these songs were adopted by the Negroes on the plantations, they thus became true Negro songs. Whether the original songs which must have inspired the composers came from Africa or originated on the plantations matters as little as whether Shakespeare invented his own plots or borrowed them from others. The thing to rejoice over is that such lovely songs exist and are sung at the present day. I, for one, am delighted by them. Just so it matters little whether the inspiration for the coming folk songs of America is derived from the Negro melodies, the songs of the creoles, the red man's chant, or the plaintive ditties of the homesick German or Norwegian. Undoubtedly the germs for the best in music lie hidden among all the races that are commingled in this great country. The music of the people is like a rare and lovely flower growing amidst encroaching weeds. Thousands pass it, while others trample it under foot, and thus the chances are that it will perish before it is seen by the one discriminating spirit who will prize it above all else. The fact that no one has as yet arisen to make the most of it does not prove that nothing is there.

New York Herald, May 21, 1893; Antonin Dvořák, "Music in America," *Harper's Weekly* (February 1895), 431–33. In the public domain.

"LIFT EVERY VOICE AND SING"—JAMES WELDON JOHNSON

James Weldon Johnson was a young writer who became an important novelist, diplomat, and crusader for civil rights. He wrote the lyrics for "Lift Every Voice and Sing," and his brother, the pianist J. Rosamond Johnson, wrote the stirring music. The song proved popular among African Americans in New York City, and in 1919, during the cultural renaissance in Harlem, the local office of the National Association for the Advancement of Colored People (NAACP) proclaimed it to be the "Negro national anthem."

> *How might this lyric be a response to African American history in the late 1800s?*
> *Was Johnson a purely genteel or middle-class lyricist?*
> *Why do you think this particular song become known as "the Negro national anthem"?*

Lift every voice and sing, till earth and Heaven ring,
Ring with the harmonies of liberty;
Let our rejoicing rise, high as the listening skies,
Let it resound loud as the rolling sea.
Sing a song full of the faith that the dark past has taught us,
Sing a song full of the hope that the present has brought us;
Facing the rising sun of our new day begun,
Let us march on till victory is won.
Stony the road we trod, bitter the chastening rod,
Felt in the days when hope unborn had died;
Yet with a steady beat, have not our weary feet,
Come to the place for which our fathers sighed?

We have come over a way that with tears has been watered,
We have come, treading our path through the blood of the slaughtered;
Out from the gloomy past, till now we stand at last
Where the white gleam of our bright star is cast.

God of our weary years, God of our silent tears,
Thou Who hast brought us thus far on the way;
Thou Who hast by Thy might, led us into the light,
Keep us forever in the path, we pray.
Lest our feet stray from the places, our God, where we met Thee.
Lest our hearts, drunk with the wine of the world, we forget Thee.
Shadowed beneath Thy hand, may we forever stand,
True to our God, true to our native land.

James Weldon Johnson and J. Rosamond Johnson, "Lift Every Voice and Sing" (1900; New York: E. B. Marks Music. Co., 1921). In the public domain.

SCOTT JOPLIN, *TREEMONISHA*

Joplin's opera, almost unknown in his lifetime and for decades afterward, is set in Reconstruction-era Arkansas. Monisha, the heroine, battles to bring education to a community. A 1970s recording of Treemonisha, *featuring this scene, is available at some online music sites.*

> *What important attitudes are Zodzetrick and Monisha representing in the opera?*
> *Is Joplin offering a reasonably authentic representation of rural black people?*
> *If* Treemonisha *had been fully staged in 1910s Harlem, would it have been a success?*

Act I, Scene 2—"The Bag of Luck"

Zodzetrick enters.

> *Zodzetrick to Monisha:* I want to sell to you dis bag o' luck, Yo' enemies it will keep away.
>
> Over yo' front do' you can hang it, An' good luck will come each day.
>
> *Monisha:* Will it drive away de blues?
>
> An' stop Ned from drinkin' booze?
>
> *Zodzetrick:* It will drive de blues, I'm thinkin',
>
> An' will stop Ned from booze-drinkin'.
>
> *Monisha, reaching for bag:* Well!

Ned, angrily: No, dat bag you'se not gwine to buy,

'Cause I know de price is high.

Zodzetrick: I mus' tell you plain an' bold,

It is worth its weight in gold.

Ned: It may be worth its weight in diamonds rare,

Or worth the earth to you.

But to me, it ain't worth a possum's hair,

Or persimmons when they're new.

Drinkin' gin I would not stop,

If dat bag was on my chin.

I'm goin' to drink an' work my crop,

'Cause I think it is no sin.

Monisha: Dis here bag will heaps o' luck bring,

An' we need here jes dis kind o' thing.

Ned: You shall not buy dat bag,

'Cause I don't want it here.

'Nough o' dat thing we've had.

'Twill do us harm, I fear. *To Zodzetrick:*

Say ole man, you won't do,

You's a stranger to me.

Tell me, who are you?

Zodzetrick: Zodzetrick—I am de Goofer dus' man

An' I's king of Goofer dus' lan'.

Strange things appear when I says "Hee hoo!"

Strange things appear when I says "Hee hoo!"

Zodzetrick starts away. Exit Ned. Monisha goes into the cabin.

Treemonisha to Zodzetrick: Wait, sir, for a few moments stay,

You should listen to what I have to say.

Please come closer to me, come along,

And I'll tell you of your great wrong.

Zodzetrick marks a cross on the ground, spits on it and turns back.

Zodzetrick: I've come back, my dear child, to hear what you say,

Go on with your story, I can't stay all day.

Treemonisha: You have lived without working for many years.

All by your tricks of conjury.

You have caused superstition and many sad tears.

You should stop, you are doing great injury.

Zodzetrick: You 'cuse me wrong

For injury I'se not done,

An' it won't be long

'Fore I'll make you from me run.

I has dese bags o' luck, 'tis true,

So take care, gal, I'll send bad luck to you.

Remus: Shut up old man, enough you've said;

You can't fool Treemonisha—she has a level head.

She is the only educated person of our race,

For many long miles far away from this place.

She'll break the spell of superstition in the neighborhood,

And all you foolish conjurors will have to be good.

To read and write she has taught me,

And I am very grateful,

I have more sense now, you can see,

And to her I'm very thankful.

You'd better quit your foolish ways

And all this useless strife,

You'd better change your ways today

And live a better life.

Zodzetrick: I don't care what you say,

I will never change my way.

Starts to leave.

I'm going now, but I'll be back soon,

Long 'fore another new moon.

D'y'all hear?

Treemonisha and Remus: Yes, and we are glad you are going.

They stand looking at Zodzetrick as he walks slowly away.

Hope he'll stay away from here always, always.

Scott Joplin, *Treemonisha: Opera in Three Acts* (New York: Scott Joplin, 1911). In the public domain.

BLUES LYRICS (1920s)

The blues swept popular music in the 1920s, and brought grassroots southern rural African American music and thought to national attention. It is impossible to capture the variety and complexity of the blues in just a few lyrics. However, in the following three selections—one by the Delta blues pioneer Charley Patton, about the great Mississippi River flood of 1927, the other two popularized by Gertrude "Ma" Rainey—we can, to an extent, compare and contrast the blues with other genres of African American music.

> *How did the blues break new ground as an expression of African Americans' thoughts and feelings?*
> *What ideas and qualities do these lyrics share with the spirituals and other black song styles?*
> *What do you think blues songs such as these meant to African American listeners in the 1920s?*

*   *   *

"High Water Everywhere," by Charley Patton (1929)

Part 1

> Well, backwater done rose all around Sumner now,
> drove me down the line
> Backwater done rose at Sumner,
> drove poor Charley down the line
> Lord, I'll tell the world the water,
> done crept through this town
>
> Lord, the whole round country,
> Lord, river has overflowed
> Lord, the whole round country,
> man, is overflowed
> You know I can't stay here,
> I'll go where it's high, boy
> I would go to the hilly country,
> but, they got me barred

Now, look-a here now at Leland,
river was risin' high
Look-a here boys around Leland tell me,
river was raisin' high
Boy, it's risin' over there, yeah
I'm gonna move to Greenville,
fore I leave, goodbye

Look-a here the water now, Lordy,
Levee broke, rose most everywhere
The water at Greenville and Leland,
Lord, it done rose everywhere
Boy, you can't never stay here
I would go down to Rosedale,
but, they tell me there's water there

Now, the water now, mama,
done took Charley's town
Well, they tell me the water,
done took Charley's town
Boy, I'm goin' to Vicksburg
Well, I'm goin' to Vicksburg,
for that high of mine

I am goin' up that water,
where lands don't never flow
Well, I'm goin' over the hill where,
water, oh don't ever flow
Boy, hit Sharkey County and everything was down in Stovall
But, that whole county was leavin',
over that Tallahatchie shore
Boy, went to Tallahatchie and got it over there

Lord, the water done rushed all over,
down old Jackson road
Lord, the water done raised,
over the Jackson road
Boy, it starched my clothes
I'm goin' back to the hilly country,
won't be worried no more

Part 2

Backwater at Blytheville, backed up all around
Backwater at Blytheville, done took Joiner town
It was fifty families and children come to sink and drown

The water was risin' up at my friend's door
The water was risin' up at my friend's door
The man said to his women folk, "Lord, we'd better go"

The water was risin', got up in my bed
Lord, the water was rollin', got up to my bed
I thought I would take a trip, Lord, out on the big ice sled

Oh, I can hear, Lord, Lord, water upon my door,
you know what I mean, look-a here
I hear the ice, Lord, Lord, was sinkin' down,
I couldn't get no boats there, Marion City gone down

So high the water was risin' our men sinkin' down
Man, the water was risin' at places all around,
boy, they's all around
It was fifty men and children come to sink and drown
Oh, Lordy, women and grown men drown

Oh, women and children sinkin' down
Lord, have mercy
I couldn't see nobody's home and wasn't no one to be found

*   *   *

"Barrelhouse Blues" by Lovie Austin (1923)

Got the barrel house blues, feeling awfully dry
Got the barrel house blues, feeling awfully dry
I can't drink moonshine 'cause I'm afraid I'd die

Papa likes his sherry, mama likes her port
Papa likes his sherry, mama likes her port
Papa likes to shimmy, mama likes to sport

Papa likes his bourbon, mama likes her gin
Papa likes his bourbon, mama likes her gin
Papa likes his outside women, mama likes outside men.

*   *   *

"Those All Night Long Blues" (1923), by J. G. Sudath

I have sent a letter away 'cause my man and I don't agree
There's no reason why he should treat me this way
'Cause the way I worry, I will soon be old and grey

Don't want to do nothing that's wrong
But can't stand this treatment long

I just lay and suffer, crying, sighing all night long
'Cause the way that I'm worried, Lordy it sure is wrong

All night long, all night long
It's this one man on my mind
Can't sleep a wink at night from crying
All night long, got my worries just renewed
And I suffer with those all night blues

All selections in the public domain.

DUKE ELLINGTON ON AFRICAN AMERICAN MUSIC

Edward Kennedy "Duke" Ellington led the famed Cotton Club Orchestra in the early 1930s, and in succeeding years became a famous composer of dance numbers and lengthier musical works. By the late 1930s, publications were asking Ellington to discuss the importance of jazz and swing to African American culture and the state of race relations in American music.

How is Ellington's opinion of black music shaped by the Harlem Renaissance and jazz history?

Is his view of black music and the status of African Americans optimistic or pessimistic?

Compare the tone of Ellington's writing and his ideas to those in the following document.

From The Negro Actor, *July 1938:* The sky-line from my windows in the Wickersham hospital is an inspiring sight. I have spent three weeks in bed here, not too ill to be thrilled daily by a view of these skyscrapers, and with plenty of time for ample meditation.

It is natural, perhaps, that I should think of many subjects, some serious, some fanciful. I spent some time comparing the marvelous sky-line to our race, likening the Chrysler tower, the Empire State building and other lofty structures to the lives of Bert Williams, Florence Mills and other immortals of the entertainment field.

I mused over the qualities that these stars possessed that enabled them to tower as far above their fellow artists as do these buildings above the skyline.

And it seemed to me, from where I was lying, that in addition to their great talent, the qualities that have made really great stars are those of simplicity, sincerity, and glory and vitality that is as rich and powerful as the sun itself. These traditions are ours to express, and will enrich our careers in proportion to the sincerity and faithfulness with which we interpret them.

Speech given in Los Angeles, February 1941: I have been asked to take as the subject of my remarks the title of a very significant poem, "We, Too, Sing America," written by the distinguished poet and author, Langston Hughes. . . .

We play more than a minority role, in singing "America." Although numerically but 10 percent of the mammoth chorus that today, with an eye overseas, sings "America" with fervor and thanksgiving, I say our 10 percent is the very heart of the chorus: the sopranos, so to speak, carrying the melody, the rhythm section of the band, the violins, pointing the way.

I contend that the Negro is the creative voice of America, is creative America, and it was a happy day in America when the first unhappy slave was landed on its shores.

There, in our tortured induction into this "land of liberty," we built its most graceful civilization. Its wealth, its flowering fields and handsome homes; its pretty traditions; its guarded leisure and its music, were all our creations.

We stirred in our shackles and our unrest awakened Justice in the hearts of a courageous few, and we re-created in America the desire for true democracy, freedom for all, the brotherhood of man, principles on which the country had been founded.

We were freed and as before, we fought America's wars, provided her labor, gave her music, kept alive her flickering conscience, prodded her on toward the yet unachieved goal, democracy—until we became more than a part of America! We—this kicking, yelling, touchy, sensitive, scrupulously demanding minority—are the personification of the ideal begun by the Pilgrims almost 350 years ago. It is our voice that sang "America" when America grew too lazy, satisfied and confident to sing . . . before the dark threats and fire-lined clouds of destruction frightened it into a thin, panicky quaver.

We are more than a few isolated instances of courage, valor, achievement. We're the injection, the shot in the arm, that has kept America and its forgotten principles alive in the fat and corrupt years intervening between our divine conception and our near tragic present.

Duke Ellington, "From Where I Lie," *The Negro Actor* 1:1 (July 15, 1938), p. 4; Duke Ellington, "We, Too, Sing 'America,'" delivered at the Annual Lincoln Day Services, Scott Methodist Church, Los Angeles, February 9, 1941, and published as "Speech of the Week" in the *California Eagle*, February 13, 1941. In the public domain.

"STRANGE FRUIT"—LEWIS ALLAN (ABEL MEEROPOL), POPULARIZED BY BILLIE HOLIDAY

This lyric, credited to a white composer but probably modified by Holiday, was a startling commentary on the lynching of black people, emerging from the gener-

ally carefree music of the swing era. It reflected both the anti-lynching activism of white and black political activists in the 1930s and Holiday's own background as a poor and abused young woman in the ghetto. The recording is available at online music sites.

    How is the attitude and style of this lyric different from earlier ones we have seen? Could the song be sung in different ways, to convey the meaning differently? How much would a song like this contribute to the growing movement for civil rights?

> Southern trees bear a strange fruit
> Blood on the leaves and blood at the root
> Black body swinging in the Southern breeze
> Strange fruit hanging from the poplar trees
>
> Pastoral scene of the gallant South
> The bulging eyes and the twisted mouth
> Scent of magnolia sweet and fresh
> and the sudden smell of burning flesh!
>
> Here is a fruit for the crows to pluck
> For the rain to gather, for the wind to suck
> For the sun to rot, for a tree to drop
> Here is a strange and bitter crop.

Lewis Allan, "Strange Fruit." Copyright © 1939 (Renewed) by Music Sales Corporation (ASCAP). International copyright secured. All rights reserved. Reprinted by permission.

PURPOSE OF THE AACM

This text is from the website of the Association for the Advancement of Creative Musicians (AACM), Chicago's major avant-garde African American jazz collective, founded in 1965. The AACM is perhaps the most important and durable of the many musicians' organizations that emerged in African American urban communities in the 1960s, during the time of riots and the Black Power and Black Arts movements.

    How much do these goals reflect the aspirations of previous generations of musicians?

    How do the goals of the AACM reflect the mood of African Americans in the 1960s?

    Can African American musicians today still promote these goals through their work?

The AACM is a tax-exempt, nonprofit organization incorporated in the State of Illinois in 1965. The organization has a nine-point mission, which has remained constant over the life of the association.

1. To cultivate young musicians and to create music of a high artistic level through programs designed to magnify creative music.
2. To create an atmosphere conducive to artistic endeavors for the artistically inclined.
3. To conduct free training for disadvantaged city youth.
4. To encourage sources of employment for musicians.
5. To set an example of high moral standards for musicians and to uplift the image of creative musicians.
6. To increase respect between creative musicians and musical trades persons.
7. To uphold the tradition of cultured musicians handed down from the past.
8. To stimulate spiritual growth in musicians.
9. To assist other complementary charitable organizations.

"Purpose of the AACM," www.aacmchicago.org/indexhold.html (accessed June 1, 2007).

OLLY WILSON, "BLACK MUSIC AS AN ART FORM," EXCERPTS

A leading African American classical composer, Olly Wilson invokes W. E. B. Du Bois's concept of "double consciousness" to explain what he calls the two traditions of black music. Wilson's essay is an interesting attempt to define the entire scope of African American music—classical and popular—in the past century.

> *Would you add or subtract anything to Wilson's list of "conceptual approaches" in black music?*
>
> *What African American music styles are, or are not, considered "art forms"? Why?*
>
> *Having read the present volume, how much do you agree or disagree with Wilson's argument?*

A thorough discussion of all of the African and, by extension, Afro-American, conceptual approaches to the process of making music is out of the purview of this paper; but a brief consideration of a few such concepts should be instructive. Among these are predilections for conceiving music in such a way that the following occur . . . :

(1) The approach to the organization of rhythm is based on the principle of rhythmic and implied metrical contrast. There is a tendency to create musical structures in which rhythmic clash or disagreement of accents is the ideal; cross-rhythm and metrical ambiguity are the accepted and expected norm.

(2) There is a tendency to approach singing or the playing of any instrument in a percussive manner. . . .

(3) There is a tendency to create musical forms in which antiphonal or call-and-response musical structures abound. . . .

(4) There is a tendency to create a high density of musical events within a relatively short musical time frame—a tendency to fill up all of the musical space.

(5) There is a common approach to music making in which a kaleidoscopic range of dramatically contrasting qualities of sound (timbre) in both vocal and instrumental music is sought after. This explains the common usage of a broad continuum of vocal sounds from speech to song. . . .

(6) There is a tendency to incorporate physical body motion as an integral part of the music making process. . . .

Black music, then, may be defined as music which is, in whole or significant degree, part of a musical tradition of peoples of African descent in which a common core of the above-mentioned conceptual approaches to music making are made manifest. . . .

Black music in the United States reflects the duality of Afro-American culture of which Du Bois speaks, "the two souls, two thoughts, two ideals." On one hand, there exists what might be described as the basic or folk African-American musical tradition. . . . It most clearly expresses the collective aesthetic values of the majority of black Americans and proceeds along a line of development that, while influenced by factors outside of Afro-American culture, is more profoundly affected by values within the culture. It is clearly music within Du Bois's veil. Hollers, cries and moans, early spirituals, rural work and play songs, rural blues, gospel music, urban blues, and soul music are the principal expressions of this tradition.

On the other hand, there exists a tradition in Afro-American music that dates from at least 1800. This tradition is characterized by a greater interaction and interpenetration of African and Euro-American elements, although the fundamental qualities that make it unique are rooted in African conceptual approaches to music making. Culturally, this tradition is a closer reflection of the second ideal to which Du Bois refers; that is, the American ideal within black consciousness. . . .

This second Afro-American music tradition finds its initial expression in the popular music of the late eighteenth- and early nineteenth-century. Beginning with the colonial practice of allowing black musicians to perform Euro-American religious, dance, and military music, it ultimately resulted in a black tradition of reshaping the Euro-American qualities of the music to African-American norms. . . . The brass bands of Frank Johnson,

A. J. Connor and others in the middle of the nineteenth century . . . continue this tradition. Finally, the post–Civil War black minstrel tradition, the black marching and circus band tradition, the black musical comedy tradition, and much of the entire jazz tradition are all expressions of this second tradition. . . .

In the first tradition, the artistic quality has to be approached in the manner associated with the African tradition; that is, the work must be judged by the capacity of its aesthetic content to achieve its functional purpose. One is concerned here not with music as an abstract object of art, but as an agent which causes something to happen. The function of the early Afro-American religious song was not simply to bring aesthetic pleasure to the listener, but to create a spiritual liaison between man and his God. . . . [H]istorically, the forms of music in the first tradition are less understood and appreciated as art by the broader American society.

The second tradition, which involves cultural transformation, is more compatible with western values. Within this tradition, music clearly exists as objects of "perceptual interest," either as entertainment or art. The fundamental criteria for artistic measure here, however, are still primarily based on African conceptual approaches to music making. . . . [G]enres of this tradition are more readily understood and accepted by the broader American society. Indeed, it is within this second tradition that most cross-cultural interaction between Euro-American music and Afro-American music has taken place.

Olly Wilson, "Black Music as an Art Form," *Black Music Research Journal* 3 (1983), 1–23. Reprinted by permission.

HIP HOP LYRICS

Since 1980, hip hop or rap music has been among the most vital and controversial forms of black popular music. Its frank and explicit commentary on poverty, race relations, injustice, and concerns within the African American community offer vivid testimony by young black musicians today.

For this exercise, visit one of the sites on the Internet that reproduces hip hop lyrics, such as The Original Hip Hop Lyrics Archive (www.ohhla.com). First examine an "old school" rap lyric from before 1987. A good example would be Grandmaster Flash & the Furious Five's "The Message" (1980).

> *Is this song a total break with the musical traditions represented in the previous documents?*
>
> *Would you say that rap is more poetry than music, or vice versa? Or is that issue meaningless?*

Are rap lyrics more authentically African American than the lyrics in earlier documents? Why?

Next, examine an example from the next "generation" of rappers, from the late 1980s and early 1990s. A classic example would be Public Enemy, "Fight the Power" (1989).

> *How does this lyric associate African American music with the struggle for justice?*
>
> *How much is this a serious political statement? How much is it entertainment?*
>
> *How do recent (post-2000) hip hop lyrics differed in significant ways from earlier rap lyrics?*

CONGRESSIONAL TESTIMONY ON HIP HOP LYRICS

In April 2007, the white radio personality Don Imus made a spontaneous comment on the air about the mostly African American women's basketball team at Rutgers University. Referring to them as "nappy-headed hoes," Imus provoked a storm of criticism and lost his national syndicated morning show. In response to this incident, a subcommittee of the United States House of Representatives held a hearing into the social consequences of racially derogatory language in the mass media.

This was not the first such hearing. For nearly twenty years members of Congress and others had sought to censor or attach consumer warnings to rap music recordings featuring words such as "nigger" and explicit sex and violence. The hearings held in September 2007 considered not only Imus's statement but similar language in the lyrics of African American hip hop artists. Therefore, the subcommittee took on the task of examining racially charged language spoken by both whites and blacks.

Two pieces of testimony before the subcommittee are excerpted below. The first testimony is from the African American hip hop performer and producer David Banner (Levell Crump), who defends his use of racially charged language. The second statement is from a sociologist at the University of Illinois, Andrew Rojecki, who argues that Don Imus and other whites have been desensitized to racial slurs by their repeated exposure to rap lyrics and other similar messages in contemporary mass culture.

> *How convincing is Banner's justification for the use of racially derogatory language in rap music?*
>
> *How much similarity is there between how earlier generations of African Americans found refuge in music, and how Banner and other young African Americans seek refuge in hip hop?*
>
> *How does Rojecki evaluate the social impact of hip hop lyrics? Does he agree or disagree with Banner?*
>
> *Based on these arguments and others you have heard, how freely do you think that racially derogatory language should be expressed in hip hop music?*

**Statement of David Banner Before the United States House of Repre-
sentatives Committee on Energy and Commerce, Subcommittee on
Commerce, Trade, and Consumer Protection, September 25, 2007:**

Good afternoon Mr. Chairman and members of the Committee. My
name is David Banner. I am an artist for SRC Recordings, a producer, and
label executive. Thank you for inviting my testimony.

This dialogue was sparked by the insulting comments made by Don
Imus concerning the Rutgers women's basketball team. Imus lost his job,
but later, may have secured a million dollar contract with another station.

While he appears to have been rewarded, the hip hop industry is left
under public scrutiny. As this "dialogue" played out in the media, the
voices of the people who create hip hop and rap music were silenced. We
were not invited to participate on any panels, nor given the opportunity
to publicly refute any of the accusations hurled at us. While Congress
lacks the power to censor, it is of the utmost importance that the people
whose livelihood is at stake be made a vital part of this process.

I am from Jackson, Mississippi. Jackson is one of the most violent cities
in the United States. . . . When I was growing up, it always ranked as one
of the top ten cities for the highest number of murders per capita. Being
located right below Chicago, a lot of kids got in trouble up there and were
sent to Jackson by their grandparents, who were from Jackson. The by-
product of this migration was violence. I was blessed to have a very
strong man for a father, and a very-very strong woman for a Mother.

Honestly, rap music is what kept me out of trouble. Statistics will never
show the positive side of rap because statistics don't reflect what you
"don't" do . . . if you "don't" commit a murder or a crime. When I would
feel angry and would think about getting revenge, I would listen to Tupac
[Shakur]. His anger in a song was a replacement for my anger. I lived vic-
ariously through his music.

Rap music is the voice of the underbelly of America. In most cases,
America wants to hide the negative that it does to its people. Hip hop is
the voice . . . and how dare America not give us the opportunity to be
heard. I am one of the few artists who went to college. I still see my
friends who, as college graduates, are unable to get a job. The truth is that
what we do sells. Often artists try to do different types of music and their
music doesn't sell. In America, the media only lifts up negativity.

People consider me a philanthropist. I give away close to a quarter of my
yearly earnings to send children from impoverished neighborhoods to different cities . . . to Disneyland. This gives them another vision. Rap music
has changed my life, and the lives of those around me. It has given us the
opportunity to eat. I remember sending 88 kids from the inner city on a
trip. I went to the local newspaper and TV station, only to be told that the

trip wasn't "newsworthy." But if I had shot somebody, it would have been all over the news. I threw the largest urban relief concert in history. That never made the front cover of a magazine. But as soon as I say something negative, rise up against my own, or become sharp at the mouth (no pun intended), I am perceived as being disrespectful to Black leaders. That negativity overshadows all of the positive things that I've done as a rap artist.

Some might argue that the content of our music serves as poison to the minds of our generation. If by some stroke of the pen hip hop was silenced, the issues would still be present in our communities. Drugs, violence, and the criminal element were around long before hip hop existed. Our consumers come from various socioeconomic backgrounds and cultures. While many are underprivileged, a large percentage are educated professionals. The responsibility for their choices does not rest on the shoulders of hip hop.

Still others raise concerns about the youth having access to our music. Much like the ratings utilized by the Motion Picture Association of America, our music is given ratings which are displayed on the packaging. These serve to inform the public of possible adult content. As such, the probability of "shocking" the unsuspecting consumer's sensibilities is virtually impossible. If the consumer is disinterested or offended by the content of our music, one could simply not purchase our CDs. The music that is played on the radio must comply with FCC guidelines. Again, this provides a safeguard. Ultimately, the burden of monitoring the music that minors listen to rests with their parents. Some argue that the verbiage used in our music is derogatory. During slavery, those in authority used the word "Nigger" as a means to degrade and emasculate. There was no push for censorship of the word back then.

The abuse that accompanied the label "Nigger" forced us to internalize it. This made the situation easier to digest. Our generation has since assumed ownership of the word. Now that we are capitalizing off the use of the word, why is it so important that it be censored? The intent and spirit of the word "Nigga" in rap music does not even remotely carry the same meaning nor historical intent. Attempting to censor the use of a word that merely depicts deep camaraderie is outrageous. People should focus less on the "offensive" words in our music, and more on the messages that are being conveyed. The same respect is often not extended to hip hop artist[s] as to those in other arenas.

Steven King and Steven Spielberg are renowned for their horrific creations. These movies are embraced as "art." Why then is our content not merely deemed horror music? Mark Twain's literary classic Huckleberry Finn is still required reading in classrooms across the United States of America. The word "Nigger" appears in the book approximately 215 times. While some may find this offensive, the book was not banned by all school districts because of its artistic value.

The same consideration should be extended to hip hop music. As consumers, we generally gravitate to and have a higher tolerance for things that we can relate to. As such, it is not surprising that the spirit of hip hop is not easily understood. In the 1971 case of *Cohen v. California*, Justice Harlan noted that "one man's vulgarity is another man's lyric. . . . " The content and verbiage illustrated in our music may be viewed as derogatory . . . or unnecessary . . . but it is a protected means of artistic expression. In 2005, Al Sharpton, who is a proponent of censorship, stated on CNN that "rappers have the right to talk about the violence they come from . . . if they're going to rap about it and sing about it, they have the First Amendment right." Much like imagery supplied via television, literature, and by other genres of music, we merely provide a product that appeals to our patrons.

Our troops are currently at war under the guise of liberating other countries, [w]hile here in America, our rights are being threatened daily. This is illustrated by homeland security, extensive phone tapping and ill placed attempts at censorship. Traditionally, multi-billion dollar industries have thrived on the premise of violence, sexuality, and derogatory content. This capitalistic trend was not created nor introduced by hip hop. It's been here. It's the American way.

I can admit that there are some problems in hip hop. But it is only a reflection of what is taking place in our society. Hip hop is sick because America is sick. Thank you.

Statement of Dr. Andrew Rojecki, University of Illinois-Chicago Circle:

The Don Imus affair is the most recent example of a pattern in the way Americans think about race. The Civil Rights movement of the 1960s not only changed the legal framework for issues of race, it also changed the way Americans spoke in public about race. In the terms of the social sciences, the norms had changed. It became socially unacceptable for white Americans to give voice to black stereotypes in anger or even in jest. By the early 1990s, the term political correctness (PC) had been coined to make fun of an exaggerated sensitivity to personal feelings attached to group identity.

The concept of PC is less important for naming a hypocritical repression of speech than for identifying an incomplete transformation. Specifically, a change in public norms has not been accompanied by a change in private attitudes. PC could not exist absent the tensions between what is expected and what is believed or felt. For example large majorities of whites say that blacks should have equal opportunity, but major American cities remain highly segregated (the ten largest at 75 percent), black children continue to get inferior education and medical care, and black unemployment remains twice as high as white.

How do whites explain these differences? In the early 1940s, surveys found that majorities of white Americans explained lower black achievement as evidence of intellectual inferiority. . . . Today, only a small minority claim that is true. . . .

The shift in perception from innate, biological differences to social injustice fueled the success of the Civil Rights movement. Unfortunately, it also gave whites license to discount discrimination as an explanation for the difference between black and white achievement. Majorities of whites now believe that the lesser position of African Americans is due to individual moral failing or flaws in black culture itself. . . . In our own research on the black image in the white mind . . . , whites we interviewed spontaneously referred to media images of sexuality and violence that supported their negative views. These images substituted for the absence of sustained contact between whites and blacks, inevitable in a society that remains segregated by race. . . . This is especially true among those persons whom we call the ambivalent majority, those whites who are sympathetic to aspirations of black Americans but who are influenced by images that highlight irresponsibility and violence. In short, majorities of white Americans have good intentions but not the settled inner convictions to put their ideals into practice, perhaps because the forms of discrimination routinely experienced by African Americans have become less visible.

[Research findings about racial perceptions] have important real world implications. In one study . . . researchers sent resumes, identical except for stereotypically white or black names to employers and found that the Greg or Emily were 50 percent more likely to get callbacks than Jamal or Lakisha. . . . More alarmingly, experimental research shows that police officers, both white and black, are more likely to shoot at black suspects than white suspects. . . .

On the issue of hip hop music, we know that Don Imus did not coin the phrase he used to describe the Rutgers women's basketball team. It is also clear that he would not have used that phrase had he thought about it for a second or two. That image was planted in his mind through a complex sequence of events that began in a culture of poverty that thrives in the black ghettos of America. Hip hop is a musical expression of a segment of lived experience that resonates with a significant number of African Americans who grew up under conditions of privation. The lived experiences of African American life have inspired a range of musical innovation and artistic expression, as in jazz and the blues. Sadness and tragedy are common to the human condition, but in the United States they have been disproportionately experienced by African Americans who have developed musical forms to give artistic expression to their lived experience.

The music industry is always on the hunt for innovative forms of music that may be marketed and sold to the largest audiences. Hip hop has for over twenty-five years been an immensely popular genre of music, and its largest audience is white. Marketing to that audience follows the path of least resistance: sensational images of sex and violence are easier to package and promote than more thoughtful and critical messages. Thus gangster rap has enjoyed much more commercial success than the more politically oriented conscious rap. DJs use a mix of hip hop to manage the mood of a club, but gangster rap is catnip to an audience more interested in sexual release than raising political consciousness.

Therein lie the incentives to artists, promoters, industry executives, and white consumers. The music industry offers one of the few paths out of poverty available to African Americans, sex and violence offer proven paths to commercial success, and black experience continues to provide vicarious thrills for white audiences. Today's suburban adolescents will in time move to influential positions within corporate America. The question this panel needs to address is whether the stream of imagery and language in gangster rap is more or less likely to get Lakisha and Jamal a callback. And if the answer is no, how can the system of incentives be changed to make that more likely.

Transcript, "From Imus to Industry: The Business of Stereotypes and Degrading Images," Subcommittee on Commerce, Trade, and Consumer Protection, September 25, 2007, energycommerce.house.gov/cmte_mtgs/ 110-ctcp-hrg.092507.Imus.to.Industry.shtml (accessed April 2008). In the public domain.

Selected Bibliography
and Discography

General surveys of the entire topic of African American music include Eileen Southern, *The Music of Black Americans*, 3rd ed. (New York: Norton, 1997), and Mellonee V. Burnim and Portia K. Maultsby, eds., *African American Music* (New York: Routledge, 2006). Both follow in the footsteps of pioneers such as Alain Locke, *The Negro and His Music* (Washington, DC: Associates in Negro Folk Education, 1936), and Maude Cuney Hare, *Negro Musicians and Their Music* (Washington, DC: Associated Publishers, 1936). Important interpretive overviews include Amiri Baraka, *Blues People* (New York: Morrow, 1963); Albert Murray, *Stomping the Blues* (New York: McGraw-Hill, 1976); Samuel A. Floyd, Jr., *The Power of Black Music* (New York: Oxford University Press, 1996); and Ronald Radano, *Lying Up a Nation* (Chicago: University of Chicago Press, 2003). Serious students of African American music should also consult issues of the *Black Music Research Journal* and *American Music*, available online through the *JSTOR* database.

African music is surveyed comprehensively in J. H. Kwabena Nketia, *The Music of Africa* (New York: Norton, 1974); *The Garland Encyclopedia of World Music*, volume 1 (New York: Garland, 1998); and "Africa," in Stanley Sadie, ed., *The New Grove Dictionary of Music and Musicians*, volume 1 (New York: Grove, 2001). (Garland and Grove are also good sources for most general subtopics in African American music.) Gerhard Kubik, *Africa and the Blues* (Jackson: University Press of Mississippi, 1999) explores the issue of the blues's origins and is an introduction to the methods of the most important ethnomusicologist of Africa. Examinations of the transmission of music from Africa to the Americas include John Storm Roberts, *Black Music of Two Worlds* (New York: Praeger, 1972); Robert Farris Thompson, *Flash of the*

Spirit (New York: Random House, 1984); and Ingrid Monson ed., *The African Diaspora* (New York: Garland, 2000). Sterling Stuckey, *Slave Culture* (New York: Oxford University Press, 1987) and Henry Louis Gates, *The Signifying Monkey* (New York: Oxford University Press, 1988) are influential interpretations of the transmission of religion and oral culture from Africa to black America, shaping the treatment of the subject in Floyd, *The Power of Black Music*, and other studies.

The study of early African American music owes much to the groundbreaking and probing research that began in the 1960s and resulted in major works such as John Lovell, *Black Song* (New York: Macmillan, 1972); Dena Epstein, *Sinful Tunes and Spirituals* (Urbana: University of Illinois Press, 1977); and Lawrence W. Levine, *Black Culture and Black Consciousness* (New York: Oxford University Press, 1977). Levine's book also offers a wide-ranging study of continuity and change in African American music and oral culture from slavery to the twentieth century. Roger D. Abrahams, *Singing the Master* (New York: Pantheon, 1992) is focused narrowly on the role of corn-shucking songs in slave music. Music in African American sermons is analyzed in Jon Michael Spencer, *Sacred Symphony* (New York: Greenwood Press, 1988).

The most comprehensive history of the Fisk Jubilee Singers is Andrew Ward, *Dark Midnight When I Rise* (New York: Farrar, Straus, and Giroux, 2000). African Americans in minstrelsy are described in Robert C. Toll, *Blacking Up* (New York: Oxford University Press, 1974). The rise of black vaudeville in New York City is related in Thomas L. Riis, *Just Before Jazz* (Washington, DC: Smithsonian Institution Press, 1989). The story of Bert Williams is told in Ann Charters, *Nobody* (New York: Macmillan, 1970) and analyzed in Louis O. Chude-Sokei, *The Last "Darky"* (Durham, NC: Duke University Press, 2006). The earliest African American recording artists are described exhaustively in Tim Brooks, *Lost Sounds* (Urbana: University of Illinois Press, 2004). James Weldon Johnson's *Black Manhattan* (New York: Knopf, 1930) and his autobiography, *Along This Way* (New York: Viking, 1933) are also valuable.

Edward A. Berlin, *Ragtime* (Berkeley: University of California Press, 1984) is a good introduction to ragtime music. Berlin's *King of Ragtime* (New York: Oxford University Press, 1994) is the best biography of Scott Joplin, while Reid Badger's *A Life in Ragtime* (New York: Oxford University Press, 1995) is an equally distinguished portrait of James Reese Europe. The migration of southern African Americans to the north is described in Carole Marks, *Farewell—We're Good and Gone* (Bloomington: Indiana University Press, 1989), and James R. Grossman, *Land of Hope* (Chicago: University of Chicago Press, 1989). Paul Oliver's *Savannah Syncopaters* (New York: Stein and Day, 1970) presaged Kubik's argument (in *Africa and the Blues*) that the blues descended from the grasslands of the

Western Sudan, while Oliver's *Songsters and Saints* (Cambridge, UK: Cambridge University Press, 1984) explores the social origins of the blues. Studies of early Delta blues include Jeff Todd Titon, *Early Downhome Blues* (Urbana: University of Illinois Press, 1977) and David Evans, *Big Road Blues* (Berkeley: University of California Press, 1982). For social context, see William Barlow, *"Looking Up at Down"* (Philadelphia: Temple University Press, 1989) and Alan Lomax, *The Land Where the Blues Began* (New York: Pantheon, 1993). The transition of the blues to northern cities is explored in Robert Palmer, *Deep Blues* (New York: Viking, 1981); Hazel Carby, "It Jus' Be's Dat Way Sometime': The Sexual Politics of Women's Blues," *Radical America* 20 (1986); Angela Y. Davis, *Blues Legacies and Black Feminism* (New York: Pantheon, 1998); and Chris Albertson, *Bessie*, revised ed. (New Haven, CT: Yale University Press, 2005).

The current standard jazz history is Ted Gioia, *The History of Jazz* (New York: Oxford University Press, 1997). On early New Orleans jazz, see Donald M. Marquis, *In Search of Buddy Bolden* (Baton Rouge: Louisiana State University Press, 1978), and Thomas Brothers, *Louis Armstrong's New Orleans* (New York: Norton, 2006). Local jazz histories include Dempsey J. Travis, *An Autobiography of Black Jazz* (Chicago: Urban Research Institute, 1983), on Chicago; Douglas Henry Daniels, *One O'Clock Jump* (Boston: Beacon, 2006), on Oklahoma City; Samuel B. Charters and Leonard Kunstadt, *Jazz* (Garden City, NY: Doubleday, 1962), on New York City; Nathan W. Pearson, *Goin' to Kansas City* (Urbana: University of Illinois Press, 1987); and Clora Bryant, ed., *Central Avenue Sounds* (Berkeley: University of California Press, 1998), on Los Angeles. On the 1920s, see Gunther Schuller, *Early Jazz* (New York: Oxford University Press, 1968); Kathy J. Ogren, *The Jazz Revolution* (New York: Oxford University Press, 1989); and Burton W. Peretti, *The Creation of Jazz* (Urbana: University of Illinois Press, 1992). The 1930s are covered in Gunther Schuller, *The Swing Era* (New York: University of Chicago Press, 1989); David W. Stowe, *Swing Changes* (Cambridge, MA: Harvard University Press, 1994); Lewis A. Erenberg, *Swingin' the Dream* (Chicago: University of Chicago Press, 1998); and Joel Dinerstein, *Swinging the Machine* (Amherst: University of Massachusetts Press, 2003). John Edward Hasse's biography of Duke Ellington, *Beyond Category* (New York: Simon & Schuster, 1993) should be supplemented by Mark Tucker, *Ellington: The Early Years* (Urbana: University of Illinois Press, 1991). Beginning with early jazz musicians, also, most prominent African American performers wrote autobiographies, which are of varying detail and insight.

Important musicological studies of jazz include Paul Berliner, *Thinking in Jazz* (Chicago: University of Chicago Press, 1994), and Ingrid Monson, *Saying Something* (Chicago: University of Chicago Press, 1996). Linda Dahl's *Stormy Weather* (New York: Pantheon, 1984) chronicles women in jazz, while her *Morning Glory* (New York: Pantheon, 1999) relates the life of Mary Lou Williams. On Billie Holiday, see Robert O'Meally, *Lady Day* (New York: Arcade, 1991). On bebop, see Thomas Owens, *Bebop* (New York: Oxford University Press, 1995), and Scott DeVeaux, *The Birth of Bebop* (Berkeley: University of California Press, 1997). Among the best studies of Miles Davis are Jack Chambers, *Milestones*, volumes 1 and 2 (Toronto: University of Toronto Press, 1985), and John Szwed, *So What* (New York: Simon & Schuster, 2002). Eric Nisenson's *Ascension* (New York: St. Martin's, 1995) explores the life of John Coltrane. Ekkehard Jost, *Free Jazz* (New York: Da Capo, 1981); John Litweiler, *The Freedom Principle* (New York: Da Capo, 1984); and Ronald Radano, *New Musical Figurations* (Chicago: University of Chicago Press, 1993) discuss jazz since 1960.

Eileen Southern, *The Music of Black Americans*, contains the most thorough coverage of African American classical composers, but it should be supplemented by David N. Baker, Lida M. Belt, and Herman C. Hudson, eds., *The Black Composer Speaks* (Metuchen, NJ: Scarecrow Press, 1978) and William C. Banfield, *Musical Landscapes in Color* (Lanham, MD: Scarecrow Press, 2003).

A useful textbook on popular music since 1950 is Larry Starr and Christopher Waterman, *American Popular Music* (New York: Oxford University Press, 2006). The history of gospel music is well-served by Anthony Heilbut, *The Gospel Sound*, revised ed. (New York: Limelight, 1985); Michael W. Harris, *The Rise of Gospel Blues* (New York: Oxford University Press, 1992); and Robert Darden, *People Get Ready!* (New York: Continuum, 2004), as well as George T. Nierenberg's documentary film *Say Amen, Somebody* (Pacific Arts Video, 1984). Robert Pruter's *Doowop* (Urbana: University of Illinois Press, 1996) charts the transition of male groups from gospel to popular music. Nelson George, *The Death of Rhythm & Blues* (New York: Pantheon, 1988) describes both the rise and the decline of the music, since the end of World War II, while Peter Guralnick, *Dream Boogie* (New York: Little, Brown, 2005) exhaustively chronicles the life of Sam Cooke. See also Guralnick's *Sweet Soul Music* (New York: Harper & Row, 1986) for a history of the Memphis soul scene and Stax Records. Phyl Garland, *The Sound of Soul* (Chicago: H. Regnery, 1969) is an early history that obviously needs updating. Leslie Gourse, *Aretha Franklin* (New York: F. Watts, 1995), and Michael Lydon, *Ray Charles* (New York: Riverhead, 1998) are useful biographies.

Studies of Motown Records include Gerald Early, *One Nation Under a Groove* (Hopewell, NJ: Ecco Press, 1995); Suzanne Smith, *Dancing in the Street* (Cambridge, MA: Harvard University Press, 1999); and Gerald Posner, *Motown* (New York: Random House, 2003). Philadelphia soul is described in John A. Jackson, *A House on Fire* (New York: Oxford University Press, 2004). James Brown has been poorly served by biographers, but for overviews of funk music, see Rickey Vincent, *Funk* (New York: St. Martin's Griffin, 1996), and Anne Danielsen, *Presence and Pleasure* (Middletown, CT: Wesleyan University Press,, 2006). Nelson George, *The Michael*

Jackson Story (New York: Dell, 1984) covers the *Thriller* years, but no serious biography of Jackson (or his family) has appeared since. Nelson George's *Post-Soul Nation* (New York: Viking, 2004) and *Hip Hop America*, revised ed. (New York: Viking, 2005) offer rich portraits of the rise of hip hop by a participant. See also Tricia Rose, *Black Noise* (Hanover, NH: Wesleyan University Press, 1994); Guthrie P. Ramsey, Jr., *Race Music* (Berkeley: University of California Press, 2003); and S. Craig Watkins, *Hip Hop Matters* (Boston: Beacon, 2005). For social context, see Bakari Kitwana, *The Hip Hop Generation* (New York: Basic Civitas, 2002), and Kyra D. Gaunt, *The Games Black Girls Play* (New York: New York University Press, 2006).

ESSENTIAL DISCOGRAPHY

It is always hazardous to recommend recordings, since issues and labels come and go frequently. Students who are keen on tracking down particular recordings are encouraged to subscribe to music file services such as Rhapsody, which feature the latest incarnations of classic albums and tracks. Whether these are obtained in CD form or as MP3 files, though, it is helpful for the listener to have a list of recommendations to work from.

It is also impossible to give a brief list of recordings that does justice to the topics covered in this book. What follows is my attempt, inevitably subjective in part, to list the most essential recordings in African American music, with record labels current as of 2007.

Explorer series, Nonesuch Records, including for example *West Africa—Drum, Chant & Instrumental Music* or *Ghana—Ancient Ceremonies: Dance Music & Songs*

Lost Sounds: Blacks and the Birth of the Recording Industry, 1891–1922 (Archeophone)—includes recordings by the Jubilee Singers, Bert Williams, George W. Johnson, Booker T. Washington, and others

Joshua Rifkin, *Scott Joplin: Piano Rags* (Nonesuch)—perhaps the most celebrated of many fine recordings of Joplin's works

Blues Masters (Rhino Records), including, for example, *Vol. 8: Mississippi Delta Blues*, or *Vol. 2: Postwar Chicago Blues*

Bessie Smith: The Collection (Sony)

Jelly Roll Morton: Birth of the Hot: The Classic "Red Hot Peppers" Sessions (RCA)

Louis Armstrong: Complete Hot Five and Hot Seven Recordings (Sony)

Duke Ellington: Complete Legendary Fargo Concert (Definitive/Spain)—a live 1940 recording that is the most exciting record of the orchestra at its peak; see also *The Duke Ellington Carnegie Hall Concerts: January 1943* (Prestige), featuring the premiere of *Black, Brown and Beige*

Art Tatum, *The Standard Sessions: 1935–1943 Broadcast Transcriptions* (Music & Arts)

Charlie Parker: A Studio Chronicle, 1940–1948 (JSP)

Miles Davis, *Birth of the Cool* (Blue Note); *Kind of Blue* (Sony); *Bitches Brew* (Sony)

Charles Mingus, *Mingus Ah Um* (Sony)

John Coltrane, *Giant Steps* (Atlantic)

Cecil Taylor, *Conquistador* (Blue Note)

Natalie Hinderas, *Piano Music by African American Composers* (CRI)

Thamyris and guest artists, *A City Called Heaven* (ACA)—featuring works by Olly Wilson, Tania León, Anthony Davis, and others

Louis Jordan & His Tympani Five (JSP)

Wade in the Water, Vol. II: African American Congregational Singing: Nineteenth-Century Roots (Smithsonian/Folkways)—representative of Bernice Johnson Reagon's important *Wade in the Water* series

Precious Lord: Recordings of the Great Gospel Songs of Thomas A. Dorsey (Sony)

When Gospel Was Gospel (Shanachie)

Ray Charles: The Birth of Soul . . . 1952–1959 (Atlantic)

Chuck Berry, *The Great Twenty-Eight* (MCA)

James Brown, *Live at the Apollo*, and *Foundations of Funk: A Brand New Bag: 1964–1969* (both Polydor)

Motown Classics: Gold (Motown)

Stax 50th Anniversary Celebration (Stax)

The Essential O'Jays (Sony) (no Philadelphia International anthology is currently in print)

Stevie Wonder, *Songs in the Key of Life* (Motown)

Michael Jackson, *Thriller* (Epic/Sony)—also available in a "special edition" featuring interviews and outtakes

Prince, *Sign 'O' the Times* (Warner)

Rapper's Delight & Other Old School Favorites (Rhino Flashback)—not nearly as good, alas, as a British Universal import compilation, *Rapper's Delight*, now out of print

Public Enemy, *Fear of a Black Planet* (Def Jam)

A Tribe Called Quest, *The Low End Theory* (Jive)

Arrested Development, *3 Years 5 Months & 2 Days in the Life of . . .* (Capitol)

The Fugees, *The Score* (Ruffhouse/Columbia)

Jay-Z, *Reasonable Doubt* (Priority)

Index

About the Author

Burton W. Peretti is professor of history and department chairperson at Western Connecticut State University. He is the author of *Nightclub City: Politics and Amusement in Manhattan* (2007); *Jazz in American Culture* (1997); *The Creation of Jazz: Music, Race, and Culture in Urban America* (1992); and numerous articles.